A
Bonfire of
Inanities

The Bible
Dismantled

VOLUME ONE

Ancestral Tales

A Bonfire of Inanities

The Bible Dismantled

VOLUME ONE

Ancestral Tales

THE REAL TRUTH
ABOUT THE ANCIENT
ROOTS OF JUDAISM
AND CHRISTIANITY

Paul McGrane

SINGULAR BOOKS

First published in 2023

Singular Books
www.paulmcgrane.co.uk

Thanks to Dave Bain for the maps

Text design by Ellipsis, Glasgow

A CIP record for this book is available from the British Library

ISBN 978-1-73939-260-4 (paperback)
ISBN 978-1-73939-261-1 (ebook)

Printed and bound by CPI Group (UK) Ltd, Croydon, CR0 4YY.

1 3 5 7 9 8 6 4 2

For Jean, David, John and Holly

Those who undertake to write histories [do so] . . . because they are concerned in the facts . . . to draw their historical facts out of darkness into light . . . on account of the great importance of the facts.

—Flavius Josephus, in his Preface to
The Antiquities of the Jews

Many would agree it is now time for a more nuanced approach, open to comparative studies and embracing archaeology, anthropology, folklore and discourse analysis – to name but a few relevant disciplines.

—John Waddell, Emeritus Professor of Archaeology at
the National University of Ireland, in his Preface to
Nikolai Tolstoy's *The Mysteries of Stonehenge*

CONTENTS

FIGURES

A Bonfire of Inanities: The Bible Dismantled

As a teenager over half a century ago, I had a brief flirtation with evangelical Christianity: the apparent certainties on offer were attractive then to the self-conscious, uncertain youth that I was. The flirtation ended very quickly during my undergraduate years, to be replaced with the atheism that I have held ever since, but the experience left me with a lifelong interest in religious faith. I retired seventeen years ago and have spent much of the time since then in revisiting Christianity from a rationalist point of view. At the heart of my approach has been what is known as 'textual criticism': a critical study of writings emphasizing a close reading and analysis of the text. Specific techniques include the identification of bias resulting from authorial belief and intent; the identification of possible errors in scribal transcription and mistranslation; and the comparison of different versions of events in different texts. All of these possibilities exist in abundance in the Bible. My own training, experience and qualification is in modern literary texts, but I decided to apply that training in critical analysis to the Bible and other contemporary texts.

I took First Class Honours in my undergraduate degree

at Ulster University, and I subsequently conducted three years' research in an archive of original manuscripts in Duke Humphrey's Reading Room at the Bodleian Library at Oxford University, before attaining my Doctorate (DPhil) from the latter. I have subsequently published peer-reviewed articles in respected academic journals. My degrees and my research have been in English Literature, specializing in the Victorian period. In the academic world this does not qualify me to write about the early history of Judaism and Christianity because, in that world, there are strict and rigid demarcation lines between academic disciplines. There is, however, a growing recognition that those divisions get in the way of real knowledge. In the case of my own research, my stance is that someone like me, trained in textual analysis and practised in working with sometimes chaotic manuscript sources, can have something to bring to the party when studying ancient scriptural texts. Of course, I am dependant on the linguistic, archaeological and historical work of experts in the field, but with my objectivity – borne of a different academic discipline, combined with a lack of supernatural preconceptions – I may be able to offer new insights into the interpretation and meaning of those scriptural texts.

I believe that my researches over the last couple of decades have uncovered a revolutionary new understanding of the roots of Judaism and Christianity. In 2017, I published a book called *The Christian Fallacy* in which I set out my initial findings. This attracted little attention and only a few readers, but undeterred, I continued my research, revised and much enlarged my previous book, and this trilogy is the end result. [That first book now forms the essence of Volume Two, although some of those original arguments, relating to the Book of Revelation and Simon Magus, can now be found in Volume Three.] The trilogy offers, for the first time, a complete, rationalistic re-interpretation of the Bible, from

Genesis to Revelation, and relates it to other contemporary texts, religious and secular, and to contemporary events and people. *Volume I: Ancestral Tales* analyses the various source texts that make up the so-called Books of Moses in the Old Testament, and in conjunction with non-Biblical records – notably the Egyptian one – is able to unravel the true roots of Jewish belief. *Volume II: Mistaken Messiahs* traces how Jewish messianic belief finds its way into the New Testament and Christianity, and identifies historical figures behind Jesus and the Apostles. *Volume III: Apocalypse Postponed* then focuses on the Christian belief in imminent apocalypse and traces how thoroughgoing misunderstanding of the relevant texts has led to two millennia of fallacious expectation.

On 7 February 1497 in Florence, the religious extremist Friar Girolamo Savonarola, held the first of his 'bonfires of the vanities' on which thousands of objects, condemned by religious authorities as 'occasions of sin', were consigned to the flames. It is high time we rationalists had our own bonfire on which to consign the sheer inanities of religious belief. This trilogy is a metaphorical bonfire of biblical fallacies. Each volume in the trilogy has been written to stand alone, but there is a natural sequence to the arguments developed, which is facilitated if they are read in order:

Vol I   *Ancestral Tales*
Vol II   *Mistaken Messiahs*
Vol III   *Apocalypse Postponed*

There has never been anything like this – in scope, in approach and in findings. It may be possible to continue in Jewish or Christian belief in the light of these three volumes, but it would be a very different kind of religious faith from the one normally espoused.

PREFACE

One of the problems I have faced in writing this book is the knowledge that, although my focus in this trilogy is Christianity, I am here reconstructing narratives that underlie the Jewish as well as the Christian faith, and that entails addressing the roots of orthodox Judaism. More particularly, some of my analysis could be seen as a slur upon those roots, and I need to address that issue right up front. I intend no disrespect to Jews, Judaism or to their founding fathers. I did not set out from a point of prejudice: I have only one interest – historical truth, insofar as it can be discovered. Prejudice apart, I also owe it to readers to set out as honestly as I can the *a priori* assumption on which my work is based. I regard all religions as irrational fairy tales, based on a belief in the supernatural that I reject. Furthermore, I regard all religions as having had, and continuing to have, a baleful influence on human civilization. I do not exempt Judaism from that judgement. In fact, from my perspective, it is a particularly pernicious set of beliefs. Jews worship a God who, from the evidence of the Bible, if taken literally, exhibits narcissistic paranoia, genocidal psychosis, and the sort of belligerent behaviour that, were He[1] a mere human being, He would have been put behind bars long ago. He drowned (virtually) the entire population of the Earth; He exhorted His followers to murder indiscriminately men, women and children in Canaan; and then He expects His 'chosen' people to submit themselves to a range of practices that separate them out from the cultures that surround them, and thus open them up to suspicion and persecution.

I am, of course, aware that many Jews today are as repulsed as I am by the descriptions of violence and genocide, incest and bigamy, that the God of the Old Testament seems to condone, if not actually delight in. The Jewish people are just like the rest of us: some good, some bad, and most something in between, just struggling to get by in the world. I believe, based on scientific fact, that all racial difference is a fiction. The genomes of a Jew and an Arab and me, who is neither, are virtually the same. The genetic differences that do exist are trivial, superficial and responsible for characteristics that create welcome diversity. The intractable differences between peoples are cultural not genetic. Racism of any kind is scientific nonsense. It is also moral degeneracy. Even if there *were* significant genetic racial differences, I would still regard racism as utterly unacceptable. Being human is a broad church, embracing huge differences in physical and mental abilities – but we are all human and equal in principle, if not in actual fact. Anything I say in this book regarding the Israelites should be read in that light.

---

[1] I shall use the honorific initial capital in references to the deity. This should not be taken for more than it is – conformity to convention.

INTRODUCTION

This is the first volume in a trilogy dividing truth from fiction in the Bible. The second volume – *Mistaken Messiahs* – will unravel events in the first century AD to discover the messianic roots of Christianity in Judaism. The third volume – *Apocalypse Postponed* – will span the Old and New Testaments to deconstruct the elements of Jewish and Christian apocalyptic fantasy. But in this first volume I will go right back to the beginning of it all – the ancient roots of both Judaism and Christianity in the early chapters of the Old Testament (or for Jews, Torah) – the five books attributed to Moses. They tell the story of the Israelites and their relationships with the tribes, peoples and nations around them, leading to the central narrative of the Jewish people: the sojourn of the Israelites as slaves in Egypt; their miraculous departure under the inspired leadership of Moses; and the triumphant arrival in the Promised Land of Canaan. Because Christianity grew out of Judaism, and in doing so embraced Jewish myths as its own, these Exodus myths feature prominently in both religions. For Christians the physical Exodus prefigures the spiritual salvation offered by Jesus Christ. In this first volume of the trilogy, I set out to solve two issues that have presented a historical enigma for many years.

The first is the difficulty of squaring the Biblical account of events with what can be gleaned from other historical sources and archaeology. Scholarly consensus has shifted several times on this over the last century or so, and right now there remains a huge disparity of view. On one hand, there is the 'Copenhagen School' of 'Minimalists' who espouse an extreme scepticism with regard to the historicity of the Biblical narratives. On the other are more conservative 'Maximalist' scholars, who regard the Biblical narratives as substantially borne out by modern investigation. I, like many others, now take a more balanced view: that these myths have their roots in *something*, and could we but strip them back to those roots we might discover some clues to history after all.

The second riddle is not a Biblical enigma at all. It concerns the mysterious 'Sea Peoples', who seem to have appeared from nowhere at the end of the Bronze Age to ravage the eastern Mediterranean and, according to a traditional view, triggered what is known by ancient historians as the 'Bronze Age Collapse' of all the Mediterranean civilisations at the time and plunged the area into a centuries-long dark age. That traditional view has been moderated by many scholars in recent years, but it will be my contention here that the revaluation has not gone far enough: the Sea Peoples have little to do with causes of the Bronze Age Collapse and everything to do with the age-old interaction and conflict between Egypt and the Levant.

These two enigmas are the province of two different scholarly disciplines – Biblical Studies and Ancient History respectively. Many or even most scholars in those disciplines act a lot of the time as if the two issues are unrelated, even tangentially. Yet I shall demonstrate here that not only are they related, but that you cannot solve one without the other: that they are two sides to one historical conundrum. I shall propose that the Exodus was not what Christians and Jews think it was, and that the Sea Peoples were not what ancient historians have hitherto proposed. In my view, modern scholarship is hampered by the isolated bunkers in which different scholarly disciplines sit. It is a major issue for human knowledge in the twenty-first century. The sheer amount of knowledge we now have requires specialisation for the human mind to grasp all the necessary detail. Yet in every specialised field you care to examine, we are coming to realise that complexity and even chaos are inherent in their operation, and that complexity sprawls across the tidy dividing lines that characterise our intellectual enquiry. In this case, I shall show that the histories of the Israelites and the Sea Peoples are part of one single but complex story about what was happening in the Bronze Age Near East. That story is a huge convoluted riddle comprising a myriad of places, tribes and nations, many of which have long disappeared into the dusts of time.

I shall try in this unravelling to simplify as much as possible, but the reader must be prepared to come to grips with at least the basic geography and the major players. The Bible is full of references to places and geographical features that are bewildering, often conflicting and, in very many cases, now impossible to locate with any certainty. Indeed, many of the old tales in the early books of the Bible, dealing as they do with deep pre-history, are there solely to provide aetiology[1] for place names. Figure 1 covers the basic geography of the region; I shall supplement it with more detailed maps as we go along.

---

[1] Aetiology is 'the investigation or attribution of the cause or reason for something, often expressed in terms of historical or mythical explanation' Capuzzi, & Stauffer, 2016.

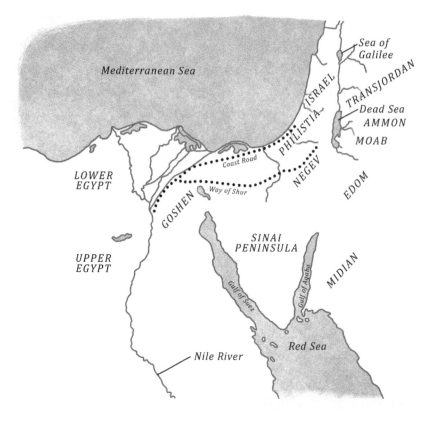

Fig. 1: Map of Egypt and the Levant

Egypt in the west of the region is defined entirely by the Nile, which flows north into the Mediterranean. All the Egyptian events in the early chapters of the Bible take place in the northern part (Lower Egypt) and more specifically in the Delta area, then known as Goshen, where the Nile divides into a number of different arms and channels as it discharges into the sea. The channels changed over time, some silting up and new ones arising, and cities built around them rose and fell accordingly. And the whole area of the Delta and the land to the east of it is characterised by wetlands – marshes, bogs and salt lakes. This area, forming the eastern boundary of Egypt, was important to defend from potential threats

4

from Asian empires, countries, armies and pirates, and many fortified towns and cities ran north–south along the border. Travelling east from Goshen into this wetland border area brings you into the Negev desert of the Sinai Peninsula, which stretches all the way from the Mediterranean south to the two gulfs of the Red Sea that stretch up either side of Sinai like two fingers – the Gulf of Suez to the west and the Gulf of Aqaba to the east. Nowadays, of course, the Gulf of Suez is connected to the Mediterranean by the Suez Canal, but in ancient times this was an area of desert punctuated by salt lakes, giving way to the wetlands of the northern coast. The two main routes from Egypt going east were the Way of Shur, which went across the desert, and the Coastal Highway. The latter was more direct, but ran through the wetland areas and was notoriously treacherous because of its bogs; it also led through the land of the Philistines who were a fierce, warlike people, probably originating in Greece, but in any case best avoided.

The Philistines lived in the area between the Negev/Sinai and the land of Canaan, which ran north–south along the Mediterranean coastline to the west and the River Jordan to the east. North of Canaan lay lands that were to become Phoenicia, or today's Lebanon, Syria and Asia Minor. The Jordan flows southwards from the freshwater Sea of Galilee into a dead end in the salty Dead Sea. The land to the east of the Jordan is mountainous, descending on the eastern slopes to the pasturelands of Transjordan, beyond which, further to the east, lay all of Asia in general and Mesopotamia in particular. Canaan itself was occupied by a number of tribes, most of whom are known today only by the Biblical references, having been supplanted by or evolved into,[2] the

---

2 The distinction between the two will be an important theme in this book.

Israelite tribes. Transjordan was home to the countries of (from north to south) Ammon, Moab and Edom, which feature heavily in the Old Testament, along with the Philistines, as enemies or rivals at one time or another of the Israelite tribes. To the north of Transjordan were Syrian lands on the eastern side of the Jordan that *were* eventually occupied by Israelite tribes. The whole of the Mediterranean coastline running south from Asia Minor down to the Sinai is often called the Levant. In this book, I shall refer to Canaan when I mean the lands traditionally associated with the twelve tribes of Israel and the Levant when I mean the wider area that takes in Phoenicia and parts of Syria.

Here, as throughout the trilogy, my approach is that of textual analysis. That, rather than Biblical studies, archaeology or history, is my scholarly base. It is a discipline that allows me to roam across all these areas of scholarly pursuit. It treats narrative texts as just that – not Scripture with messages, either overt or hidden, from a deity, nor dry academic exercises, but living, breathing stories that were considered valuable enough to hand down through generations and preserve in writing. I believe that if one approaches these precious ancient texts with the care and attention they merit, and one views them without the preconceptions of faith – Christian or Jewish – one can find them surprisingly informative. It should be a source of wonder and gratitude that these texts, several millennia old, not only survive but have been subjected over the last few hundred years to extensive, skilled analysis and deconstruction. This book rests heavily on the powerful legacy of Biblical scholars whose knowledge of ancient history and ancient languages far surpasses my own. I believe the scholarly tools needed to put all the pieces of the jigsaw together and construct reasonable hypotheses about what it all means have been available for a long time.

And it is vitally important to do so. Our western civilisation is under attack on many fronts. Its roots lie in these texts and, as supernatural faith fades away, we need to reinterpret those roots for our own post-religious times.

I shall argue in this book that the racial myths on which Israel is based, are just that – myths. Hardly a stunningly original conclusion, you might well say. But there is more to it than that. Putting matters of faith to one side, the Books of Moses are an incredible set of texts dating back at least three millennia. They are quite unique in their scale and their manuscript richness. As such, they are worthy of historical and literary study for what they can tell us about the times in which they were written and redacted. In my view, there is historical evidence to be gleaned from the Old Testament account. As Richard Friedman (an eminent biblical scholar, of whom more later) has commented, if the Bible texts were only just discovered, we would be more inclined to treat them seriously as sources of information, rather than dismiss them as fables. We must not let over-familiarity with those stories, or the religious history of the last two millennia, get in the way of us regarding these texts in that light. The evidence they provide suggests a racial narrative very different indeed from that taught in western Bible classes and Israeli nurseries alike. The true narrative does involve Canaanites in Egypt; a number of separate Exoduses; and even *perhaps* key characters like Joseph, Jacob and Moses. But it happened in a very different way to that which the writers of the Bible would have you believe, and it intersects with secular ancient history in a way that has never been properly understood before.

CHAPTER I

The Exodus Enigma

What Christians call the *Old* Testament, for Jews represents *The* Testament. It contains many different elements, but threaded through it is a narrative of the Jewish people, handed down generation to generation. It is possible to abstract from it a simple story that, stripped of its attributions of natural and supernatural causality, runs as follows:

1. Mankind's beginnings in **Eden.**
2. The **Great Flood,** by which all animal life is wiped out.
3. A New Beginning with the offspring of **Noah.**
4. The founding of the Jewish people by **Abraham**[1] and his descendants, notably **Isaac, Jacob** and **Joseph.** Then, at an unspecified time later:
5. The escape (**Exodus**) of those people from slavery in

---

[1] Abraham is originally called Abram; the god Yahweh changes his name and similarly changes his wife Sarai's name to Sarah. For convenience, I use Abraham and Sarah throughout.

9

Egypt under the leadership of **Moses** and **Aaron** and their 40 years wandering in the Sinai Desert.

6. Their entry into and **Conquest** of the **Promised Land** of Canaan under the leadership of **Joshua**.

7. Their organisation into a **Northern Kingdom (Israel)** and a **Southern Kingdom (Judah)**.

8. The period when the people were ruled by **Judges**.

9. The subsequent period of a **United Kingdom** under kings, notably **Saul, David** and **Solomon**, centred on **Jerusalem** (after its capture by David).

10. Schism back into Israel and Judah again under **Jereboam** and **Rehoboam**, respectively.

11. The conquest and disappearance of the **Ten Tribes of Israel** by **Assyria,** who also subjugate Judah.

12. The conquest and **exile** of the Two **Tribes** of Judah and Benjamin by **Babylon**.

13. The **return** from Exile and the rebuilding of the **New Temple** in **Jerusalem**.

14. The evolution of the Jewish state that became the Roman province of **Judaea,** down to the **1st century** AD when it was finally shattered and scattered by the **Roman Empire**.

To square this story with non-Biblical history requires dates to be assigned to each of these topics. Relying on the narratives themselves for this produces considerable difficulty because, of course, no dates as such are provided, and references to external history are often vague. The most relevant such history is Egyptian, which – because of the length of that civilisation, its relative stability, the propensity of its kings to record their triumphs in stone, and the record keeping of its priesthood – has been retrieved with considerable success by Egyptologists. Although, as we shall see, the picture gets confused at periods and the consensus is not without its challengers.[2] There is one key date that all are agreed upon because it is well attested in independent sources: the Babylonian Exile (No. 12 above), which took place over a number of years, beginning in 597 BC. Unfortunately, the eleven topics before that grow increasingly difficult to date as one moves back in time, and unless you are a Biblical fundamentalist, the dating of the first three topics at least is meaningless.

Nonetheless, through much detective work, educated guesses and generation counting, most Biblical scholars would broadly agree on a 'standard' chronology, based on the clues provided by the Bible itself. This would have Abraham born around the turn of the second millennium BC; the Israelite Sojourn in Egypt from around 1800 BC (or later); the Exodus in about 1450 (or earlier or later); the United Kingdom from about the beginning of the first millennium BC; the schism back to two nations in about 900 BC; the Assyrian conquest of Israel in 722 BC and the Babylonian Exile in 597 BC. But all this is shifting sand. Estimates of the length of the Sojourn are a particular bugbear, ranging from around 400 years (the 'long' Sojourn theory) to about 120 years (the 'short' Sojourn theory) and of course, whichever you plump for has a knock-on effect to the rest of the timeline – particularly the date of the Exodus. The uncertainties around the dates of the Sojourn and the Exodus are crucial. There is, as we shall see, inconvenient evidence in the Bible and elsewhere that calls into question the dates given above. But any other dates create problems with the overall chronology; put simply, the history of the Israelites set out in the Bible requires dates like these or something very like them, or it cannot all be fitted in. The

---

2 One notable such is David Rohl, who has proposed a radical revision to the standard Egyptian chronology. This remains a minority view and I have ignored it here, although I suspect some of my conclusions here may explain some of the anomalies on which Rohl's arguments rest

issue before us is whether any of this can be squared with chronologies established *externally* to the Bible.

I have already alluded to the Egyptian chronology and its weaknesses. The timelines of different scholars for the periods of most relevance to this book can vary by hundreds of years. In this book I shall develop my own chronology of events, but at this stage, to give a benchmark timeline, I give below that of Kenneth Kitchen:

Middle Kingdom	Dynasties 11–12	2106–1786 BC
Second Intermediate Period	Dynasties 13–17	1786–1550 BC
New Kingdom	Dynasties 18–20	1550–1069 BC

Professor Kitchen, born in 1932, is now retired after a long and distinguished academic career based at Liverpool University, in which, most unusually, he has made major contributions to both Biblical and Egyptian studies. He has never been awarded a doctorate (proudly styling himself 'Mr') and is a strong evangelical Christian, both of which perhaps have contributed to a somewhat maverick reputation and a taste for controversy. But he must be respected for his dogged determination to square the Biblical account with other sources: his expertise in the period that concerns us in this book is unparalleled, and one disagrees with him at one's peril. We shall encounter him again in this book.

The period of Abraham, Isaac, Jacob and Joseph as dated above coincides pretty much with the Middle Kingdom in Egypt. On the same basis, the Sojourn would have coincided with the Intermediate Period that followed. The five dynasties of that period (Dynasties 13–17) were not consecutive: they overlap because Egypt had broken into two parts. Upper Egypt in the south remained under Egyptian governance, but Lower Egypt in the north was for long periods ruled by people of Canaanite origin, who are known as the Hyksos. This, of course, begs the question of whether the Israelite Sojourn is connected in some way with those Canaanite rulers. Many think so, although Israelite slaves and Canaanite rulers are very different things.

The big problem is dating the Exodus, assuming that such an event took place. The key evidence from the Bible itself is the following passage from the 1st Book of Kings:

> And it came to pass in the four hundred and eightieth year after the children of Israel were come out of the land of Egypt, in the fourth year of Solomon's reign over Israel, in the month Zif, which is the second month, that he began to build the house of the LORD.[3]

The fourth year of Solomon's reign is usually dated to 966 BC, so 480 years before that would be 1446 BC – hence the standard chronology dating for the Exodus of *c*.1450. This dating falls in the middle of the reign of an Egyptian Pharaoh called Thutmose III, who created the largest overseas empire that Egypt had ever seen, including Canaan, from whence he exacted annual tribute. There is no record in his reign of anything like the Exodus, and he did not die with his army in the Red Sea as related in the Bible, but many are happy to accept the identification nonetheless.

But, if the Hyksos parallel is valid, then the Exodus might be, and is by some scholars presumed to reflect the ejection of the Hyksos from Egypt. This took place around the mid-16th century BC under the first New Kingdom pharaoh, Ahmose I, founder of the 18th Dynasty. But this is a century *earlier* than the 1450 BC date given above. And others would argue for a *later* date. The Israelites are described in the Bible

---

3 1 Kings 6.1.

as being forced as slaves to build the city of 'Raamses'.[4] This is Pi-Ramesses, the new Egyptian capital, built in the Delta by the 19th Dynasty pharoah, Ramesses II ('The Great') sometime in the early to mid-13th century BC. For this reason, some commentators have argued for Ramesses II as the pharaoh of the Exodus. Others have argued for a slightly later date for the Exodus in the *late* 13th century BC. This date was proposed in the 1930s on the basis of archaeological evidence discovered then; we shall turn to the archaeological evidence in the next chapter. It has been championed in more recent times by Kenneth Kitchen, despite the adherence of most other evangelicals to the 1446 BC date. The 1956 film *The Ten Commandments*, which starred Yul Brynner as pharaoh, haunts the imagination of many. This was based on popular novels of the time that identified the Exodus Pharaoh as the founder of the 19th Dynasty, Ramesses I, who reigned from 1292-1290 BC. Some scholars suggest that Pi-Ramesses was begun in the reign of Ramesses I, reinforcing the argument from the Pi-Ramesses evidence. I shall unpack all this over the course of this book, and provide regnal charts to help you get your head around the bewildering lists of pharaohs, kingdoms and dynasties. Here we must simply note the key point that *there is no agreement at all about the date of the Exodus*; the hypotheses range over a 350-year period from the mid-16th century BC to the late 13th century BC. But any date other than *c.*1450 creates problems elsewhere in the chronology. Part of the solution to all this, as we shall see, is to separate secular history from religious history. If the Exodus is regarded not as a major historical event as described in the Bible, but as a major event in the history of religious ideas, chronology is preserved and the circle can be squared.

---

4 Exodus 1:11.

Another way of measuring chronology is to follow the terminology of archaeologists who find their evidence in layers/strata in the ground, datable from pottery styles and sometimes scientific analysis. In this case, the situation is reversed. The periods and dates do not refer to specific people and events: they are invented by archaeologists to categorise their findings, and the problem then is to fit the historical record into the archaeological bands. Those of relevance to this book are as follows:

MIDDLE BRONZE AGE

MBA I	2100–2000 BC
MBA IIA	2000–1750 BC
MBA IIB	1750–1650 BC
MBA IIC	1650–1550 BC

LATE BRONZE AGE

LBA I	1550–1400 BC
LBA IIA	1400–1300 BC
LBA IIB	1300–1200 BC

IRON AGE	1200–

The Israelite Sojourn in Egypt, on the above basis, took place in the Middle to Late Bronze Ages and the Exodus, however you date it, in the Late Bronze Age. Between the Late Bronze Age and the Iron Age, what archaeologists and historians refer to as the Bronze Age Collapse occurred. This was a dark age when, right across the Mediterranean and elsewhere, the hitherto heights of civilisation reached by that time suddenly fell apart in what has been described as a 'perfect storm' of natural and cultural events. Centuries later, the Iron Age then had to rediscover much that was lost during this period. A related issue is the mysterious, so-called Sea Peoples, who emerged from nowhere at the time of the Collapse and were either involved in its causes – or were a result of them. The coincidence of the Exodus, the Collapse at the end of the Bronze Age, and the Sea Peoples will be the subject of this book.

Most fundamentally, the argument of this book concerns the historicity or otherwise of the foundational narrative of the Jews. We are looking for answers to questions such as:

- Where did the stories about Eden, the Flood and Babel originate, and how did they filter into the Jewish narrative?
- Is there any truth at all in the stories of Abraham, Isaac, Jacob and Joseph, and how does that relate to events in Egypt?
- Were the Hyksos the source of the Exodus story? And if so, why the mismatch in essential elements and dates?
- Common sense would suggest that millions of Israelites could not have wandered the Sinai for forty years as the Bible tells the story: what is the source of that myth?
- Did the Conquest of Canaan happen as described?
- When and how did the nation of Israel come into being?
- How and when did the distinctive monotheistic religion of the Israelites originate?
- Were the events of the Exodus and Conquest in any way connected to wider events in the Levant and Egypt – notably, the Sea Peoples and the Bronze Age Collapse? And if so, how?

First let us see what the archaeological record can tell us.

CHAPTER 2

The Archaeological Record

I referred in the Introduction to the Biblical Minimalists, who argue that there is nothing of historical value in the Bible, and conservative Biblical Maximalists, who regard archaeology as having triumphantly vindicated the Biblical narrative. Their polarised debate has dominated the field for the last three decades at least, and their irreconcilable differences can leave the poor layman bewildered and exasperated. If equally respected scholars can take such diametrically opposed positions, what are the rest of us to conclude? Of course, for most of the last two thousand years, everyone (just about) was a Maximalist. The Bible was regarded as infallible as a record of history, and scientific enquiry had to fit itself into that paradigm. But as the Bible came under fire from all directions in the 19th century – from biology, geology, and textual criticism – the great hope became that the emerging field of archaeology would come to the rescue.

Archaeology, as a scientific discipline as opposed to antiquarian conjecture or treasure seeking, only got underway in the early 19th century. Early interest centred on Mesopotamia, Egypt and the Aegean, but by the end of the century it became the turn of the Levant. The hunt was on to find evidence in the ground for the historical claims of the Old Testament.

Unfortunately, the mindset was still driven by the perspective of faith, rather than scientific objectivity. It was reaction against this bias, more than anything else, that culminated in the rise of Minimalism in the 1990s. Niels Peter Lemche and Thomas L. Thompson at the University of Copenhagen led the charge,[1] resulting in the movement being dubbed the Copenhagen School. They argued that the Bible should not be used as an arbiter of archaeological interpretation and were extremely sceptical of its historical validity. Their extremism met with a united counter-charge from archaeologists and biblical historians, who took the opposite extreme and became known as Maximalists. The most prominent Maximalist has been, predictably, Kenneth Kitchen, who has ploughed his own furrow through the mass of conflicting data to arrive at his own evangelical conclusions.

The Minimalists were, of course, right to fight for scientific objectivity, and the Maximalists can be forgiven for their championing of the particular archaeological evidence that was, in fact, supportive of the Biblical account. More balanced scholars in the decades since have, on the whole, taken a more central view. Rather than engage directly in this debate, my aim in this chapter is to review briefly what archaeologists have actually found in the ground, deferring for the moment how that might or might not square with the historical sources available to us. (This chapter is not concerned with *written* sources uncovered by archaeological excavation; from our point of view, *how* these sources were discovered is irrelevant, and their content will be considered alongside other surviving written sources.) Throughout the Levant there are hundreds of mounds known as 'tells' that

---

1 Swiftly followed by the late Philip Davies, sometime Professor Emeritus of Biblical Studies at the University of Sheffield.

are the remains of walled cities where occupation often stretches back millennia. Walled cities facilitate archaeology, because the walls themselves retain the stratified remains of each generation in a compact form that preserves datable pottery, bones, etc., in layers that can be read and codified. Before looking at what has been found in these tells, however, it is vitally important to emphasize that most archaeology can therefore only tell us about cities – a severe shortcoming in a region and at a time when much life was conducted outside such walls.[2]

This is not to say that the cities were not numerous and important and that most recorded history derives from them. But as we shall see, the Israelites in particular did not come from those cities. Their founding fathers were, according to the Bible, more like the Bedouin of today – itinerant or nomadic dwellers in tents who counted their riches in terms of their livestock. Such people leave little if any mark on the landscape for archaeologists to discover. Contemporary sources in Egypt and Mesopotamia are full of references to these peoples, all of which are hard to interpret because, quite literally, they seek to identify moving targets. Historians are faced with conflicting accounts of tribal names and territories, the resolution of which receives little or no support from archaeology. Moreover, between the nomads and the cities, many others lived in unwalled settlements and villages that also leave little trace in the sand. Wherever people lived, their primary allegiance in any case was to the extended family unit, and beyond that to the wider tribe from which their family traced its descent. Bronze Age

---

2 A bit like the old joke about the man on his knees under a lamp post, looking for a lost coin. When asked where he lost it, he replied: 'Over there, but the light is better here.'

tribes were, therefore not defined geographically[3] but gene-alogically, and they were bound together by religious affiliations and mutual protection, rather than by local or national politics. In summary, therefore, this creates an extremely confused and overlapping culture of affiliations that can be very hard indeed to interpret through the written sources – let alone through the dumb evidence of archaeology.

The main techniques of scientific archaeology – the identification of strata with datable remains and careful recording of such – were becoming established by the time archaeologists turned their attention to Palestine. However, as noted above, scientific objectivity was, from the beginning, in short supply and the legitimacy of archaeology in the area has been undermined throughout by the prejudices of the archaeologists themselves about what they would find, based on their preconceived views about the historicity or otherwise of the Biblical narratives. Indeed, the very impetus of these early archaeologists was less objective truth and more their romantic desire to find evidence for ancient myth. In the 1870s, Heinrich Schliemann (1822–1890) set the precedent with his excavations at Troy and Mycenae, in which he was in a tearing hurry to locate Homer's cities; as a result, he carelessly ripped through strata in the search for romantic artefacts and jumped to Homeric conclusions with scant regard for the facts. Similarly in Palestine, the motivation and interpretation were Biblical. The very earliest excavators were sceptics; Biblical criticism and source analysis (of which more later) led them to expect to find little to substantiate

---

3 This may come as a surprise to those familiar with the Biblical account of the twelve tribes of Israel, who each had territory in Canaan allotted to them by Moses: but this was a later Iron Age development and the story is, as we shall see, in any case aetiological.

what they regarded as pure myth. The next generation of scholars, in the first half of the twentieth century, swung the other way – they did begin to find evidence that there might be some truth behind the myths after all. In more modern times, the Copenhagen School has sought to reverse the pendulum again. At the end of the day, the desire to use archaeology to 'prove' Bible narratives, one way or the other, is misguided. The very most archaeology can do is shed some light on the background to the Biblical narratives and, as we shall now see, very occasionally provide specific evidence that places and events found in written sources are historically tenable or otherwise.

One such piece of evidence is the Biblical Flood. One of the early archaeologists working in Mesopotamia, the British excavator Sir Charles Leonard Woolley (1880–1960), believed that he had found 'the Flood' in a ten-foot-deep layer of sediment at the ancient city of Ur in Mesopotamia. He dated this to 4000 BC, which fit nicely into the fundamentalist chronology that many creationists subscribe to – that the Earth is about 6,000 years old. Subsequently, other such deposits have been discovered at other sites in Mesopotamia, although unfortunately for fundamentalists their dates vary over several millennia. The truth is that Mesopotamia, as its name derives, is the area between two great rivers – the Tigris and the Euphrates – which on the one hand made it a perfect homeland for the evolution of agriculture, fixed human settlement and civilization, but on the other, a most unfortunate location for those very settlements, given its propensity for catastrophic flooding. This provides the *background* to the Biblical Flood, and its equivalent Mesopotamian narratives, but it provides no *proof* of a universal Flood destroying all living creatures on the Earth. Woolley's excavations at Ur have, in a similar way, provided background to the

Biblical story of Abraham, whose family according to one of the sources of Genesis, originated in 'Ur of the Chaldees'. We shall explore the Mesopotamian origins of the Israelites later.

Archaeology in Egypt is largely driven by the interests of Egyptologists rather than Biblical studies, but it has nevertheless revealed information useful in understanding the background to the Biblical narrative of the Israelite Sojourn in Egypt and the subsequent Exodus. For example, the Biblical narrative describes the Israelites as slaves in the Nile Delta area, building the cities of Pi-Ramesses and Pithom. Much excavation has been done in the Eastern Delta where both were located, with the result that the site of Pi-Ramesses has been identified with some confidence although Pithom remains uncertain. Their location can help understand some details of the route the Israelites took in the Exodus narrative as they headed east from their Delta homeland, but again, their existence in no way 'proves' that narrative is true. In fact, it has been argued that Pi-Ramesses itself is proof that the Exodus narrative cannot be correct. It was built at the beginning of the 13th century BC, which would rule out earlier (i.e. mid-16th- or mid-15th-century BC) dates for the Exodus. On the other hand, as Kitchen has argued, it could be consistent with a late-13th-century BC date. The Bible narrative itself seems inconsistent: it says that Joseph's family were settled there[4] but also that it was built by Joseph's enslaved descendants.[5] Of course, both passages were written centuries later than either, so the earlier reference may just be a case of the writer referring to an area by the name by which it came to be known. But the issue here is the date of the Exodus, and archaeology offers no evidence either way. Nor

---

4 Genesis 47:11.

5 Exodus 1:11.

can it offer anything in relation to the wanderings of the Israelites in the desert for forty years. No evidence has been found, but then, as we noted above, evidence of nomadic peoples should not be expected in the archaeological record.

It is an interesting thought, nevertheless, that there might be evidence of a *negative* sort. Jewish tradition has it that several million people were involved in the Exodus, and this can be calculated from figures provided in the Biblical account. We are told, in Numbers 1:44, that Moses took a census of the number of able-bodied men involved in the Exodus – a total of 603,550 (a rather precise number). Various calculations can be done using this base figure, producing results anywhere between two and four million men, women and children. This just is not credible without huge suspension of disbelief. The logistics alone of such a mass movement of people and belongings would be a nightmare – even allowing for some supernatural assistance. And as has been observed by many, if there really had been millions of Israelites and their livestock roaming the Negev for a generation of forty years, the human and animal excrement would have been on such a scale that the desert sand would have become fertile soil by the end! Needless to say, desert it remains.

In Palestine itself, archaeology has focused on Jerusalem and 'tells' identified as ancient Canaanite cities. The first great excavator of the latter, and indeed, the 'father' of modern Biblical archaeology, was William Foxwell Albright (1891–1971). At the outset of his career, influenced by modern textual criticism of the Bible, he was a Minimalist in outlook, but over time, he became, in effect, a Maximalist before such terms existed. When modern evangelical Christians naively claim that the Bible is 'proved' by archaeology, it is Albright's work and views that fundamentally influence them. And indeed, Albright's most important contribution to knowledge – his development of a standard pottery typology for the Levant – remains a lasting legacy. But when he departed from strict scientific description into speculation about connections between what he found in the ground and the Biblical account, he strayed into controversy. In particular, during the 1930s he conducted pioneering archaeology at three sites in Palestine: Tell Beit Mirsim, Beitin and Lachish. The first two he misidentified, as is now believed, as Biblical Debir and Bethel; the third is known and recognised. All three have violent destruction layers that Albright dated to around 1200 BC, and on the basis of which he argued for them as evidence of the Conquest, implying a late-13th-century date for the Exodus itself. As noted above, in more recent times Kenneth Kitchen has thrown his weight behind that date. Yet most of those scholars who argue that the Exodus was historical – and also most Christians – reject this in favour of the date suggested by the Bible itself – the mid-15th-century. Can modern archaeology since Albright throw light on this?

The Biblical Book of Joshua is the main source for the narrative of the Conquest but although it purports to tell that story, it is in reality a hotchpotch of ancient tales and other material and only narrates in any detail the conquest of a few, individual Canaanite cities. The Book of Joshua specifically mentions just three cities that were burnt to the ground by Joshua and his invading forces – Ai, Hazor and Jericho. This is potentially important because destruction from burning can be identified and dated reasonably securely in the archaeological record.

Fig. 2 Map of Archaeological Sites in Canaan

In the case of Ai, the Hebrew name simply means the same as the Arabic 'tell', so the story of its conquest may simply be an aetiological explanation for a prominent mound on the landscape. There is such a mound very close to the site of

Bethel, which, as we shall see later, was a hugely important cultic site in the Israelite narrative, and the current Arabic name for it is El Tell. That site has been excavated but shows no sign of occupation after the Early Bronze Age. However, in my view there is no convincing evidence that Ai has yet been identified, so we should look elsewhere for evidence. Another city recorded as having been burnt – Hazor – is more promising. It was first excavated in the 1950s by Yigael Yadin and today it is the largest archaeological site in Israel, sprawling over 200 acres. In the Middle Bronze Age, it was the largest fortified city in Canaan, with tens of thousands of inhabitants. This would fit with the Biblical account that Hazor led a confederation of Canaanites against the incoming Israelites. And the excavations of the city have indeed found a destruction layer consistent with fire, after which the city was no more than a village until it rose again around the time of Solomon, much later in the Iron Age. That layer – a metre deep – has been dated to around 1200 BC. This matches well with Albright's findings of the 1930s elsewhere in Canaan and has been taken by many as the final corroboration of an Exodus and Conquest at that time.

But any celebrations would have been premature: what of the third city to be destroyed by fire, Jericho? Jericho is, of course, more famous than all the others put together; the story of Joshua at the falling walls of Jericho is a beloved Bible story, narrated in great detail in the Bible. The city was first excavated in 1868, but Albright did not excavate there and the first excavation to use modern techniques was not conducted until the 1950s, by Kathleen Kenyon (1906–1978). There has been much more work done since then, including carbon dating, but Kenyon's basic findings emerge pretty unscathed. In essence, the site has been occupied since 10,000 BC – the Stone Age – but reached its pinnacle as a city, like Hazor, in the Middle Bronze Age, by when it had massive walls and other complex fortifications. The Bible story clearly preserves a memory of this. However, it was destroyed in the mid-16th century and remained a small, insignificant settlement throughout subsequent centuries. So, Jericho was destroyed in the 16th century BC and Hazor in the 13th century BC. Each can be used in evidence for one of the hypothesised dates for the Exodus – but with over three centuries between them, they cannot both have been part of a single historical event. And in those two dates lies in stark contrast the problem that faces those who want to believe in the Conquest. Wherever the archaeologists look in Bronze Age Canaan, there is no consistent evidence of a single Conquest as described in the Bible.

Canaan was a land lying between Egypt and the mighty civilizations of Asia and Asia Minor. As the balance of power shifted back and forth, Canaan was the buffer zone, sometimes the unfortunate victim of other peoples' wars, and sometimes a player in its own right; sometimes a vassal state of Egypt, providing protection against incursions from the north and east, and sometimes, as in the time of the Hyksos, taking control itself. So, cities came and went; some were destroyed, never to rise again; some were knocked down and picked themselves up again time after time. If there is a balance of evidence for such upheavals in the late 13th century BC (apart from Jericho), it might be tempting to see them as evidence of an Exodus and Conquest at that time. (Indeed, it might be particularly convenient for me to see it that way because, like Kitchen, I will argue in this book for such a late dating). But therein lies precisely the danger of false logic that drives so many Maximalists. The late 13th century BC and early 12th century is the time of the Bronze Age Collapse. We shall investigate its causes and effects in a later chapter, but if one is looking for the 'cause' of so much destruction in

Canaan at that time, there is absolutely no need to cite a putative Exodus and Conquest as evidence: given the widespread Collapse, it is not at all surprising to see evidence of disruption at that time, without the need to cite a specific Levantine invasion from Egypt.

On this basis, many scholars are agreed that there was no Conquest as described in the Bible; that the descriptions in the Book of Joshua and elsewhere of victories over peoples and cities reflect not a single campaign of occupation, but a millennium of conflicts and destructions, remembered by Iron Age Israelites as myths and legends that were gathered together into coherent narratives in support of a racial foundation myth that had no basis in reality. But the question then remains – who exactly were the Israelites and, if not by Conquest, how did they come to be in Canaan? Common sense suggests that there are just three possibilities. One solution proposed by many is that they were already there: that the Israelites were just Canaanites that grew to distinguish themselves from others by virtue of their distinctive religious beliefs. Or, alternatively, it has been proposed that the Israelites *did* come from Egypt, but it was never a massive, hostile invasion as portrayed in the Bible, but a smaller group that infiltrated Canaan over time and grew to dominance in the region. A third possibility is, of course, a combination of both: that a small group with a distinctive religion spread their message throughout Canaan and, over time, Canaanites came to self-identify as Israelites.

The earliest evidence that we have of an 'Israel' in Canaan is from an Egyptian inscription,[6] of around 1207 BC. We do not know what 'Israel' meant in this context, and we do not know how long it had been in existence before 1207 BC. If the Exodus can be pinned to that period and it was a smaller

---

6 The *Merneptah Stele*, of which, much more later.

scale affair than the Bible suggests, then a connection could be argued, consistent with a limited but hostile invasion of Asiatic refugees from Egypt, either in isolation or in tandem with an introduction of a new religion. But as I said at the beginning of this chapter, archaeology cannot do any more than give us the background. The destruction levels of Jericho and Hazor are no proof of anything. They are certainly consistent with the Minimalist view that the Conquest never happened. But they are also consistent with a more nuanced view that the Biblical account does contain material of historical significance. It may confuse people, places and times, but there are clues to how that can be unpicked if you look for them, and as we turn to look at the Biblical accounts themselves in the next chapter, we will begin to see some of the tools at our disposal to do so.

CHAPTER 3

The Biblical Sources

The Biblical texts in question are mainly what are known as the five books of Moses. These are the first five books of the Old Testament in the Christian Bible, known as the Pentateuch from the Greek for 'five scrolls'. In Judaism, these books are known as Torah, meaning 'to guide/teach'. Their authorship by Moses is attested by references in the Old Testament to a 'book of Moses' or a 'book of the law of Moses'.[1] Many orthodox Jews and fundamentalist Christians, because they believe in Scripture as the inerrant word of God, take this at face value. Virtually all reputable scholars on the other hand reject this as patently absurd. We shall, of course, return to the question of authorship but suffice to say here that, like the rest of the Bible, these texts are the product of many hands and many layers of redaction over very many years.

In Hebrew, these books have different names from those in the Christian Bible, each taken from the first Hebrew word that appears in the book. They are, in order, as follows:

---

1 E.g. Joshua 8:31-32; Ezra 6:18.

GENESIS, or Bereishit (תִּישָׁאֵרְבּ), meaning 'In the beginning': describes the Creation, the Garden of Eden, the Flood, the Tower of Babel, and the lives of Abraham, Isaac/Israel, Jacob and Joseph.

EXODUS, or Shemot (תוֹמְשׁ), meaning 'Names': starts by naming the eleven tribes that went with Jacob into Egypt and then tells the story of the Exodus under Moses.

LEVITICUS, or Vayikra (אָרְקִיַּו), meaning 'And He called': begins with God calling Moses but then deals with matters of ritual and religious law.

NUMBERS, or BaMidbar (רְבִדְמַּב), meaning 'In the wilderness': chronicles the Israelites' journey through the wilderness.

DEUTERONOMY, or Devarim (סיִרָבְד), meaning 'Words': essentially another version of the story told in Numbers, and the laws in Leviticus, with differences and additions.[2]

Whether or not any of the above means anything to you will depend on your religious education. The narrative of these five books was drummed into us at Sunday School and religious instruction classes at school when I was a boy,[3] but I assume they will be far less familiar to the average reader today. In the next few chapters I shall recount that narrative, not as it now appears in the Bible, but as it grew from its constituent parts.

As far back as the seventeenth century, it was becoming apparent to Renaissance minds, now with unfettered access to Scripture in their native tongues as well as in Hebrew and Greek, that the attribution of these texts to Moses was absurd. They were clearly based on very old oral tales, but

---

2 An obvious indication that we are dealing with more than one author here!

3 Over half a century ago. I attended normal state schools, but at that time it was considered acceptable to indoctrinate all children in such fairy tales, alongside science and maths.

who exactly first wrote them down, and when? And as the discipline of textual criticism – applied at first to the classics but then to Scripture itself – flourished from the mid-eighteenth century onwards, Biblical scholars came to recognise the composite nature of the Old Testament. Even for a lay person, the evidence is not hard to find: the texts are littered with repetition,[4] parallel accounts of the same stories, inconsistencies between them, and digressions in all directions, betraying the insertion of new material into existing texts. Moreover, the hand of one or more redactors is often evident from the conjunctive verses that seek to deal with these anomalies. Scholars found less obvious but nonetheless compelling further evidence as they deconstructed the texts: notably, changes in style and vocabulary, particularly on key matters such as the name of God.

At first, two main sources were thus identified, weaving their way in and out of the Pentateuch. One seemed to refer to God as YHVH. This is known as the Tetragrammaton – the ineffable name of the Jewish deity. The ancient Hebrew alphabet only contained consonants, so its pronunciation is uncertain. It used to be rendered in English as 'Jehovah', so the texts that used YHVH were dubbed 'Jehovist', usually shortened to the J Source. Modern scholarship regards 'Yahweh' as the more likely rendering, but J Source it remains (so Jahvist). The other source had a different name entirely for God. It refers to Him as 'El' and so is known as the 'Elohist' now referred to as the E Source. Both Gods – El and Yahweh – were male, patriarchal figures intimately concerned with the doings of their creation and ruling it through direct intervention. Later, it was recognised that the E source itself had elements within it of another source entirely, which seemed obsessed with matters mainly of interest to, and for

---

4 Scholars refer to the same story told twice as a 'doublet'.

the benefit of, priests. This was dubbed the Priestly Source, now known as **P**. And since the Book of Deuteronomy stood out from the other three as having no signs of **J**, **E** or **P**, it was given a source of its own – the Deuteronomist, or **D**. All these texts date from the Iron Age – no scholar would suggest otherwise, no matter how they might disagree on detail. So they all post-date the Bronze Age characters and events they describe by centuries, and the long dark age of the Bronze Age Collapse is a yawning chasm that separates record from reality.

All this was brought together and formalised in the 1870s and 1880s by a brilliant German scholar – Julius Wellhausen (1844–1918); his Documentary Hypothesis remains the basis of scholarly understanding of these texts to this day, a remarkable achievement. Indeed, there was no real challenge to his hypothesis until the end of the twentieth century, when a range of scholars, including notably, Kenneth Kitchen, began to push back. For the last 50 years, controversy has raged about Wellhausen's dating and the detail of his attributions. This has resulted in considerable refinement of the Hypothesis, but in my view Wellhausen's central ideas remain intact. Fundamentalists of both Christian and Jewish persuasion feel threatened by it, and some radical scholars would argue for later and more fragmented sources (and if one looks at their individual arguments in isolation, they can seem plausible). But no other hypothesis fits all the facts anything like as well as some form of Wellhausen's Documentary Hypothesis. In his seminal 1991 book, *The Unauthorised Version*,[5] the distinguished scholar of ancient history Robin Lane Fox opens his Introduction with these words:

My views of the early history of the Hebrew Scriptures have been formed by the insights of J. Wellhausen, more than a

---

5 See Bibliography.

century ago. Modern attempts to depart from their main principles have mostly confirmed me in the widely shared acceptance that Wellhausen was right.

With all due respect to the redoubtable Mr Kitchen, I concur.

THE J[AHWIST] SOURCE

Wellhausen argued that this was the earliest source, dating from the period of Israel's great kings – Saul, David and Solomon; this is usually assigned to around the 10th century BC. More recent scholars have argued for dates that range between the 5th and 9th centuries BC. However, the key characteristic of J, and Wellhausen's original insight about him, remain unaffected: the overwhelming evidence is that the author was a citizen of the southern tribe/nation of Judah, and his interests are wholly focused there. For J, the name of God was Yahweh, and this name was known as such to the Israelites from the very beginning. His God was a personal God – one who could be spoken to and who could be expected to respond; one who could be reasoned with and influenced. He is the God of Creation, so was certainly omnipotent – but whether He was the sole God, or whether He ruled over other Gods is, for the present, a moot point. Unquestionably, He was the God of Judah – one who had chosen the descendants of Abraham to be His special people, and to whom He had made a special prophecy regarding the land of Canaan.

This prophecy represented a pact between Yahweh and Abraham – a promise by Yahweh that if Abraham's people were faithful to Him, He would eventually provide for them a homeland of their own, 'flowing with milk and honey'. We are so used to this promise that we fail to notice how unusual it is. Pacts between peoples and their tribal gods are usually based on an assumption that they already have a homeland: the pact is usually about protecting it and rendering it fruitful. The Israelites did not have a homeland; they were itinerant pastoralists, living as guests in the homelands of other, more settled peoples. As noted above, such pastoralists leave little if any record of their existence. What made the Israelites different in this respect? How did they self-identify and why did their racial story survive? In many cultures (like Egypt, for example), myths of racial and cultural origins are preserved by priests. I shall show that that is the case here – **E**, **P** and **D** all have priestly connections. But, for the moment, we must observe that the other important characteristic to note about **J** specifically is that he is, unlike all the other sources, probably not a member of a priestly grouping; he has little interest in the paraphernalia of ritual, worship and sacrifice. This means that the **J** Source is not only the earliest we have, but it is remarkably free from the priestly biases that can affect the later ones. This last characteristic is of importance in relation to the Exodus narratives, as we shall see.

THE E[LOHIST] SOURCE

Wellhausen argued that **E** was a little later than **J** – a ninth-century text deriving, in contrast with **J**, from the *north* of Canaan: it is concerned with northern tribes, patriarchs and heroes. It also bears some traits that would suggest, unlike **J**, origins in northern *priestly* traditions. The **E** text almost certainly found its way south with refugees after the Assyrian conquest and dismemberment of the northern kingdom, so most modern scholars place it in the 8th or 9th century BC. Wellhausen argued that at some later time a redactor, **RJE**, combined J and E to create a single text. There are two broad, modern challenges to the Wellhausen view about the status of E and its relationship with J. The 'supplementary' hypotheses see J as the fundamental document to which other E sections have been added at different times. The 'fragmentary' hypotheses deny that either J or E were ever coherent documents and argue for a gradual accretion of many individual blocks of material over the centuries. However, whatever view you want to take on these matters, Wellhausen's original insights concerning E's northern origins and use of 'El' to refer to God remain true, and it is useful to refer to J and E as unitary 'sources' whatever view one takes about their ultimate origins and degree of coherence or fragmentation.

When the redactor **RJE** combined the J and E texts he[6] did not seek to reconcile the differing biases of the two sources. He seems to have been content to let them sit side by side. In particular, the rivalry between the north and the south, between Israel and Judah, was intense and runs as a strong current through these narratives.[7] This rivalry can be relatively easily discerned when you separate out the J and E narratives. They each celebrate the patriarchs, heroes and places of their respective regions and, as openly as they dare, denigrate those of the opposite side. What this says about historicity or otherwise of their differing accounts is hard to determine, but where we can discern parochial concerns, we should be on our guard for biased reporting at the very least.

---

6 I shall refer to all the sources and redactors as 'he'. In truth, we cannot be sure what sex they all were, so with apologies to female readers, I shall take the easy route of the masculine pronoun singular. Like the debate over the unitary nature of the different sources, this issue has no implications for the arguments in this book.

7 The rivalry, of course, continued right down to the Christian era, when Roman Judaea in the south looked down its nose at the (in their view) bastardized and degenerate religion of the northern Samaria, as evidenced in Jesus' parable of the Good Samaritan.

THE P[RIESTLY] SOURCE

There is less dissension among scholars about this source: it is quite clearly distinct from the other sources and relatively easy to pick out because of its overriding obsession with matters of interest mainly to priests – matters such as rules, rituals and regalia. Wellhausen argued that it is later than J and E – dating to the sixth century – and although some modern scholars have argued for dates earlier than J and E, the strong consensus as I write still seems to be in Wellhausen's favour. I shall take the view in this book that wherever P provides information missing from J and E, it is a later addition and must be viewed as suspect historically – particularly when that information serves to support the interests of the priestly caste to which P belongs. The obsession with priestly matters is very specifically orientated towards justification of the role of Aaron and his descendants as the only priests allowed to perform key rituals – a distinction within the wider priestly ranks that is presented by P as instituted at the very beginning by Moses, but in reality emerged much later.[8]

THE D[EUTERONOMIST] SOURCE

This source is also more clear-cut than J and E, and scholars are largely agreed that it dates to the sixth or seventh century – and, critically, it post-dates the destruction of the northern tribes. It bridges between the Pentateuch and the subsequent narratives contained in the Books of Joshua, Judges, Samuel and Kings, all of which betray the hallmark

---

8 We shall describe Moses and Aaron in later chapters. In the traditional story, Moses led the Exodus but died before the Conquest, which was then led by his successor, Joshua.

of **D**, and which relate events leading up to the northern disaster in terms that emphasize God's Covenant with His chosen people, and their continual breaching of that Covenant as the reason for the disasters that overtake them. The Book of Deuteronomy is thus both the last book of the Pentateuch and the first book of what is known as the Deuteronomic History. **D** was almost certainly a Levite and therefore a member of the priestly caste. But he makes no mention at all of Aaron or the Aaronide privileges championed by **P**. Just as **J** and **E** are characterised by the antagonism between north and south, **P** and **D** are characterised by the antagonism between two competing priestly groups associated with those rival territories. For **E** and **D**, all Levites – members of the tribe of Levi – are hereditary priests, entitled to officiate at rites carried out in the various cult sites scattered across Canaan. Moses was a Levite, and their priesthood was named 'Mushite' after him. But for **J** and **P**, only the Levite descendants of Aaron were true priests, and other Levites were only allowed a minor, supporting role. The narratives of the four sources are often distinguishable as much by this intense rivalry as by the north/south divide. Aaronide texts take the minor character of Aaron and build up his role and authority, while the other camp play him down and focus on Moses as the main hero.

The fact that there is so much scholarly disagreement about the detail of Wellhausen's original hypothesis, and that arguably no new consensus can yet be discerned as arising from all the challenges to it, presents a methodological problem for this book. I have neither the expertise nor the presumption definitively to resolve all the issues, although I of course have my own views. In any case, the purpose of this book is not to propound a new hypothesis: it is to propound a new historical understanding of these narratives, based on the insights that all the foregoing textual analysis makes possible. Right now, I think the focus needs to shift from the minutiae of the model, or from arguments over dating, and take a broader view about what it all *means*. In this context, I do not think that dating the various sources is particularly critical to the arguments that I want to present in this book. The key point I need to emphasize here about dating is that *none of the sources are contemporary with the people and events they describe*. To emphasize the point: the earliest date attributed to any of the sources is the tenth century BC, two centuries after the destruction of Hazor and five hundred years after the Hyksos left Egypt. And in the period between the Exodus, whatever date you assign to it, and the earliest of these sources was the Bronze Age Collapse, when upheavals across the Mediterranean generally, and the Levant in particular, meant that virtually all records were lost.

However, for the purposes of this book I do need to work from a convenient and coherent source model. I have, therefore, chosen to follow the synthesis of the American Biblical scholar Richard Elliott Friedman (1946–) who, through a series of books published in the last couple of decades,[9] has established a foremost reputation in the field. Friedman broadly agrees with Wellhausen on J and E, but differs from his JEDP model by arguing that D dates to the late seventh century BC, and P to the early seventh century BC, thus reversing P and D to produce a JEPD model. Friedman has his critics, but most, if not all, are agreed that his overall approach represents a coherent, central view.

In the chapters that follow, I shall deal with each source according to Friedman's published deconstruction, and making considerable use of his insights, for which I am deeply indebted. It is Friedman's contention that when

---

9 See Select Bibliography

extracted and consolidated, each source does in fact constitute a coherent narrative that stands up in its own right; that the coherence we can still see is evidence that these were actual, discrete and whole texts as envisaged by Wellhausen. I think he is right, as hopefully the following chapters will demonstrate. Of course, at the end of the day it is impossible to say whether those coherent source narratives represent an original document in its entirety – the appearance of coherence may be a coincidence and redactors might have removed duplicate material to create a new coherence. But as we shall see, duplication of material occurs throughout the Pentateuch, so does not seem to have concerned the redactors overmuch; perhaps we can take absence of material in one source compared to another at the very least as an indication that something is worth careful attention. I shall, therefore, treat each source as if it is a continuous, coherent narrative with nothing missing. Where this issue matters, I shall allude to it, but, in general, it will be convenient to tell each source's story as if there are no missing pieces.

What I am trying to unearth by this process is what narratives we can (and cannot) accept as, in some sense, a record of historical events. Written history always betrays the viewpoint of the writer to some degree. Modern historians strive in the main to achieve as much objectivity as their unconscious assumptions will allow, but the writers of these texts had very different concerns. The 'truth' they sought to convey was religious in nature and could be found as readily in myth and symbolism as in actual historical events. What did it matter to them whether Abraham 'actually' killed his own son Isaac – a possibility that we shall consider; the story illustrates an eternal 'truth' about God and obedience, whatever the factual reality. This disparity of intention between modern historical method and ancient religious writers of purportedly historical texts bedevils attempts to interpret the

New as well as the Old Testament, as I shall show in the second and third volumes of this trilogy. There I shall demonstrate that the narrative of the life of Jesus was compiled from Old Testament stories originally applied to other persons and contexts entirely. Here, the problem is different. There are no older texts to compare – just the existing texts, compiled by unknown redactors.[10] But there are clues, nonetheless, and I would suggest that the following rationalist criteria can indicate the *possibility* of historicity or otherwise:

1. **If a narrative has clear evidence of authorial intention other than objective history.** We need to listen out for the sound of axes grinding. The four sources outlined above constantly betray their geographical and ideological prejudices and these not only distort their narratives but, in many cases, are the reason why those narratives exist. More generally, it is clearly a central concern of Genesis to provide genealogical 'evidence' to support the assertion that the tribes of Israel and Canaan were descended from Adam, via different patriarchs (Shem and Ham): that the Israelites were a holy, separate nation from the outset, not to be confused in any way with the Canaanite tribes among whom they dwelt, or the Arab and Gentile nations surrounding them.

2. **If a narrative depends entirely upon divine intervention in history.** This is, of course, as I declared in the Introduction, my own prejudice. The attribution of events to the gods is irrational and often obscures other reasons for a narrative's existence. I am also prejudiced against modern day 'scientific' explanations for recorded

---

10 The final redaction is in fact the first such attempt at writing a continuous historical narrative to have survived from ancient times.

miracles, as, for example, red algae being responsible for the Nile turning to blood, or an earthquake causing the Red Sea to part. These almost always do not match up with the detail of the miracle as described and distract from an understanding of what is really going on in the text.

3. **If a narrative only appears in one of the four sources.** The corollary of this is that if all sources are agreed, then we should pay close attention because there must be a reason why the narrative concerned is so widespread and compelling.

4. **If a narrative appears to have an aetiological function.** That is, its raison d'être would appear to be to provide a 'folk' explanation of the subject of the narrative. This is often the real reason for stories that are presented as miracles and, indeed, provides explanation for much of the Books of Moses. Many stories seem to be told purely to provide explanations, usually of dubious etymological value, of geographical places and features surviving at the time the Pentateuch was redacted.

5. **If there is more than one version of the same story.** But that story is applied to different people, places or times. We shall come across this time and again – in the creation accounts, in stories about wives being taken for sisters, in stories of infertility and of brothers who usurp their sibling's inheritance or birthright. Genesis in particular is riddled with such, betraying its composite nature and probable confusion of ancient stories overlapping with each other.

6. **If one version of a story differs substantively from another.** For example, we shall see that there are no less than four versions of the miracle of the parting of the Red Sea, and only one of them – the latest – describes anything like the miracle of popular imagination.

7. **If a story is obviously physically impossible or conflicts with a certain fact proved elsewhere.** Did the patriarchs really live to 100 years and beyond, and can we really base chronology on them? Did millions of Israelites wander in the desert for forty years and leave no trace?

8. **If a story contains obvious digression from the main narrative.** In Genesis, the stories of Lot and Joseph stick out like a sore thumb. The former is a seemingly unnecessary digression from the main genealogical story, and the latter is a genealogical irrelevance.

9. **Claims to knowledge of past people or events that seem impossible.** For example, the Creation, by definition, could not have been witnessed by Moses or any other human being. Indeed, any knowledge of people or events predating the Flood would surely not have survived that questionable worldwide catastrophe.

10. **Claims to knowledge of future events.** It is a central concern of the Books of Moses to foreshadow the future greatness of the nation of Israel, under the aegis of a favourable God's Promise, handed down the generations. When God tells Abraham that his descendants will be held captive in Egypt for a specific period of time, is it not more likely that a later writer has inserted his own chronological beliefs into the narrative? The 20/20 vision of hindsight is the most likely

explanation of apparent prophecy, as I shall demonstrate comprehensively in Volume 3 of this trilogy.

None of these criteria alone constitute certainty about the historicity of a narrative, and even if a narrative survives all these criteria that would still not constitute proof of anything. But that is the realm of knowledge in which we are finding our way in this book. Even modern science hesitates to accept anything as proven for certain – we still talk about the theories of evolution or relativity, not because scientists don't use those theories every day to explain the phenomena they observe, but because they remain open to the possibility that something better might come along. I leave to the reader to judge for themselves the likely validity of the conclusions I reach, and I offer them not as proven facts, but as a plausible contribution to the ongoing historical project.

CHAPTER 4

Origins

Genesis, as we have it in the Bible, falls naturally into two parts. The first part, and the subject of this chapter, tells the primeval story of the Creation of the world and of mankind, and the destruction of that Creation by the Flood. The second part, from Chapter 12 onwards, is the ancestral 'history' of the Israelites. However, the first part sets out some basic themes that are then developed in the second part, and those themes are the *raison d'être* of Genesis. They have nothing to do with history but everything to do with establishing the racial *bona fides* of the Jewish nation. The main line of argument runs through an ancient genealogy that descends from Adam, through Noah, and then from Abraham through Jacob. A lot of space is given to stories about Lot, Ishmael, Isaac and Joseph, none of whom play an important role in the main genealogy. Identifying why those stories are incorporated into the main Genesis narrative will tell us much about the interests of the different sources of the text, but it will also provide some important clues to the real history behind the narrative of the Books of Moses.

The early chapters of Genesis, dealing with the Creation, Eden, and the Flood are (apart from Chapter 1) all from

J, for whom Yahweh is a universal deity: they are about the origins of all mankind, not the Israelites, who do not feature until Yahweh singles out Abraham and his descendants for special favour. J's narrative starts at Genesis 2:4:

> These are the generations of the heavens and of the earth when they were created, in the day that the Lord God made the earth and the heavens.[1]

Note the phrase 'Lord God'. In the original Hebrew this is 'YHWH God'. 'Lord' is how the King James Version translates the Tetragrammaton.[2] This is the key discriminator for identifying J texts; various names are used for God in other texts, but for J this is the sole name of God, revealed by Him to His Creation from the very beginning. Most modern English translations, like the King James Version, obscure the issue of the different names of God in the Bible, but understanding the distinctions and why they arise is key to locating the real history underlying these texts. Yahweh in J is portrayed anthropomorphically: He walks in His Garden of Eden; He likes the smell of burnt offerings; He regrets things and changes His mind; He is influenced by His emotions of

---

1 Throughout this trilogy, all Biblical quotation will be from the King James Authorised Version. It is the preferred version of many evangelical Christians and I do not wish my arguments to founder on accusations of translation bias. But the truth is, I personally prefer it. Its language, along with Shakespeare's, weaves its way throughout the great literature of the English-speaking peoples, and just as I prefer to read Shakespeare as he wrote it, so I prefer the Bible as it was read by the great writers of English prose and poetry right down to modern times. Its translation, is of course, affected by the beliefs of its translators – but so too are more modern translations!

2 Some redactor has added the word 'God' after 'Yahweh' because, as we shall see, P is also a source for these early chapters and P always calls God 'El', and the double name helps to blur the distinction.

love, anger and jealousy; and He chats and interacts with Adam and Eve and their descendants more like a Greek god than the omnipotent, omniscient and omnipresent God of modern Christian and Jewish imagination.

There is no mention at all in J of a six-day creation and a day of rest – just 'the day' of Creation. In the space of a few verses, Yahweh creates everything, waters it all like a good gardener and then creates (unnamed) Man from dust and plants him in the Garden of Eden. We know now, of course, that humankind originated in Africa and migrated north into the rest of the world. J locates mankind's origins in 'Eden' and a great deal of paper and ink has been wasted over the years trying to identify its location. For those so inclined, a clue is in the names of the four rivers that J says[3] flow out of Eden from a single source. Two of them are easy – the Tigris[4] and the Euphrates, the twin rivers that frame the land of Mesopotamia, where we now know that agriculture probably originated. The other two – the Gihon and the Pishon – are more problematical. The Gihon is, in my view, probably the Nile and, also in my view, the Pishon is probably the Jordan: but there are dozens of other identifications that scholars have made over the years. None of them make any modern geographical sense: a glance at any atlas will discover that even the Tigris and Euphrates do not have a single source,[5] whatever the identity of the other two. But geography is not the point here. Eden is not a real place. It is a paradise, paralleling others such, as in the ancient literature of the Mediterranean and Middle East. And the single source

---

3 Genesis 2: 10-14.

4 In Hebrew, 'Hiddekel', from the original Sumerian word for 'running water'.

5 Their sources are 50 miles apart in eastern Turkey.

is like the mythical 'Great River' known as Oceanus that the classical world of Greece and Egypt wrongly believed circled the lands of the Mediterranean and connected all the major rivers they knew.

According to J, when Adam and Eve, the first humans, are expelled from Eden, re-entry is barred by an angel with a fiery sword. We may as well seek that angel on Earth as Eden itself. Its location is unknowable and to seek it misses the point. We are dealing with myths about early human settlement rather than ultimate origins. What we should notice here, however, is the likely Mesopotamian origin of this narrative: why would an Israelite writer, concerned with Israelite history, place his creation story in the Tigris/Euphrates area unless his sources ultimately derived from that area? The first eleven chapters of Genesis, before we are introduced to Abraham (who himself comes from Mesopotamia) in Chapter 12, are saturated in Mesopotamian myths, recovered by archaeologists from surviving tablets originating in the great Asian Bronze Age civilizations. There are two such myths we should note in passing. The first is the *Enuma Elish*, the creation myth of Babylon: its accounts of the creation of the Heavens and the Earth and the creation of man, have many parallels with Genesis. It is also true that there are differences, and the precise relationship between the two is a matter of scholarly debate, but the basic parallels are undeniable. Much the same is true of the second Mesopotamian myth: the *Atra-Hasis*. This contains both a creation account and a Flood myth, which was then the basis for the later Flood story told in the Babylonian Epic of Gilgamesh that provides close parallels to both the Flood itself and to the story of Noah and his Ark.

Fig. 3: Map of Mesopotamia and Eastern Mediterranean

We need not be concerned here with the detail. The point is that all the 'origins' stories in Genesis 2–11 – Creation, Eden, Adam and the Flood – can be found also in Mesopotamian narratives that predate Genesis. We are then told, in Genesis Chapter 12, that Abraham, the founder of the Israelite people, originated in Ur of the Chaldees in Mesopotamia. Genesis is very clear that the Israelites were not originally from Canaan, and their relationship with the aboriginal occupants of the Levant was thus problematical from the start. For me at least, it takes some very special pleading indeed to ignore the obvious: that the people who became the Israelites came to Egypt, and ultimately Canaan, from Mesopotamia and brought these stories with them. As their own racial myths and distinctive religious beliefs developed, those stories were adapted to fit – hence the differences that arose – but the common origin seems inescapable. The question that then arises is what Mesopotamian people/tribe/

nation did Abraham come from? The answer will become clear as we continue with the Genesis account.

Adam and Eve upset God and are ejected from Eden to fend for themselves. They then have two children, Cain and Abel. Cain grows up to be a 'tiller of the ground' and Abel a shepherd[6] – clearly therefore symbolic of settled farmers and pastoralists respectively. Cain murders his brother for reasons not clearly stated and goes off into the world to found a dynasty of his own. The story is told for a purpose. When Abraham later enters the story, he, like Abel, is a pastoralist – he measures his wealth by the size of his flocks. The same is true of his early descendants, and his racial origins are with nomadic herdsmen. These people live their lives moving around between settlements – villages, towns and cities – where the inhabitants are settled farmers. Abel the shepherd is thus the 'goody' and Cain the farmer is the 'baddy'. The early Israelites aligned themselves with the former and often found themselves in conflict with the latter, who not unreasonably could feel threatened by nomadic outsiders. The story of Cain and Abel is told by J; the redactor **RJE** then inserts a passage about a third son – Seth – and his many offspring, followed by the last words of Chapter 4:

. . . then began men to call upon the name of the Lord.

This should, of course, be translated as 'the name of Yahweh' and is an explicit statement that for **J**, God's name was Yahweh from the beginning. There follows a long passage, known as 'The Book of Names', of unknown authorship, in which the nine generations between Adam and Noah are detailed.[7]

---

6 Genesis 4:2.

7 Genesis 5.

Next comes the Mesopotamian story of Noah and the Flood. Noah's ancestry is a contradiction. He is the son of Lamech, but the latter is described by J as being descended from Cain,[8] and in 'The Book of Names' he is listed as descending from Seth.[9] The redactor inserted the reference to the birth of Seth to connect the two, but the incompatibilities remain. In the time of Noah, it seems wickedness has abounded in the world, and Yahweh decides to destroy all life – not just sinful men and animals but fallen angelic beings too – by the Flood. The only exception is Noah, who 'found grace' in His eyes.[10] J as we have it provides no more explanation than this. Yahweh tells Noah to build an 'Ark' for his family and mating pairs of all animals. In addition, he is to take extra pairs of 'clean' animals because he will need these for sacrifice when the Flood is over. Then the rains come and the resulting flood lasts forty days and, as promised, wipes out all animal life.[11] Noah lands the Ark and makes sacrifice with some of the 'pure' animals and Yahweh is so pleased with the 'sweet savour' that He promises never to do it again.

The story then swiftly moves on to the next generation and, in the first of many such parallels, Noah, like Adam, also has three sons – Shem, Ham and Japheth. J says that these three sons are then the fathers of all the nations of the Earth.[12] All of these patriarchs live to a great age – over a hundred – presumably reflecting the purity of these early ages of man. Lifespans decrease over succeeding generations

---

8 Cain – Enoch – Irad – Mehujael – Methusael – Lamech (Genesis 4:17–18).

9 Seth – Enos – Cainan – Mahalaleel – Jared – Enoch – Methuselah – Lamech – Noah (Genesis 5:3–29).

10 Genesis 6:8.

11 A recurrent number in these texts, as we shall see.

12 Genesis 9:19.

as sin spreads and pollutes the world. Shem's descendants are the 'S[h]emites' named after him; in Jewish tradition, they eventually become the Jews and other Semitic peoples. Ham's son is Canaan, and their descendants are the Hamites; tradition ascribed to them the aboriginal peoples of Canaan, Africa and Arabia. This distinction is central to the Genesis narrative. Historically, the definition of a Semite is someone who speaks a version of a group of languages linguists refer to (after the Biblical account) as Semitic. Genesis wants us to understand that the Semitic Israelites were entirely distinct from the Hamitic Canaanites: the former are destined to eject the latter from Canaan. But as we have seen, there is no evidence for a Conquest from the archaeological record. In reality, Canaan was a melting pot of Asian and Semitic peoples speaking a variety of languages – Semitic and non-Semitic. The story of Shem and Ham is told not as history but as a mythical justification for a distinction that is central to Israelite/ Jewish self-identity, and it probably has no basis at all in historical reality.

J does not specifically mention Japheth's descendants, pre- sumably because his sole interest is in telling the story of the future struggle between the S[h]emite and the Hamite tribes for possession of Canaan. The Japhethites were regarded as basically everyone else in the Gentile world, so beyond the concerns of the writer, and indeed of the Bible, until we get to the New Testament, when the Apostle Paul widens God's affections to embrace Gentiles. The descendants of Shem and Ham are next listed, and it is clear that the names represent the patriarchs of all the nations of the Earth known to the writer at the time. Precise identifications are sometimes dis- puted but what is important here is the principle – that these are the people that gradually repopulated the planet after the Flood. In order to stop them all getting too big for their boots, Yahweh makes sure that they all speak different languages in the aetiological Tower of Babel incident.[13] Many of the stories told in the Books of Moses are there for aetiological reasons – they are *post hoc* explanations, based on oral traditions and folk tales, of the names of people places, and tribes. Rabbis and reverends have and do extract moral and religious lessons from the tale of Babel, but its aetiological purpose is to explain the multiplicity of languages. It too has its roots in Mesopotamia; probably inspired by Etemenanki, the ziggurat dedicated to the god Marduk in Babylon (hence 'Babel'), it is paralleled like the Flood story in similar myths from Sumer and Assyria.

Turning now to the other component of the early chapters of Genesis, the P[riestly] Source, which is so named because virtually all its concerns centre around the importance of priests and priestly matters: ritual worship; the origin of rituals and the shrines in which they are performed; and most important of all, exactly who can be a priest – Aaronide or Mushite; and the hierarchy of priests. This is immediately apparent in Chapter 1 of Genesis, which is entirely the work of **P**. It starts with the creation of the world and the cosmos by God 'in the beginning' when 'the earth was without form and void'.[14] The creation account here is based on a cosmology that we know to be nonsense:

> And God said, Let there be a firmament in the midst of the waters, and let it divide the waters from the waters. And God made the firmament, and divided the waters which were under the firmament from the waters which were above the firmament: and it was so.[15]

---

13 Genesis 11:1-9 – if you want/need to read the story.

14 Genesis 1:1-2.

15 Genesis 1:6-7.

As with **J**, that cosmology is unmistakeably Mesopotamian. The same parallels with Mesopotamian myth can be identified, but it is hardly necessary: Mesopotamian civilization is based on and defined by the great rivers Tigris and Euphrates. In similar fashion, **P** sees creation as essentially involving division of primeval waters by land. The sky is blue because it is a sort of membrane layer ('firmament') holding water above it. This is the source of all the water that creates Noah's Flood. I suspect it is also the source of the river that flows out of Eden that **J** believes feeds the four rivers of Eden. **P** describes how God made everything in six days and ceased on the seventh. Included in this is the creation of all living creatures on the fifth and sixth days, and, at last, humanity:

> And God said, Let us make man in our image, after our likeness: and let them have dominion over the fish of the sea, and over the fowl of the air, and over the cattle, and over all the earth, and over every creeping thing that creepeth upon the earth. So God created man in his own image, in the image of God created he him; male and female created he them.[16]

But as we saw, **J** tells a totally different story: in **J**, after God has rested he waters his creation and only then, we are told, does he create man from dust. He puts him into the garden of Eden, and then realizes that man will be lonely on his own, so he sets about creating – not a woman – but:

> . . . every beast of the field, and every fowl of the air; and brought *them* unto Adam[17] . . . but for Adam there was not found an help meet for him. And the LORD God caused a

---

16 Genesis 1:26-7.

17 The first mention of his name.

deep sleep to fall upon Adam, and he slept: and he took one
of his ribs, and closed up the flesh instead thereof; And the
rib, which the LORD God had taken from man, made he a
woman, and brought her unto the man. And Adam said, This
is now bone of my bones, and flesh of my flesh: she shall be
called Woman, because she was taken out of Man.[18]

The two stories of **J** and **P** differ in all major respects about
how, and in what order, God created animal and human life.
They have been jammed together by the redactor, who presumably wanted to preserve both. We are so familiar with all
of this we forget the most fundamental thing of all about **P**'s
particular vision of Creation – its division into days of the
week and its emphasis on the importance of the seventh day
– the Sabbath. This is what matters to **P** because, of course,
observance of the Sabbath underpins the role of priests in
Israelite life.

After this chunk of narrative at the very start of Genesis,
the use of **P** thereafter in that book is sporadic and episodic,
to the extent that one of the main attacks on the Documentary Hypothesis has come from those who argue that **P** was
never a single, coherent narrative, but more an editorial
expansion of **RJE** by a later priestly redactor. The first of
these contributions, either from the **P** Source or by a priestly
redactor (depending on your point of view), are parts of the
story of Noah and the Flood, leading to the Covenant that
God makes with Noah that, provided mankind follows a few
simple rules of righteous behaviour, God will never again
destroy animal life. That Covenant, and more particularly,
those rules, are what priests exist to police on behalf of God.
Next, **P** provides about half of the genealogies of Shem, Ham
and Japheth – the rest coming from **J**. Genealogies were also

---

18 Genesis 2:19-23.

important to priests because they reflect on the purity of the race, and ritual purity is a central concern of **P**.

We have skated very swiftly over these early chapters of Genesis because, up until this point at least, it would be very hard to discern anything remotely 'historical' in the stories of J and P, and assigning any sort of dates to them is pointless. Judeo-Christian fundamentalists may choose to believe in Adam and Eve, the Garden of Eden, the Tower of Babel and the Flood, but without the viewpoint of faith, the rational view must be that these are ancient myths that represent a primitive explanation for creation, suffering and the proliferation of separate nations in the ancient world, rather than historical people or events. We can identify parallel myths in other ancient peoples, some of which must have influenced or been a source for the Biblical narrative, but this is a very long way from saying that Genesis is somehow 'proved' by their existence. However, as the Genesis narrative now moves into the 'brave new world' after the Flood, we might perhaps begin to hope that traces of real history will show themselves. And, furthermore, as the narrative now focuses on Abraham, it becomes important to make the attempt, because it is the 'Promise' that God makes to Abraham and to his descendants that underlies the central story of Judaism itself.

CHAPTER 5

Abraham

The redacted narrative of the Israelites as we now have it combines elements from **J**, **E** and **P**. It will be recalled that **J** was the only source not to derive from some sort of priestly background. So, in the **J** Source, Abraham suddenly appears in the narrative after the story of the Tower of Babel, with no introduction or genealogical back story as would have been expected from a priestly writer. In the final redaction of the narrative, the genealogy is supplied by an unknown source who traces the descent from Shem down to Abraham's father, Terah.[1] The priestly **P** provides more details of Abraham's ancestry. He lived in 'Ur of the Chaldees'[2] with his father Terah and their extended family (See Fig. 3, p. 49). We know where this was – on the Euphrates River in Mesopotamia near the Persian Gulf.[3] We are told that Terah decided to take his family westwards into Canaan. The well-trodden caravan trade route from Ur to Canaan, following the contours of the land and available fresh water supplies, did not

---

1 Shem – Arphaxad – Salah – Eber – Peleg – Reu – Serug – Nahor – Terah – Abraham.

2 Genesis 11:31.

3 Its location was discovered by the archaeologist Leonard Woolley in the 1930s at Tell el Mukkayer.

go directly from east to west, but diverted north-west first to Haran, before descending south through Canaan. Haran – now modern Harran – means 'crossroads' and it was an important city that stood at a junction where the ancient east–west trade route coming from India and China via Mesopotamia met the north–south route that went down the coast of Canaan into Egypt and up into Asia Minor and beyond. This seems further evidence that we are touching something really historical here. The migration of Terah and his family accords not only with the Israelite racial tradition that they originated in Mesopotamia, but it makes historical sense as well. We are told by **P** that Terah 'dwelt' in Haran for a while.

J, however, seems to know none of this; he starts immediately with Abraham in Haran and with his calling and Promise from Yahweh:

> Get thee out of thy country, and from thy kindred, and from thy father's house, unto a land that I will shew thee: And I will make of thee a great nation, and I will bless thee, and make thy name great; and thou shalt be a blessing: And I will bless them that bless thee, and curse him that curseth thee: and in thee shall all families of the earth be blessed.[4]

In obedience, Abraham travels to the Promised Land of Canaan, and arrives at 'the place of Sichem, unto the plain of Moreh'.

---

4 Genesis 12:1-3.

Fig. 4: The Travels of Abraham in Canaan

'Sichem' is Shechem – an old Canaanite city sited on the main trade route running north from Jerusalem. The 'plain of Moreh' is better translated as the '[oak] tree of Moreh' and was a cultic shrine to the Canaanite god, El. There were other pagan gods recognized in Canaan, representing different elements of nature, but El was the head of the Canaanite pantheon. He was worshipped in tree groves like Moreh, referred to as the 'High Places'. The significance of this location is important. Shechem was to become the capital city of the northern kingdom of Israel, located in the territory of the tribe of Ephraim. But the southern J Source cannot leave his hero in the north, so he has Abraham leave Shechem and journey south to Bethel, another important cultic centre on the border between the northern and southern tribes of later times. The name Bethel means 'House of El': J may have worshipped Yahweh, but his Canaanite sources betray an earlier divine name.

We now learn from J that a famine in Canaan drives Abraham further south and west into Egypt. Much of Genesis from this point on takes place in Egypt. And famine also plays a recurring role. So, long before the stories of Joseph, Moses and the Exodus from Egypt, that country winds its way in and out of the Genesis narrative, and the relationship of the Israelites with Egypt dates right back to the founding patriarch. Traffic between Canaan and Egypt was an every-day occurrence in the first and second millennia BC. Indeed, so important was that trade route that Egypt regarded it as a national strategic imperative for much of that period to control Canaan as a buffer area between its own civilization and those to its east and north: armies could travel the route into Egypt as easily as traders and goods. The way Egypt protected its borders varied over time. In the African area south of Egypt, the border was secured through direct Egyptian rule exercised by a formal viceroy. In Canaan, it was less formally exercised through client local rulers who were kept in line by occasional military excursions as need arose. In addition to normal trade, famine was often the incentive for southwards migration: famine was not unknown in Egypt but the civilization there was founded on the annual inundation of the soil by the Nile, which was more regular and largely dependable than the climate in Canaan.

Abraham is accompanied south into Egypt by his wife Sarah and family, among whom his nephew Lot is singled out for special mention, for reasons we shall see presently. Abraham amasses considerable wealth in Egypt. As the J narrative runs, this derives from Pharaoh (unnamed) who, believing Sarah to be Abraham's sister, wants her as a concubine and pays Abraham handsomely for the privilege. When the truth emerges, he sends Abraham, Sarah and Lot packing and an enriched Abraham travels back out of Egypt again, back to Bethel. As we shall see, this story of mistaken identity is repeated about different patriarchs at different times and is part of an obsession within the Pentateuch about familial relationships and birth rights. Lot now separates from Abraham, apparently because, as potential patriarchs, they each need a land of their own. Lot 'chose him all the plain of Jordan' to the east of Bethel; we shall see exactly where this is in a moment. By contrast, Abraham travels to 'the plain of Mamre, which is in Hebron', where he builds another altar to Yahweh and yet again receives Yahweh's Promise that his seed will be countless and will occupy Canaan. Mamre was another important cultic shrine to El, based around 'great trees',[5] and Hebron was to become the capital city of the southern tribe of Judah. So, by the end of Chapter 13, Abraham has turned his back on the northern kingdom and has travelled with Yahweh's blessing to settle in the heart of the southern kingdom – the home of J. From J's point of view, that is a neat outcome.

A passage of uncertain origin gives a little more detail about Yahweh's Promise that one day Abraham's descendants will occupy Canaan:

> And he said unto Abraham, Know of a surety that thy seed shall be a stranger in a land *that is* not theirs, and shall serve them; and they shall afflict them four hundred years; And also that nation, whom they shall serve, will I judge: and

---

5 Genesis 13:18.

afterward shall they come out with great substance. And thou shalt go to thy fathers in peace; thou shalt be buried in a good old age. But in the fourth generation they shall come hither again: for the iniquity of the Amorites is not yet full.[6]

The prophecy, of course, concerns the Israelites' future Sojourn as slaves in Egypt. It is, however, ambiguous. On the one hand, the prophecy seems to be that the Sojourn will last for around 400 years – a figure that Jewish and Christian fundamentalists like to take at face value. However, the prophecy also says that the Israelites will inherit God's Promise of Canaan 'in the fourth generation'. Fundamentalists will point to the long lives attributed to these patriarchs, so four generations might indeed equate to 400 years. This is known as the 'long Sojourn' theory. Alternatively, the four generations could be taken as support for a 'short Sojourn' theory: four normal generations would equate to about 120 years. In fact, the second half of this passage is almost certainly an insertion by a late redactor, so the conflict arises from two narratives by two different authors being shoehorned together. The reference to the Amorites is key to what this is all about: the redactor is pain-fully aware of the need to explain the long delay between the Promise and its fulfilment and blames it on the 'iniquity of the Amorites'. In this context, Amorites are synonymous with Canaanites generally, although we shall see later that things were not that simple. The idea that God delays punishment to allow sin to run its course is found elsewhere in the Bible – it is a useful explanation for delays in God's judgement on the oppressors of the Israelites/Jews. It is difficult to use the length of the Sojourn – long or short – to date anything in these nar-ratives, because of course we have no idea of the date of the Exodus, or of the original arrival in Egypt.

---

6 Genesis 15:13-16.

We now get to the heart of the Abraham story: Abraham is getting old and his wife Sarah seems to be barren. How then is the Promise to be fulfilled if Abraham is to have no descendants? The name Sarah comes from the same Hebrew consonantal root as 'Isra' in Israel. It means to fight or contend with someone. Presumably this is an aetiological explanation for the story that follows, in which she fights with Yahweh over her apparent inability to have children. As J tells the story, she comes up with her own solution: she tells Abraham to have sex with Hagar, her Egyptian handmaid, and Abraham willingly obliges. Unfortunately, but predictably, Hagar gets uppity about her new station in life as a concubine, and as a result Sarah 'ill treats' her with Abraham's implicit consent. Hagar runs away, but an angel sent from Yahweh persuades her to return with a promise of her own: that she will give birth to a son called Ishmael, who will also be the patriarch of a nation. Ishmael means 'God hears', and is again an aetiological reference to Sarah's desire for a child. The angel prophesies that Ishmael will become a 'wild man' and an 'enemy' to all. Thus, it was not Ishmael's descendants who were to inherit God's Promise of Canaan: he was to become the patriarch of the Arab tribes of Arabia. Instead, now at last God intervenes in Sarah's childlessness, and at the advanced age of 90 she bears Abraham a son called Isaac, who becomes the patriarch of the Israelite tribes. In these stories we have the mythic origin of the Arab and Jewish races. Like Abraham's, Isaac's name is aetiological. It means 'he laughs'. J is aware of this and attributes the name to Sarah who, being past childbearing age, laughs when she is told she is to have a son.[7]

The first nineteen chapters of Genesis are largely the work of J, but from the beginning of Chapter 20, following Abraham's

---

7 Genesis 18:10-15.

return from Egypt, the redactor begins to use E extensively. E relates four separate stories about Abraham. The first tells how Abraham and Sarah, between the births of Ishmael and Isaac, move south again to a place called Gerar, between Kadesh and Shur in the land of the Philistines on the coast of the south of Canaan. The Kadesh here is Kadesh Barnea on the southern border of Canaan (not to be confused with the Kadesh further north in Syria) and Shur was somewhere to the east of the Nile Delta. So, the location of Gerar seems to have been on the borders of Canaan and the Sinai Peninsula – the area now known as the Negev Desert.[8] Here Abraham and Sarah pretend they are brother and sister. As a result, King Abimelech of the Philistines takes Sarah as a concubine, but before he can sleep with her God warns him of the deception. Abimelech upbraids Abraham, who points out that Sarah is in fact his half-sister (on his father's side) as well as his wife. The story ends with reconciliation and Abimelech enriching Abraham. If this story rings a bell, it certainly should. It is a parallel version of almost exactly the same story earlier told about Abraham, Sarah and *Pharaoh*. We shall see presently that essentially the same story is told yet again about Abraham's son Isaac and *his* wife and Abimelech.[9] Either this is a favourite con trick of Abraham's family, and Abimelech is stupid enough to fall for it twice, or we must conclude that we are dealing here in Genesis with a number of individual mythical stories about various patriarchs rather than history. The same stories get transferred between patriarchs over the centuries and fitted into an emerging narrative in various different ways.

---

8 Gerar was probably at the site of Tel Haror in the Negev – the remains of a large Bronze Age city, about 40 acres across.

9 See page 83.

God's name in this story is given as El or the plural, Elo-
him.[10] The E Source is called that because of this characteristic; E stands for Elohist and E refers to God in this way. E
is retelling old Canaanite stories about Canaanite patriarchs.
How and when Yahweh was introduced to Canaan, and
where He came from originally are matters to which we
shall return. But clearly, for E, Yahweh was not a name he
wished to use in these early tales. It is not that E was
unaware of Yahweh; it is just that in the northern tribes at
this time, Yahweh was not used sufficiently to warrant
changing from El in these ancient stories he is retelling. The
corollary of this, of course, is that in the southern tribes
Yahweh *was* current and J used it exclusively as a result. It
would be wrong, however, to assume that because El seems
to be a more ancient name for God (in Canaan at least) that
He was in some way a less sophisticated conception. In fact,
Yahweh as presented by J seems a lot more primitive in conception. As we have noted, J's Yahweh embodies a very
anthropomorphic idea of the divine – He walks and talks
with men as if He was one of them. E's El, on the other
hand, seems a more remote divinity. In this story, he converses with Abimelech only through a dream and Abraham
communicates with his God through prayer rather than
human conversation. As we shall see in later E narratives,
when El is not communicating through dreams He likes to
use angels as intermediaries, preferring to keep a modicum
of distance from His Creation. So, the transition from El to
Yahweh does not represent a refinement of theology, or a
maturing concept of the nature of the divine. El and Yahweh
are rival deities, presumably deriving from different Middle

---

10 Yahweh is mentioned in the final verse (18) but this is clearly a later insertion
to gloss verse 17.

Eastern peoples, who came to be associated with each other. We know that El was Canaanite; we shall discover later where Yahweh originated.[11]

Three more separate stories about Abraham follow. The next story involves Hagar and Ishmael fleeing from Abraham's family. It parallels the same story told by J, but with sufficient changes to present is as a sequel, although one suspects that these are two versions of the same single myth. In E's version, Ishmael 'mocks' Sarah, who complains to Abraham, who in turn sends Hagar and Ishmael away into the desert. El reassures Abraham that all will be well: Isaac will carry on Abraham's destiny, but Ishmael will found a nation of his own. The next story again concerns Abimelech, King of the Philistines. Abimelech is worried about Abraham's intentions, living in his land, and eventually they fall out over ownership of a well. The disagreement is serious because Abimelech's army commander, Phicol, is involved. However, peace is negotiated, a treaty is signed in Beersheba and Abraham lives in the area for a long time. Yet again, this story is parallelled a few chapters later when, with Abraham dead, we are told that, following the other parallel story involving Abimelech, of Rebekah as wife and sister, *Isaac* also falls out with Abimelech over wells; Phicol also appears as a threat, and a peace treaty is signed in Beersheba. This second story is told by J, and he (or a redactor) covers up the parallel by saying that the squabble was over the original wells that Abraham had dug and that after Abraham's death the Philistines had blocked them up again. But this is a very

---

11 Scholars refer to this propensity for deities to merge with one another as 'syncretism'. Many readers will be familiar with something similar in the classical world, where Greek gods are associated with Roman counterparts – Zeus becomes Jupiter, Ares becomes Mars, and so on. The identification of Israelite Yahweh with Canaanite El is implicit in the Pentateuch; the problem is tracing how and when it took place.

thin disguise: these events take place in the Negev desert where water is scarce and where a well, once discovered, is surely unlikely to be stopped up again. Why would anyone do that? Surely what we have here, as with the sister/wife stories and the Hagar/Ishmael stories, are parallel myths that different narrators have attributed to different people – Abraham and Isaac – who themselves may have had no distinct historical reality.

The third and final story by E in this section concerns the sacrifice of Isaac; we shall discuss it in the next chapter when we examine Isaac's story.

So, is any of the Abraham story historical? Abraham himself is clearly not a historical figure. His very name betrays his symbolic identity. Abraham founds the Jewish nation and the root of his name is, appropriately, 'father'. In fact, the Bible quite explicitly states this. According to P, God changes his name from Abram to Abraham because 'a father of many nations I have made thee'.[12] Did Abraham found the cultic 'high places' at Shechem, Bethel and Hebron? Highly unlikely – these stories too are aetiological. By the time J was writing his narrative about Abraham, these had long been special cultic centres, originally orientated to El, but later to Yahweh. J and the other sources place their heroes and events concerning them in such places as a way of both grounding their tales in sacred geography and incorporating that geography into the central religious myths upon which worship of Yahweh was based.

It will also now be apparent that it is very difficult to separate stories about Israelites from stories about Canaanites. Abraham was clearly not originally a Canaanite, but in that case, what was he? He seems to move around a lot with his family and livestock, gradually enriching himself, and,

---

12 Genesis 17:5.

beyond that, his sole purpose in the narrative is to produce offspring to inherit Yahweh's Promise. I mentioned earlier the importance of the conflict between the itinerant pastoralist, symbolised by Abel, and the settled agriculturalist, symbolised by Cain. The nomadic, pastoralist nature of Abraham's lifestyle – he seems to exist on the fringes of Canaanite and Egyptian society – reflects this and, together with the earlier story, seems to be one clue as to the background of Abraham and his descendants. What also seems potentially convincing, because it is so specific, are his Mesopotamian roots – particularly in the context of the other Mesopotamian influences on the early Genesis stories.

For me, and for many scholars, this suggests very strongly that the story of Abraham is, in fact, the story of a people known as Amorites. We saw them previously, in the reference to the Sojourn being necessary because of the 'sins of the Amorites'. In that Iron Age reference, the Amorites are synonymous with Canaanites. But long before that, the Amorites were a Bronze Age people and their story is more complex than it appears. The Amorites were a Semitic, pastoralist people who indeed originated in western Asia – Canaan and Syria – but who in the second millennium BC, long before the time of Abraham, moved into large parts of Mesopotamia. There, some of them became rich, established major cities and changed their lifestyles accordingly. The most notable such city was Babylon: it was an Amorite king of Babylon, Hammurabi, who gave the world its first codified set of laws, which many scholars regard as a source for the Ten Commandments and associated laws, supposedly received by Moses from Yahweh on Mount Sinai (also called Mount Horeb).[13] The deity of the Amorites – Amurru – was, like Yahweh, a mountain God. His wife was Ashterah, who

---

13 The Sinai/Horeb confusion will be dealt with later.

also appears in the Bible as the wife of El. These parallels support the case for the Amorites being the origin of the Israelites.

We know a great deal about the Amorites because of a cache of cuneiform tablets found at Mari – an Amorite city in the mid-Euphrates area. These make it clear that although some Amorites became city dwellers, many kept to the old pastoralist ways. With the fall of the Amorite cities to other Asian peoples in the first millennium BC, nomadic tribalism again became the Amorite norm, and they fell back to their original homelands in the west. These lands were of course now occupied by others, so the Amorites, repeating their past in Mesopotamia, would force themselves and their herds on the Canaanite inhabitants as immigrant nomads, sometimes becoming rich in the process. The story of Abraham almost certainly reflects this. By the time of the Exodus and Conquest, the Amorites were essentially synonymous with the Canaanites. The Bible speaks of other inhabitants in Canaan – as we have seen, its position between Egypt and Asia made it a melting pot. But, at times, the Bible speaks quite explicitly as if Canaanites and Amorites are indistinguishable. For the Israelites, however, descended from Abraham as the Biblical account has it, these Amorite roots had been forgotten. The Israelites no longer thought of themselves as Amorite, but as a wholly different nation with its own racial myths involving an Egyptian Sojourn and a divine Promise. The Amorites were now the Canaanite enemy. The story of Shem and Ham was invented to drive a wedge between Semite Israelites and Hamitic Canaanites, but in reality, both had common roots in the Amorites. And that origin nonetheless betrays itself in the Mesopotamian connection, the nomadic way of life, the worship of a God who dwells on a mountain, and a founding 'father' who, like the Amorite nation, leaves behind the Mesopotamian city of Ur for a nomadic pastoral life in the west, becomes rich and founds a dynasty.

Central to the Israelite racial story is that Abraham's descendants formed the twelve tribes of Israel that displaced the Canaanites/Amorites. If this was true, of course, there should be no trace of those twelve tribes found in Canaan until after the Exodus and the Conquest. Intriguingly, one prominent Amorite nomadic group that features in the Mari tablets and who we are told there, fiercely maintained their independence from the Amorite city states in Mesopotamia, were the Banu-Yamina. This sounds suspiciously like the Israelite tribe of Benjamin, who we are told are descended from Abraham. As we shall see, when we examine these Abrahamic descendants in detail, Benjamin has a special place in the Genesis story, perhaps reflecting the antiquity of traditions about him. But how can the tribe of Benjamin have existed a millennium before the life of the man from whom they are supposed to descend? We shall also see evidence that other Israelite tribes existed in Canaan before the Exodus and Conquest. The solution to this conundrum, as I foreshadowed earlier, is to separate racial and religious origins. The Israelites existed in Canaan from way back; they only came to self-identify as Israelites when they acquired a set of beliefs about themselves as Yahweh's people of Promise. The enigma to be solved thus becomes not when and how the Israelites arrived in Canaan – in other words, when was the Exodus – but rather, when and how they replaced El with the syncretic Yahweh and redefined themselves as a people in the wake of that religious innovation.

Before moving on to the next generation in the Israelite story, that of Isaac and Ishmael, we need to deal here with an apparently gratuitous digression from the main story, which concerns Abraham's nephew Lot. J is tracing the history of the Israelites; Lot as Abraham's nephew is just a side shoot in that genealogy, so why does J suddenly intrude this apparent irrelevance into the story? The reason, as we shall now also digress to unravel, is that the story of Lot is an ancient racial slur upon the Hamite peoples living to the east of the southern Jordan river, in the area known as Transjordan and nowadays partly occupied by the Emirate of Jordan. This area was known as Moab. It is worthwhile for us to follow this Moabite digression because it throws into sharp relief the mythological and partisan nature of these early patriarchal tales.[14]

---

14 It is also very funny and I can't resist pealing back this particular onion.

CHAPTER 6

Lot

Fig. 5: Map of Lot and the Cities of the Plain

It is significant that it is southern J that tells the story of Lot: Judah is the southern Israelite tribe adjoining the Transjordan area and the ancient enmity between Judah and

Moab lies behind the Lot narrative. We are told that Abraham heads for Mamre in Hebron, but Lot settles among the 'cities of the plain', near Sodom, in the area that later became known as Moab. The Lot narrative begins with Abraham sitting at the entrance to his tent by the shrine of Mamre, when three men approach. We discover that one of these is J's anthropomorphic Yahweh visiting Abraham for a chat, as He did with Abraham's ancestors. The other two are apparently angels who eventually leave in the direction of Sodom because Yahweh has decided that Sodom's sinfulness is so great that he needs to have the angels investigate so he can decide what to do.[1]

The action then moves to Sodom, where the two angels find Lot sitting at the city gate. He invites them home for bed and breakfast, to which they reluctantly agree. That night, something occurs that is one of the strangest events in the Bible. Lot's house is besieged by the male population of Sodom who, not to put too fine a point on it, want to bugger the visitors. Whether this is common practice in Sodom or the Sodomites[2] are excited by the thought of buggering a couple of angels is not disclosed. But Lot resists and the scene gets ugly. Lot, less than heroically, offers his two virgin daughters to the mob for them to do whatever they want with – presumably some kind of gang rape – but the mob won't be put off even with this. So, the angels finally intervene and strike the mob blind; they also warn Lot to take his family and escape the city because Yahweh is now intent on destroying it. In the morning the angels lead Lot, his wife and two daughters out of the city and it is agreed that Lot will flee to a nearby small town called Zoar,[3] and that town

---

1 So much for omniscience then.

2 This story is, of course, where the term 'sodomy' originates.

3 *Zoara* means 'small' or 'insignificant' in Hebrew.

will be spared the destruction that is coming. Lot is also warned that no one in the party should look back on the destruction. Lot's wife does so and is turned into a pillar of salt. When Lot and his two daughters reach safety in Zoar, Yahweh rains burning sulphur down on Sodom and another city, Gomorrah, and the rest of the plain.

This story is clearly in part an aetiological explanation for the desert geography and geology of the area. The story of Lot's wife is also solely to provide an aetiology for a geographical feature that seems to have existed at the time, but it provides a clue as to where all this is taking place, because salt pillars are a feature of the highly salted Dead Sea area. Elsewhere,[4] we learn that Zoar was in Moab on the eastern shore of the Dead Sea. Between that sea and the mountain range that runs north–south further east, there are plains that were the location of Sodom, Gomorrah and Zoar, all in Moab. And Moab was, throughout the history of the Israelites, a major thorn in their flesh. Israelite tribes settled to the west of the Jordan and to the north-east, but Moab was an enemy never conquered. The Old Testament is littered with negative references to Moab, and the Israelites were often at war with their Moabite neighbours. The true point of J's story of Lot is to libel Judah's neighbours, the Moabite people, as the descendants of, if not practitioners of, deviant sexual practices. The story of buggery in Sodom is only one layer to this, as we shall now see.

We are told that after the destruction of the cities of the Moab plain, and with his wife now dead, Lot, motivated by fear, moves with his two virgin daughters to live in a cave in the hills to the east. This is not exactly conducive to social intercourse and, in particular, the girls start to worry that they will never have sex. So, on two consecutive nights, they

---

4 Isaiah 15:5.

get Lot drunk, deliberately sleep with him and get pregnant incestuously. One can only suppose that if Lot considered offering those daughters up for gang rape was acceptable morality, then a little father/daughter incest must have been regarded as a minor peccadillo in Lot's family. The Bible speaks approvingly of all these events, so one must suppose that Yahweh was comfortable with it too – whatever his reservations by the time we get to the New Testament! The eldest daughter bears a son, aetiologically named Moab, who becomes the patriarch of the Moabites, and the youngest has a son called Ben-Ammi, who is to become the patriarch of the Ammonites – the nation living just north of the Moabites (not to be confused with the Amorites[5]), whose relationship with Judah was similarly negative. So, what we have here is another layer to the racial libel: not only were these peoples descended from Sodomites, but the descent then continues through father/daughter incest. Lot himself is supposedly innocent in all this – the incest takes place without his knowledge or consent. But the racial slur does not even end there, as we shall now see.

Another insertion into J's narrative about Lot,[6] presumably by one of the redactors, is an old story from an unknown source. That story was placed here because Lot plays a minor role in it and it links to more layers of the libel. It tells of a war:

> And it came to pass in the days of Amraphel king of Shinar, Arioch king of Ellasar, Chedorlaomer king of Elam, and Tidal king of nations; *That these* made war with Bera king of Sodom, and with Birsha king of Gomorrah, Shinab king of

---

5 Or perhaps so? Benjamin/Ben-Ammi/Banu-Yamina. Amorite/Ammonite. These names slide around.

6 Genesis 14.

Admah, and Shemeber king of Zeboiim, and the king of Bela, which is Zoar. All these were joined together in the vale of Siddim, which is the salt sea.[7]

This needs some unpacking. First, the alliance between the kings of Shinar, Ellasar, Elam and 'nations'. The first three are all ancient nations from Southern Mesopotamia; the word translated here as 'nations' is *goyim*, which either means another similar nation or is a description of the other three because it is the Hebrew for 'Gentile'. This alliance of Gentile Asian nations makes war with Sodom, Gomorrah, Admah, Zeboiim, and Bela/Zoar. We have met three of these five 'cities of the plain'; the other two were presumably in the same area – the 'vale of Siddim' – where we are told there are 'slime pits'.[8] This describes the area to the south of the Dead Sea in Moab, where there are indeed large tar deposits, presumably the aetiological remnant of Yahweh's sulphuric destruction of the area. The ostensible reason for telling the story here is that the Mesopotamian alliance of kings wins the battle and carries off the spoils of war, including poor old Lot and his possessions. This abduction of his nephew brings Abraham into the war. He pursues the alliance north, defeats them and recaptures Lot. Abraham makes it clear that he wants nothing from the cities of the plain in recompense, and the implication is that he would be sullying his purity to take anything from such wicked people. For his actions and his piety, Abraham is blessed by Melchizedek, the king and chief priest of Salem – or Jerusalem the future capital of Judah. And Lot is neatly disassociated from all the sinfulness across the Jordan.

But there is a deeper meaning here. Remember that the nation of Moab is centuries in the future, and we so far have

---

7 Genesis 14:1-3.

8 Genesis 14:10.

only been told the names of the five old cities of the plain. What were the nations that inhabited those cities at the time of Abraham? We are told:

> In the fourteenth year, came Chedorlaomer, [the King of Elam] and the kings that were, and smote the Rephaims . . . the Zuzims . . . the Emims . . . And the Horites . . .[9]

To unpack this, we need to jump to Deuteronomy (not the work of J, but useful here nonetheless). Deuteronomy takes up the story of the Conquest of Canaan (so centuries ahead in time) at a point when the Israelites are in the land to the east of the Jordan – the lands we have been discussing. As they drive north, Yahweh tells them not to attack the Moabites, as they are by now known:

> And the LORD said unto me [Moses], Distress not the Moabites, neither contend with them in battle: for I will not give thee of their land for a possession; because I have given Ar [in Moab] unto the children of Lot for a possession. The Emims dwelt therein in times past, a people great, and many, and tall, as the Anakims; Which also were accounted giants, as the Anakims; but the Moabites call them Emims. The Horims also dwelt in Seir before time; but the children of Esau succeeded them, when they had destroyed them from before them, and dwelt in their stead; as Israel did unto the land of his possession, which the LORD gave unto them. [10]

I recognise that this is all getting very complicated, but in simple terms we now know from this passage that the

---

9 Genesis 14:5-6

10 Deuteronomy 2:9-12.

ancient inhabitants of Moab were called Rephaim/Rephaites, Emims/Emites, Anakims/Anakites, and Horims/Horites, and that they were all renowned for being 'giants'. In another passage, in Numbers, set like the previous passage at the time of the Israelite Conquest of Canaan, Moses sends out scouts who report back about the frightening, giant stature of the inhabitants. J says there:

> And there we saw the giants, the sons of Anak, which come of the giants: and we were in our own sight as grasshoppers, and so we were in their sight.[11]

The sons of Anak are the Anakites, and the word translated here as 'giants' is Nephilim. And with that, we come at last to the libel here intended, and it goes right back to the very beginning of everything: the Flood. Yahweh destroyed life on Earth because of human wickedness. But J tells us that there was more to it than that:

> And it came to pass, when men began to multiply on the face of the earth, and daughters were born unto them, that the sons of God saw the daughters of men that they *were* *f*air; and they took them wives of all which they chose. . . There were giants in the earth in those days; and also after that, when the sons of God came in unto the daughters of men, and they bare *children* to them, the same *became* mighty men which *were* of old, men of renown.[12]

This obscure passage has fascinated fantasists for centuries, as evidence of angelic beings mating with human women to produce monstrous offspring – giants remembered as mighty

---

11 Numbers 13:33.

12 Genesis 6:1-4.

men of myth. The story, of course, recalls Greek and Roman myths of similar unnatural sexual congress and the resulting demi-god heroes like Hercules. And it has about as much to do with reality as Hercules. The 'giants' who became mighty ancient men of renown were the Nephilim – the word is translated as 'giant' because of the associations we have been tracking. So, to cut a very long story short, J and the other sources present the inhabitants of the lands to the east of the Jordan, lands that the Israelites never occupied and which they regarded as occupied by their enemies, as descended originally from the unnatural mating of fallen angels with human women; then from sodomites; and, finally, from father/daughter incest: three layers of sexual deviancy.

How did the original Nephilim survive the flood? Were the Canaanites and Moabites that the Israelites encountered of large stature? Is there any historical truth in any of this? Who knows? There are enough references in the Pentateuch to giant men[13] to suggest that there was perhaps some genetic truth behind the stories. And the idea of Rephaim can be traced to the religious beliefs of the Amorites. Texts in an Amorite dialect, Ugaritic, have been found referring to 'rpum', who were semi-deified deceased ancestors – the most likely etymology for Rephaim and for the stories of ancient 'men of renown'. Indeed, in many later Biblical texts,[14] the Rephaim are referred to in exactly that way: not as giants, but as revered, dead ancestors, 'mighty men of old'. The idea that they came from unnatural conjoining of fallen angels with human women probably came from a folk etymology that saw the Hebrew 'npl', meaning 'to fall', behind Nephilim.

---

13 E.g., the Philistine Goliath that David killed with his slingshot; or again, Og 'of the remnant of the Rephaim' [Deuteronomy 3:11] whose bed was of iron and 13ft long by 6ft wide.

14 Isaiah 14:9, 26:14, 26:19; Psalms 88:10; Proverbs 2:18, 9:18, 21:16; Job 26:5, and possibly 2 Chronicles 16:1.

But all that is to miss the point. A racial slur passed down the centuries is behind these stories, and that slur is the reason why the central narrative about Abraham is interrupted by these strange stories about Lot. Like so much else in the Bible,[15] today's religious beliefs, not to mention the wild speculations of modern supernatural fantasists, turn out to be founded on parochial, trivial jealousies and animosities, revealing themselves in wordplay and malicious rumour.

---

15 For example, the reality behind the Beast with the number 666 and the Antichrist, of the Book of Revelation. See Vol. 3: *Apocalypse Postponed* for details.

CHAPTER 7

Isaac and Ishmael

It will be recalled that discussion of the fourth and final story told by E about Abraham was postponed to this chapter because it is the story of Abraham's intended sacrifice of Isaac. E narrates that El instructs Abraham to take Isaac to Moriah and sacrifice him by burning him on an altar. As the story appears in Genesis, El intervenes at the last moment and stops Abraham. But it is by no means clear that this is what happened in the original story. Here is E's account:

> And Abraham stretched forth his hand, and took the knife to slay his son . . . And said, By myself have I sworn, saith the LORD, for because thou hast done this thing, and hast not withheld thy son, thine only son: That in blessing I will bless thee, and in multiplying I will multiply thy seed as the stars of the heaven, and as the sand which is upon the sea shore; and thy seed shall possess the gate of his enemies; And in thy seed shall all the nations of the earth be blessed; because thou hast obeyed my voice.[1]

---

1 Genesis 22:10; 16-18.

The lacuna in the first line is filled in Genesis with the account of God's intervention to save Isaac. But this is the work of the redactor **RJE**, as is the phrase 'saith the Lord' (i.e. Yahweh) in the second line. In E's original narrative there is no such intervention – Abraham apparently *does* sacrifice Isaac and receives El's (not Yahweh's) blessing as a result.

There are a number of things to note here. First, J does not tell this story at all. Either it was not current in the southern tribes or, if it was, child sacrifice was not considered to be required by Yahweh. We know that child sacrifice *was* practised in Canaan, and it is the Bible itself that provides the evidence. There are many references in the Old Testament to the practice and it is true that in every one of them God forbids the abominable act. But these very passages attest to this as a relatively common Canaanite practice, otherwise, why so many texts fulminating against it? And second, Abraham does not for a moment argue with the original command to kill Isaac – he just sets off to do it. This would imply that there was nothing unusual in the command. The centre for this cultic practice was in the south of Canaan, in a place called Tophet, located in a valley surrounding the old city of Jerusalem. Children were ritually burnt there to appease Canaanite gods. Abraham is told to carry out the sacrifice in Moriah, and Mount Moriah was also in Jerusalem – the site of the first Temple, built there by Solomon. In my view, there can be no doubt that E's story preserves an ancient Jerusalem-based, southern narrative of a Canaanite rite, involving child sacrifice to El by fire. E tells it as it is; J omits it; and **RJE** includes it but adds a passage reducing it to a divine test rather than a divine offering.

The main J narrative continues with the need to get Abraham's legitimate son Isaac married before he dies. But Isaac must keep the race pure: he is not to marry a Canaanite woman, even though that is where he lives, presumably because when his descendants inherit Canaan their bloodline must not be tainted by that of the tribes they are destined to oust. The solution, as often in the Books of Moses, was to be a little spot of incest, with age difference and parentage no obstacle. Abraham sends a servant off to his original home country to find a wife for Isaac. The servant travels to northern Mesopotamia, where Abraham's brother Nahor still lives, presumably not having migrated further west with the rest of the family. Nahor has a son called Bethuel, and Bethuel has a son called Laban and a daughter called Rebekah. The servant brings Rebekah, Isaac's cousin's daughter, back to Isaac. Abraham and Sarah die and Isaac and Rebekah settle down to married life by a well called Lahai-Roi.[2] This was 'between Kadesh and Bered',[3] and in the 'south country'.[4] In other words, in the area of the Negev desert, to the south of Canaan and bordering Egypt. This was the area occupied by the Philistines, and the friction between the nascent Israelites and the Philistines surrounding them will continue to be a recurrent theme as the narrative progresses.

In another replay of the Abraham narrative there is a famine in the Negev, and Isaac, rather than go down into Egypt like his father, and on direct instruction from Yahweh, instead seeks help from the Philistine king, Abimelech, in Gerar in the Negev area. While in Gerar, Isaac pretends that the beautiful Rebekah is his sister; since she is his cousin's daughter, this may be less a deception than it seems! This is, of course, a third version of Abraham's identical twin encounters with Pharaoh, and then Abimelech. Isaac secures

---

2 Genesis 25:11.

3 Genesis 16:14.

4 Genesis 24:62.

Abimelech's favour and, like Abraham, becomes very rich as a result – in fact, so rich that, like his father before him, Abimelech sends him away for having become too powerful. In the end, Isaac and Abimelech make peace, swear oaths, and Isaac and his family settle in Beersheba, at the southernmost extremity of the Negev, where Isaac grows into old age.[5]

Isaac is the most shadowy of these patriarchs. He hardly gets a mention before the focus switches to his sons, Jacob and Esau, and he gets much less space devoted to him than Ishmael, or even Lot. Most of the Isaac story is just echoing Abraham's identical one with Abimelech, and the only entirely new story is that of Isaac being sacrificed – a story that, I have argued, probably originally ended in Isaac's untimely death, which would certainly explain why we seem to hear so little about him! It is also very strange that God should have wanted to kill Isaac. We are told over and over again that Abraham's descendants are to inherit the Promise. A great deal is then made of Sarah's infertility, which seems to threaten the Promise. God then intervenes with the miracle of Isaac's birth in Sarah's old age. Why then, after all that, does God tell Abraham to kill Isaac? It makes no sense in a narrative about the importance of genealogy. Of course, in the final redaction, Sarah's miracle and Abraham's obedience become object lessons in the need for faith in the face of impossible odds. But I believe the reality is that an old Canaanite tale about child sacrifice has been hijacked by **E** to fill out the otherwise very thin account of Isaac. The only

---

5 Beer means 'well' or 'spring'. Sheba means either 'seven' or 'oath'. I would suggest that the place was originally called Seven Wells. The stories involving Abimelech, of stopped wells and oaths, are aetiological. I also suspect (but with no evidence) that Solomon's Queen of Sheba did not come from Saba in present-day Yemen as usually suggested; she was a Queen of the South from Sheba in the Negev.

rational conclusion is that Isaac never existed. In fact, he seems to exist in the narrative solely because it requires Abraham to have two sons/patriarchs; Ishmael is treated at some length, but Isaac is skipped over because his genealogical role is really taken by his son Jacob, to whom we shall now turn.

CHAPTER 8

Jacob and Esau

In yet another parallel story, a replay of the story of Abraham and Sarah, Isaac's wife Rebekah also turns out to be barren. But this time, Yahweh intervenes without delay and she becomes pregnant with twin sons who J tells us are, like Isaac and Ishmael in the previous generation, to become the patriarchs of two nations. Rebekah feels them fighting in her womb and is told that this foreshadows their future antagonistic roles. Esau, the eldest, will found Edom, the land immediately to the south of Lot's Moab; and Jacob, the youngest, will found the Israelites. In doing so, Jacob will supplant his older brother's genealogical birthright – and in Hebrew, the root of 'Jacob' means to 'supplant'. J tells two parallel aetiological tales in which Jacob the younger tricks Esau the elder to obtain the latter's primogeniture rights. Both are curiously strange stories, the purpose of which is to explain why Jacob the younger twin is to become the patriarch of the Israelite tribes, which in ordinary circumstances would be the birthright of the eldest. Birthright was an important economic issue. The first-born son would inherit the largest part of the inheritance when a father died. This was traditionally double what any other brothers received. But in these stories which concern themselves with lineages, the birthright is also something more intangible: the passing of the religious expectations of the race down the main adult line. Yahweh's Promise to Abraham is passed down in this way, as were priestly rights.

We are told that Esau is 'hairy'; the name Esau probably comes from an Arabic root meaning just that. Esau is also born 'red all over', and in Hebrew the word for red is 'Edom', the land that Esau is to found and rule. In the first story, Jacob tricks Esau into swapping his birthright for a bowl of '*red* pottage' (lentil stew). In the second story, using a fur skin to emulate his brother's hairy skin, Jacob tricks Isaac into giving him a blessing, thinking he is Esau. Apparently, all this leaves Esau disinherited and nothing can be done about it. All very unlikely, and Jacob hardly emerges from it with any honour – but that isn't the point: this is not history, as the aetiological names and events show. Esau gets married first to *two* Hittite[1] women: apparently bigamy was no more taboo than incest for these early patriarchs. This went against the grain with Isaac and, over time, a feud broke out between Esau and Jacob (paralleling the Cain and Abel story), resulting in Jacob fleeing Canaan to his mother's brother, Laban, in Haran. On the way, he stops at Bethel and, like Abraham before him, receives Yahweh's Promise. Jacob ends up marrying Laban's daughter (his mother's niece), called Rachel. However, all is not plain sailing from there. Rachel has an elder sister, Leah, and their father, Laban, needs to see her married off as well, so by trickery he gets Jacob to marry her too: all very cosy! Jacob stays for some years in Haran with his bigamous wives, working for Laban as a shepherd.

What then follows is another example of Jacob's trickery. He wants, and Yahweh instructs him, to go back to his

---

[1] The Hittites were a significant nation to the north of Canaan.

brother Esau, but he falls out with Laban over what he is due for his years of work, so he manages the breeding of the flock so that he ends up with the best stock and Laban is left with the rest. Then Jacob sets off to be reconciled with Esau, who, by this time, seems to be living in a place called Seir,[2] in what later became Edom. The E Source tells us that, to placate his father for having married the two Hittite women, Esau had then incestuously married Ishmael's daughter, Mahalath, in neighbouring Arabia and at some point moved his family to 'the land of Seir, the country of Edom'.[3] Seir was a mountainous region of Arabia, south-east of Canaan and stretching between the Dead Sea and the Gulf of Aqaba, inhabited by the 'giant' Horites. It sat right on the border between Egypt and Canaan. Esau's descendants intermarried with the Horites, and the region came to be known as Edom. The nation of Edom and the nation of Israel were close neighbours, and throughout the first millennium BC their fates were intermingled. And coming into the Christian era, Herod the Great, the persecutor of the infant Jesus, was an Idumean – that is, coming from Edom. Edom and Seir are very important to our story as it unfolds, particularly when we get to the Exodus and the story of Moses. Meanwhile, Jacob's reconciliation with Esau eventually takes place, and Jacob subsequently departs back to Canaan and settles in the mountains on the high road north from Jerusalem at Shechem which, it will be recalled, was to become the first capital of the northern

---

2 The Bible mentions two distinct geographical areas named Seir: a 'land of Seir' and 'Mount Seir' in the south, and another 'Mount Seir' further north, on the northern boundary of Judah. Given the context, Esau was living in the *southern* land of Seir, in what was to become Edom. We came across this land earlier, in the Lot narrative, where we were told that Mount Seir was the home of the Horites. Elsewhere (Genesis 36:20) we learn that it was named after 'Seir the Horite', whose offspring inhabited the area.

3 Genesis 32:3.

kingdom of Israel, (before King David later conquered Jerusalem itself). It will also be remembered that according to J, Abraham is supposed to have built an altar there.

Jacob, as the patriarch of the twelve tribes of Israel, is destined to have twelve sons to provide the appropriate racial descent. But yet again the genealogical narrative turns out to have several twists and turns. First, we discover that, like Rebekah and Sarah before her, Rachel also turns out to be barren. What are the chances – three wives in three generations, all with the same fertility problem? Surely we are dealing with one story, attaching itself to three different people. In this case it is the second wife, Rachel's elder sister Leah, who has the initial childbearing success. She bears Jacob four sons: **Reuben, Simeon, Levi** and **Judah.** These are the patriarchs of the first four tribes of Israel. Not to be outdone, Rachel takes a leaf out of Sarah's book and gets Jacob to sleep with her maidservant, Bilhah, who then has two sons by Jacob, **Dan** and **Naphtali:** the patriarchs of the fifth and sixth tribes. By this time, Bilhah is past childbearing age, so, not to be outdone by Leah's four sons, Rachel tells Jacob to sleep with another of her maidservants, Zilpah. She too has two sons – **Gad** and **Asher:** numbers seven and eight. Now it was Leah's turn again. Not to be outdone by Rachel's stratagem of using her two handmaids, she sleeps with Jacob again and has **Issachar** and **Zebulun.** So now we have ten sons of Jacob, all tribal patriarchs, and none by his wife Rachel.

The point of this whole convoluted story, which is told by the northerner **E,** is that each of these ten sons founds one of the ten tribes of the *northern* kingdom of Israel, all descended from Jacob by three different women. The other two tribes are to descend from 'legitimate' sons of Jacob by Rachel, made possible despite her barrenness because God steps in again and deals, as he did with Sarah, with Rachel's infertility. She gives birth to the last two of Jacob's sons –

Joseph, the patriarch of the eleventh tribe, and **Benjamin,** the twelfth. So we neatly arrive at the point[4] where Jacob has twelve sons, representing the traditional twelve tribes of Israel. And to reinforce the point, God renews the Abrahamic Promise yet again and changes Jacob's name to the symbolic 'Israel'. All straightforward – or is it? Figure 6 shows a map of the tribal allotments following the Exodus and Conquest.

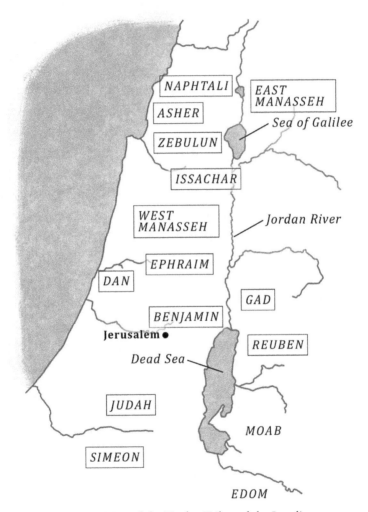

NAPHTALI

EAST MANASSEH

ASHER

Sea of Galilee

ZEBULUN

ISSACHAR

WEST MANASSEH

Jordan River

EPHRAIM

DAN

GAD

BENJAMIN

Jerusalem ●

REUBEN

Dead Sea

JUDAH

MOAB

SIMEON

EDOM

Fig. 6: Map of the Twelve Tribes of the Israelites

---

4 Genesis 31.

Notice that Levi and Joseph are missing, and there are new tribes not accounted for among Jacob's sons – East and West Manasseh, and Ephraim. What happened to Levi, and where did the Manassehs and Ephraim come from? As we shall presently see, the descendants of Levi became priests to the whole nation and were not allotted a single territory. But the chief fly in the ointment here is Joseph. In Genesis as we now have it, the well-known story of Joseph's captivity in Egypt and his eventual triumph is inserted at this point. Yet a moment's reflection will indicate that this makes little sense in the context of the genealogical narrative. Like the Lot narrative, this is a digression from the main line of argument. The main line of descent goes down through Judah, the son of Leah, not Joseph, the son of Rachel. The ten northern tribes are driven from history by the Assyrians, and it is southern Judah that eventually evolves into the Jewish nation. To understand what is going on here, we need to jump now to the end of Genesis, which deals with Jacob's deathbed blessing of the twelve sons. In doing so, we jump over the whole story of Joseph in Egypt, to which we shall return separately in the next chapter.

Jacob's blessing involves a number of 'prophesies' made by Jacob to his sons, as follows:

REUBEN. In a story told earlier by southern J, this brother sleeps with Bilhah, his father's concubine and mother of some of his brothers. This scurrilous story is told to denigrate the northern firstborn son, making the way clear for the pre-eminence of the southern Judah. The prophecy is that as a punishment, the tribe of Reuben will not 'excel' – in other words, their patriarch's sexual behaviour means that they have forfeited their birth right.

SIMEON AND LEVI. In another scurrilous story told by J, these two brothers slaughter a large but unspecified number of Canaanite men in Shechem in revenge for a rape apparently perpetrated by one of the Canaanites on their sister, Dinah.[5] E makes no mention of this – the story is told by J, and as with the Reuben incest, it is in pursuance of his interest in downplaying the northern tribes that would otherwise take precedence over the later-born Judah. The prophecy is that, as a punishment, the tribes of Simeon and Levi are to be 'scattered' in Canaan. This reflects the future role of the Levites, who are not allotted Canaanite land by Moses but are to become priests to all the other tribes. Likewise, Simeon's allotment is eventually swallowed up within adjacent Judah.

JUDAH. With Reuben, Simeon and Levi neatly disposed of, Judah gets more lines devoted to him here than any of the other brothers, reflecting the future importance of his tribe as the ultimate source of the Jewish nation. We are told that he will hold the 'sceptre' and 'staff' of a ruler and king and that the other sons will bow down before him. This seems very strange indeed. We shall look at the story of Joseph in the next chapter, but those readers already familiar with this (from the Lloyd-Webber musical, *Joseph and the Amazing Technicolor Dreamcoat,* if nowhere else) will know this was precisely the role of Joseph in Egypt, expressed in the same language in Joseph's prophetic dreams. Here, J downplays northern Joseph and give the birthright to southern Judah.

ZEBULUN will be a 'haven of ships' – and indeed, that tribe was located on the Canaan coast, just south of Galilee. This tribe will turn out to be important when we come in Chapter 15, to identify specific Sea Peoples.

---

5 Simeon, Levi and Dinah are all daughters of Leah.

ISSACHAR will be an 'ass . . . between two burdens' and a 'servant unto tribute'. The two burdens are the areas of East and West Manasseh, between which the area occupied by Issachar was sandwiched. Read on for the story of Manasseh.

DAN shall 'judge his people'. Dan means 'judge' in Hebrew. After the Exodus, and before the tribes were united under kings, they were ruled by judges, the most famous of whom was Samson, who was of the tribe of Dan.

GAD means either 'troop' or 'fortune' in Hebrew. The prophecy is that Gad will be overcome by a troop or by fortune but will itself overcome at last. The tribe of Gad fought with the Israelites in Canaan to the bitter end, despite the fact that they asked for, and were eventually granted, land to the east of the Jordan, bordering on that of the Ammonites. Friction on that border was eventually resolved with the destruction of the Ammonites by Israel.

ASHER was assigned land in the north between Galilee and the Coast, a region with comparatively low temperature, and much rainfall, making it some of the most fertile land in Canaan, with rich pasture, wooded hills and orchards. This explains their prophecy here: 'Out of Asher his bread will be fat'. This tribe will also feature in Chapter 15: the Sea Peoples.

NAPHTALI was assigned the land later known as Galilee, which is located in the Canaan highlands – hence the prophecy that 'Naphtali is a hind (presumably a mountain deer of some kind) let loose'.

JOSEPH is 'a fruitful bough'. This is a reference to Joseph's two sons, **Manasseh** and **Ephraim**. It is these that become patriarchs of tribes, as shown on the map. There will be no tribe of Joseph, but two separate tribes that bear his sons' names. This, of course, implies that there were thirteen tribes, not twelve; we shall resolve this issue too in the next chapter.

But before doing so, there is one more story about Judah, told by J and inserted into the Joseph narrative, which yet again reinforces his, rather than Joseph's, centrality in the Israelite descent narrative. J describes how Judah marries a Canaanite woman and they have three sons. The eldest son, Er, marries a woman called Tamar, but Yahweh decides he is sinful and kills him. No explanation is given – Yahweh, it seems, is just like that! The second son, Onan, marries the widowed Tamar as a familial duty (as was the tradition). This could have substantial economic repercussions for Onan who, as the surviving eldest son, would normally stand to inherit the double birthright from Judah; but any son born to Tamar would be deemed the heir of the deceased Er, and able to claim the double share instead of Onan. So, wholly understandably, Onan practises birth control through *coitus interruptus*. But Yahweh is not to be thwarted in this way and kills him as well.[6] Not surprisingly, afraid that if his third son, Shelah, dutifully marries the twice-widowed Tamar, he too will be killed by Yahweh, Judah sends Tamar back to her father. Later on, tiring of widowhood and determined to have a child, Tamar poses as a prostitute and incestuously seduces Judah,[7] first having inveigled from him some proofs of his identity – including a 'cord'. When as

---

6 Onan's sin has been interpreted as either masturbation, or birth control or both, and this story has been used by the Christian Church to condemn both practices – a good example of Christian ignorance about Jewish practice.

7 Some commentators, keen to excuse Judah, interpret this as cultic/temple prostitution, practised by Canaanites but not Israelites; there is nothing in the text to suggest this.

tribal leader, Judah sentences her to death for prostitution, she reveals the proofs and Judah is forced to acquit her. At the end of this convoluted and unlikely story of divine malignancy and incestuous deception, Tamar bears twin sons. One of them, Zerah, is partially born but then withdraws into the womb, leaving the other twin, Perez, to be born first: Zerah is identified by a red cord tied round his wrist by the midwife before he withdraws.

Details here matter. Zerah's cord echoes the cord that Judah gives to Tamar as proof of identity. But more important is its red colour. Remember that Esau was born 'red all over'. Esau founds Edom; red is the colour of Edom; the word 'edom' in Hebrew means 'red'. Perez usurps Zerah's primogeniture and therefore his birth right. Later in the Bible we learn that King David (and, ultimately, Jesus Christ),[8] are descended from Perez – so Perez is the founder of the royal line. Zerah on the other hand, is more puzzling. Genesis describes two people called Zerah. In the passage in Chapter 38 that we have been examining, written by J, Zerah is clearly an Israelite by his descent from Judah. But in one of P's genealogical tables in Genesis 36 there is a Zerah listed who is a tribal chief in Edom but is identified as a grandson of Esau, the patriarch of the Edomites.[9] There can be no doubt that they are one and the same person – J's story of the red cord is clearly intended to show that his Zerah became an Edomite. So, two traditions, both recognizing Zerah as an Edomite, but why does J tell his highly unlikely and convoluted tale about a prenatal fraternal struggle, rather than P's much simpler one? The struggle in the womb between Zerah and Perez is obviously meant to echo the

---

8 Matthew 1:3 and Luke 3:33 both provide genealogies for Jesus that descend from Perez.

9 Esau marries Basemath; their son, Reuel, has Zerah. Tamar is not mentioned.

similar prenatal struggle between Jacob and Esau – it will be recalled that Rebekah felt them fighting in her womb: then, Jacob founded the Israelites and Esau founded the Edomites. This is, therefore, almost certainly another case of an old story finding its way into two different contexts. But there is more to it than that. J is aware that Judah, not Joseph, founded the southern tribe that, through David, eventually became the Jewish nation. From that point of view, even though the story of Joseph dominates the rest of Genesis, something needed to be inserted as a marker for the importance of Judah – and the story of his twin sons not only sets that down, but it does so in a way that directly echoes the story of Jacob and Esau and their disputed birth right. Why does J take up so much time with the founding of Edom? Because he comes from the tribe of Judah – the closest tribe to Edom, bordering it at the southern end of the Dead Sea. So, the concern here is parochial: future rivalry between Judah and Edom symbolised by both Jacob and Esau and by Zerah and Perez – two sets of twins whose conflict even in the womb foreshadows the relationship between the two nations.[10]

But now, let us turn at last to that story of Joseph that we skipped over earlier.

---

10 King Henry VIII divorced Katherine of Aragon because he argued she had been his brother's wife. This tale could be taken as confirmation of Yahweh's hatred of such marriage - but in fact, Levirate marriage as it is known was encouraged (Deuteronomy 25.5-10). Henry primarily relied on Leviticus 18 and 20 but those texts refer to sexual relations with a brother's wife - not his widow.

CHAPTER 9

Joseph

Both J and E contribute large parts of the Joseph story and the story itself occupies over ten chapters – that is twenty per cent of the whole Genesis narrative. Later, we shall identify its likely origin. Unfortunately, whatever its provenance, it provided problems for both textual sources in terms of their prime narrative concerns. J's problem with Joseph is obvious enough. Joseph is the hero of the north: his sons Ephraim and Manasseh founded the two largest and most important of the northern tribes. So, J loses no opportunity to downgrade Joseph's reputation and advance that of the southern hero, Judah. E on the other hand, writing from a northern bias, is concerned throughout to do the opposite. Yet he too has a problem. All of Jacob's sons continue to feature in the Books of Moses through the Israelite tribes that they found. But there is no tribe of Joseph, and after Genesis his famous name just fades away.

The story of Joseph must predate both J and E and must have been so popular and well known that neither could ignore it. Yet it makes no sense at all in the racial narrative they are both trying to describe. The line of descent of the Israelites comes down from Abraham to Jacob and it is Jacob who is the patriarch of the twelve tribes: God even changes his name to 'Israel' to emphasize this. The story of Joseph is just not needed in this context, and both J and E have to go to considerable lengths to shoehorn him in. Both J and E do manage to 'fit' the Joseph story into their narratives to explain how and why the Israelites come to spend centuries in Egypt rather than in Canaan. But it remains implausible and begs alternative explanation. I suspect that because the Exodus did not happen as the Bible tells it, so the Joseph story 'fits' in a different place. We need, as this book progresses, to explain exactly who Joseph was, why the narrative focuses on him rather than Jacob, and the most likely real sequence of events.

But for now, J's version has Joseph tending Jacob's flocks with his half-brothers. He tells them of dreams in which the symbolism seems to suggest that they, together with their father and mother, will at some time in the future bow down before him.[1] Not surprisingly, no one is happy with this prophecy, and his half-brothers plot to kill him. However, for J, Judah is the good guy in all this as he suggests a change of plan: not to murder Joseph, but to sell him into slavery instead, with a passing band of 'Ishmaelites' – or nowadays, Arabs – who are travelling with trade goods down to Egypt. The brothers smear Joseph's coat in goat's blood and, returning to Jacob with this 'evidence', persuade him that Joseph has been killed by a wild animal. For J, it is important that it is Judah that prevents the killing of Joseph – for the obvious reason that Judah's future tribe was to become the founder of the Jewish people.

J is used by the redactor to tell much of this story, but E has some interesting variances. The first is easily explained: J portrays the southern hero Judah as the kind brother who

---

[1] Remember that in Jacob's Blessing, it is Judah who is prophesied to fulfil this role.

persuades the others to sell Joseph rather than kill him. E emphasizes the northern hero Reuben, who also tries to save Joseph's life by having him sold into slavery. But another variance is less obvious: J has Joseph sold into slavery with Ishmaelites; E has him sold to Midianites. (RJE includes both references without reconciliation). We shall see later that for E who, it will be remembered, had a priestly background, Midian had associations with Moses and Yahweh. We shall have much more to say about Midian as this book progresses.

Joseph is sold on in Egypt to Potiphar, an officer in Pharaoh's guard. Joseph prospers and rises to become overseer of the household, but when he rejects the sexual advances of Potiphar's wife she accuses him of impropriety, and he is imprisoned. It is significant that it is J who tells the story this way, as the logic of the narrative does not require the story of Potiphar's wife at all. Joseph enters Egypt already a slave and it is his subsequent elevation by Pharaoh that is the heart of the story; the intrusion of Potiphar's wife is superfluous. Later in Joseph's story, the E Source tells us that as a reward for his actions, Pharaoh gives Joseph a wife – the daughter of an Egyptian priest – and her name is Potipherah. It seems obvious that the two stories arise from a common myth, but you can hear axes being ground clearly in each. The northern E tells a positive story about the northern hero Joseph, but J tells a scurrilous tale of a humiliating sexual assault, accusation and imprisonment.

At this point, the Genesis narrative is taken up by the E Source, presumably because the redactor of J and E chose the more positive version. Joseph gains favour generally by interpreting dreams in prison and two years later, at the age of thirty, comes to the attention of Pharaoh, who is himself troubled by recurring dreams. Joseph interprets them to mean that seven years of famine are coming but will be preceded by seven years of good harvests. He recommends building large grain stores and filling them during the good years to see the people through the coming famine. All of this is nonsense of course. Famine was a fact of life in the Near East; Egypt's resilience in that regard was an important factor in its economy and local influence, and no Pharaoh would have needed a Canaanite immigrant to teach him anything about storing and exporting grain surpluses. Nevertheless, as a result, Joseph becomes Pharaoh's overseer:

> Thou shalt be over my house, and according unto thy word shall all my people be ruled: only in the throne will I be greater than thou. And Pharaoh said unto Joseph, See, I have set thee over all the land of Egypt. And Pharaoh took off his ring from his hand, and put it upon Joseph's hand, and arrayed him in vestures of fine linen, and put a gold chain about his neck; And he made him to ride in the second chariot which he had; and they cried before him, Bow the knee: and he made him *ruler* over all the land of Egypt. And Pharaoh said unto Joseph, I *am* Pharaoh, and without thee shall no man lift up his hand or foot in all the land of Egypt. And Pharaoh called Joseph's name Zaphnathpaaneah; and he gave him to wife Asenath the daughter of Potipherah priest of On.[2]

This also looks unlikely on the face of it. If we are to take this passage at face value, Joseph became, in effect, a Pharaoh himself in all but name. Pharaohs did indeed rule though powerful civil servants and priests, and Egyptian viziers did have substantial executive powers. But for an Asiatic immigrant to be given that much power is almost unheard of – almost, but in fact not unknown. We shall

---

2 Genesis 41:40-45.

return to this later; it will turn out to be very important because it points strongly towards the real historical figure behind 'Joseph'.

Over the next fourteen years, everything pans out as Joseph had predicted, and this reinforces his position and power. The Joseph story now switches back and forth between J and E, and each time the respective prejudices intrude. In essence, the redacted tale runs thus: Joseph's family in Canaan are suffering under the famine and travel down to Egypt for relief; Joseph toys with them and then reveals his identity to much joyous celebration. But southern J, being no fan of northern Joseph, emphasizes the way in which Joseph heartlessly pretends not to recognize his family, plays cruel games with them, and contrives to bring Rachel's other son and Joseph's full brother, Benjamin, into the heart of the story. Centuries later, it will be the tribe of Benjamin alone that will stand by Judah when the northern tribes secede from the united monarchy. Northern E on the other hand, has Reuben, the eldest son and northern hero, berating his brothers for their actions and protecting Benjamin, and emphasizes the kindness of Joseph in filling the brothers' saddlebags with money. Following the big reveal, and with Pharaoh's agreement, Joseph moves the whole family to Goshen – a particularly fertile area in the eastern Nile Delta – to be near him. This area was, years later, where we are told that the Israelites were held in slavery until Moses led them out. And that is really the end of the Genesis story: Exodus starts with the Israelites in Goshen.

But before Genesis ends, as we saw earlier, it focuses on all the sons of Jacob, and at this point we need to address again the issue of those sons. The E narrative provided the full information about the twelve sons and their various mothers. The J Source, however, tells us of only six brothers: Reuben, Simeon, Levi, Judah, Joseph and Benjamin. J knows about the other six of course: when also in **J**, the brothers describe themselves to Joseph, unaware of his identity,[3] they describe twelve brothers in all – one 'dead' (Joseph) and one at home (Benjamin). So why is **J** reticent about the other six? Because they are all destined to become the patriarchs of the northern tribes. As we saw, **J** denigrates the other brothers as best he can, and plays up the role of Judah wherever he can, to the extent of describing him in terms that **E** applies to Joseph. But there remains another problem: it is time now to resolve the issue identified in the last chapter, of the twelve or thirteen tribes and the disappearance of the tribe of Joseph.

Just before Jacob's blessing of his twelve sons, **E** relates a different version of Jacob's deathbed blessings – one that allots the double share of birthright to Joseph rather than Judah through the expedient of bringing the 'fruit of his bough' into the equation – his two sons, **Manasseh** and **Ephraim**. Joseph brings the two boys to Jacob, who tells Joseph that he will regard these two in the same way as his own firstborn sons, Reuben and Simeon – effectively, as if they were his own sons, not grandsons. But we are now treated to yet *another* story of mis-identity and usurped birthright. Jacob is blind in his old age, and mistakes the younger son, Ephraim, for the elder, Manasseh. He gives his blessing to the former instead of the latter. First, Jacob fore-tells that both will father tribes. And indeed, as the story continues to the Conquest of Canaan, there seems to be no tribe of Joseph at all – but the two tribes of Manasseh and Ephraim. This means, of course, that there are thirteen tribes, not twelve. The solution to this conundrum is that Levi

---

3 Joseph's hidden identity and his bloodstained coat echo earlier tales of decep-tion – of Noah's sons covering themselves in a coat to hide themselves, and Jacob wearing a fur coat to deceive his father Isaac that he is Esau.

became regarded as having founded a 'tribe', but following the Conquest they were not allotted land of their own. Their role will emerge later, but for now, this squares the circle: just twelve landed tribes plus the landless Levites.

Jacob goes on to foretell, in an exact echo of Esau and Jacob before them, that although Manasseh was the first-born, it will be Ephraim's descendants that will be greater and will father 'a multitude of nations'. As we shall see, Joshua, the leader of the Conquest after Moses' death, descends from Ephraim; later still, Jeroboam, the breakaway King of Israel, was an Ephraimite; and Shechem, the capital of the north, was in Ephraim territory – hence its pre-eminence. Manasseh occupied a huge area of Canaan – so much so, that it was divided into West Manasseh and East Manasseh. The two sons of Joseph also suggest a further layer of meaning to the story of Judah's twins, Zerah and Perez, which is located in the middle of the long Joseph narrative. Judah's twins found the Davidic royal line and an important Edomite tribe; this is effectively one-upmanship by J, who is saying that anything the northern hero Joseph and his two offspring can do, so can the twin offspring of the southern hero Judah.

But right now, let us pause and consider what should by now be patently obvious: J's narrative is full, from start to finish, of parallel stories. These cannot be explained away by reference to different sources for the same story – J seems to have deliberately written it this way. But why? The first parallel concerns all the incestuous relationships, culminating in the father-in-law/daughter-in-law mating of Judah and Tamar. Yahweh clearly disapproves of sodomy and the withdrawal method of contraception but is not ill-disposed towards keeping it in the family, if that is what is needed to preserve inheritance and racial purity. But the second set of parallels is harder to account for, and concerns barren women, concubines, trickery, concealed identity, and conflicting birthrights

– between siblings, and especially between twins. Behind all this seems to be a recurring message that just being the natural firstborn of a first wife does not necessarily mean automatic inheritance: Yahweh will choose his favourites irrespective of their birth. It is not Cain or Abel that founded the Israelites – it is Seth, the thirdborn. Abraham's firstborn is Ishmael, but his fate is to found the Arab nations and it is Isaac, the second son, who is the patriarch of the Israelites. Isaac's firstborn is Esau, who founds the Edomite nation; it is Jacob, the secondborn, who steals Esau's birthright and carries on the Israelite descent. And in his turn, Jacob's first son is Reuben, but he sleeps with his father's concubine; and, although he, like his brothers, founds an Israelite tribe, it is, as a direct result, prophesied by Jacob to be a minor one.[4] It is Jacob's later son, Joseph, who is destined to receive a multitude of blessings.[5] And Judah's sons reverse the normal order – Zerah's birthright is usurped even in the womb by Perez, the ancestor of King David.

But there is a more general theme running through all this, going right back to the sons of Noah – the ultimate patriarchs. It will be remembered that Shem was the ancestor of the Semite Israelites and Ham was the patriarch of the Arab peoples. Right up until the Conquest of Canaan by the Israelites after their Exodus from Egypt, Canaan is occupied by Hamite tribes. We are not told the order of birth of Noah's sons, but it is Ham's descendants who seem to have primogeniture: Ham's son is called Canaan. Yet it is Shem's descendants who receive the Promise and eventually seize Canaan from the Hamite tribes. Much of J's narrative is formed by this wider picture: he is building up the case for the Conquest of Canaan. That is what all these stories about sibling

---

4 Genesis 49:3-4.

5 Genesis 49:22-26.

rivalry, squabbling twins and usurpation of birthrights is really all about – justifying the otherwise morally reprehensible Conquest. It is all making clear that the Israelite right to Canaan is not based on 'finders, keepers' but on the divine will of Yahweh, who has chosen Shem's people over Ham's. When Yahweh instructs Moses and Joshua to kill every Canaanite, this ethnic cleansing is justified by the Israelite Promise, which itself is founded, not on accident of birth, but the sovereign and unfettered will of Yahweh.

The Joseph story is inserted into the narrative of Jacob and his twelve sons in a way that interrupts the narrative flow. He is the racial hero of the north, and, by the time Genesis was set down, the northern tribes had become the 'lost' ten tribes of Christian myth, scattered by the Assyrian Empire. The lineage of the Jewish nation does not flow from Joseph, and he is effectively replaced at the end of Genesis by his two sons, who founded the last two of the twelve tribes: there is no tribe of Joseph. The fact that, nevertheless, both J and E and their redactors felt the need to include the Joseph narrative must point to its currency throughout Israel and Judah. It must also point to an importance about Joseph that, frankly, narrative entertainment apart, seems to be absent. Everything in the Book of Genesis is there for a reason. Even the most obscure passages and episodes are there to drive the main argument along. If Joseph gets in the way of this, there has to be a reason – but what? I shall argue that the story of Joseph belongs in a different time and context entirely, and to locate him we must move on as the Bible does, from Genesis to Exodus.

CHAPTER 10

Moses according to J

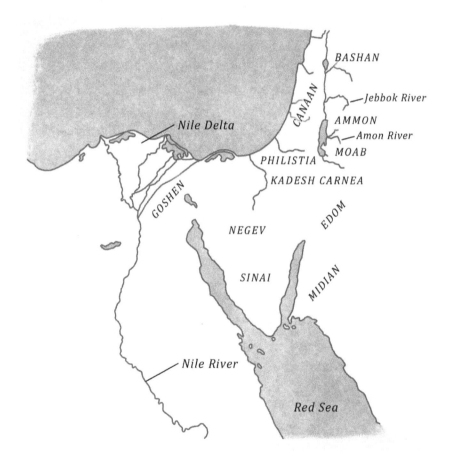

Fig. 7: Map of the Exodus

Genesis must not be judged as history. All three of its authors and its redactors have their different axes to grind, but they are all united in overall purpose: to establish the divine right of the Israelites to the land of Canaan, irrespective of its previous occupants. When viewed from this perspective, so much of Genesis that would otherwise appear anecdotal, digressive, repetitive and obsessive, falls naturally into place. Genealogies, family relationships, descendants, disputes and usurpations are all grist to this overriding mill. From a historical perspective, the Conquest of Canaan and the associated genocide of its inhabitants is a story of human aggression and acquisition; from the perspective set out in inordinate and repetitive length in Genesis, the Conquest becomes an expression of the free, unfettered will of God in choosing the descendants of one man to inherit a Promised Land, flowing with milk and honey. The story of Adam and Eve, and of their sons, Cain, Abel and Seth, is just the first step in setting out this fundamental religious and racial thesis. The peoples deriving from these first patriarchs are, of course, wiped out in the story of the Flood. From a historical perspective, this makes as much sense as the idea that all mankind is descended, presumably incestuously, from just one mating couple, but that perspective is irrelevant. The only issue here is God's relationship with mankind and how, over time, he separates out the Israelites as a special nation, dedicated to Himself.

The **J** narrative now moves on to the story of Moses, found in the second book of the Pentateuch – Exodus. Apparently, we have moved on an unspecified period of time and the Israelites are now slaves in Egypt. What happened to change their fortunes, and over what length of time, are key issues we need to determine – but **J** provides no clues, only that Pharaoh decrees that Israelite male children should be drowned in the Nile – undoubtedly the origin of the story about Herod's similar action in the first century AD. And so begins the story of 'Moses in the Bullrushes' which, besides the Nativity of Jesus and the story of Joseph, must be the most beloved of Bible stories for children. A married couple from the Levite tribe (it is important to note the tribe here), have a male child and the wife makes an 'ark' (recalling the Noah story) of bullrushes and lays it by the side of the Nile, leaving 'his sister' hidden to watch what happens. A daughter of Pharaoh comes down to wash at the river, and seeing the child, recognizes immediately that this must be 'one of the Hebrews' children'.[1] The sister then offers to find the child a Hebrew wet nurse; Pharaoh's daughter agrees, and the Levite mother is introduced in the role. Eventually, the child is adopted by Pharaoh's daughter and brought up at court. There is a familiar pattern in myth – the royal child abandoned, brought up in ignorance of his origins, who then regains his inheritance. Here, that myth is strangely inverted: the child is from poor origins but is brought up in wealth. Why this tortuous inversion of a familiar story? Because the writer wants us to know that the child has a sort of dual nationality – both Egyptian but also Israelite, of the tribe of Levi.

There is a similar duality in the child's name. The princess calls him Moses, 'because I drew him out of the water'.[2] This folk etymology, based on the Hebrew root 'mashah' meaning 'to draw out', is strange given that it is the Egyptian princess doing the naming, and it is unlikely to say the least that she would have known any Hebrew. The true etymology is, as has been recognized for centuries, an Egyptian one. The root is 'msy' meaning 'child of'. Many pharaohs' names end in 'messes' or 'mesy', linked always to a god of the Egyptian

---

1 The designation 'Hebrew' will be discussed in a later chapter.

2 Exodus 2:10.

pantheon: hence, for example, Ra-messes means 'child of Ra'. Without the god's, or any other, paternal name, the name is meaningless, so 'Moses' is clearly a corruption – but what is beyond doubt is that it is Egyptian, not Hebrew.

Moses grows up at the Egyptian court; we are given no details and it seems unclear whether he knows of his Levite heritage. But in any case, he kills an Egyptian who is ill-treating a Hebrew slave and, in fear of retribution, flees to the land of 'Midian'. Midianites feature largely in the story of Moses and elsewhere[3] in these books. The E Source says that after Sarah's death, Abraham married again to a woman called Keturah, with whom he had another six sons, all of whom received their inheritance and were sent away by Abraham to the east.[4] Midian was one of these sons of Abraham by Keturah, and the Midianites seem to have lived in Arabia – more specifically it seems, in the north-west of the Arabian Peninsula, south of Edom, on the east shore of the Gulf of Aqaba on the Red Sea – so, very close to a trade route out of Egypt. However, it seems likely that there was no such 'land'. Midianite was a term for the Arab tribes – nomadic shepherds and traders – who lived there. The normal social unit for these peoples – Israelite, Canaanite, Arabian – was the extended family and, when settled for a period, their 'village'. Their 'tribe' was a much looser association, claiming their allegiance for purposes of war and for collective cultic worship. Some scholars, therefore, argue that Midian was not a place at all but a 'tribal league' or 'cultic collective'. The word 'midian', in fact, comes from the Hebrew 'madon' meaning 'strife', and as we shall see as the narrative proceeds, worship and war intermingle endlessly in the ancestral tales we are dealing with.

---

3 As in E's version of Joseph being sold into slavery – to 'Midianites'.

4 Genesis 25:1-6.

In Midian, Moses meets a Midianite priest called Reuel[5] and marries his daughter Zipporah. Meanwhile, 'Pharaoh' (unspecified) dies and Yahweh recruits Moses to the task of confronting the new Pharaoh (also unspecified) by famously appearing to him in a burning bush. He renews the Promise originally made to Abraham an unknown number of years before, of a land flowing with milk and honey – the land of 'the Canaanites, and the Hittites, and the Amorites, and the Perizzites, and the Hivites, and the Jebusites'.[6] Before proceeding with the story, it would be best if we pause to notice who these peoples are:

- **Canaanites:** In Hebrew, *KənáƏan*, Canaan was one of Ham's sons[7] and the patriarch of the various tribes of the land named after him. From the same root comes the Levantine nomadic tribe of Kenites, who were coppersmiths and metalworkers. One of the seven names (see footnote below) of Moses' Midianite father-in-law was Keni, and he was apparently a Kenite.[8]
- **Hittites:** This one is easy now, though about a 150 years ago it would have been a puzzle. Since then, archaeology and Biblical texts together have uncovered an important Late Bronze Age civilization north of Canaan in Asia Minor, centred on its capital Hattusa. Its influence stretched south into Canaan, parts of which it occupied at times. Because Egypt was likewise expanding its sphere of influence north into Canaan, the Hit-

---

5 In fact, he goes by seven different names in different parts of the Bible: Reuel, Jether, Jethro, Hobab, Heber, Keni and Putiel. Fundamentalists tie themselves in knots reconciling this one. Presumably the earlier Reuel, son of Esau and father of Zerah, is someone different. Or perhaps not – who knows?

6 Exodus 3:8.

7 Genesis 10:6, 15-18.

8 Judges 1:16.

tites and Egyptians vied and often fought with one another during the first and second millennium BC.

- **Amorites**: We dealt with these earlier: the people that ultimately became synonymous in the Bible with Canaanites and were probably the racial origin of the Israelites.
- **Perizzites**: These are unknown outside of the Bible and were therefore probably not a tribe at all, but rather a nomadic people occupying the mountainous areas of Canaan: the Hebrew derivation of their name seems to mean something like 'rural people'.
- **Hivites**: Much the same can be said of this people – only referenced in the Bible and probably hill-dwelling nomads – their name seems to mean something like 'tent-dwellers'.
- **Jebusites**: Much like the Hivites and Perizzites, but centred on Jerusalem, which did not become an Israelite city until much later, under King David.

  Elsewhere[9] we are told of one other tribe in Canaan at the time:
- **Girgashites**: Even more obscure than the others, but perhaps to be identified with the Qaraqisha, who were a people from Asia Minor allied to the Hittites.

All these Hamite tribes are now to be ejected by the Israelites so they can take up their ancient Promise, first made to Abraham. Yahweh reassures Moses that those who sought his life are now dead, so he packs up his wife and sons and heads for Egypt. At some point he is joined by someone called Aaron. Both Hebrew and Egyptian etymologies have been suggested for this name, with various possible meanings. On balance, the Egyptian derivation is probably more

---

9 Deuteronomy 7:1.

plausible and his association with Moses makes this more likely, in which case the meaning would be something like 'warrior lion'. But J gives no backstory and at this point RJE abandons J for several chapters. The narrative, as supplied by others, involves Moses forcing Pharaoh to let the Israelites leave Egypt by invoking a series of plagues and Pharaoh's change of mind and hot pursuit of the fleeing horde, followed by the famous miracle of the parting of the Red Sea. The J Source does not re-enter the narrative until, in Chapter 14, the Israelites have left Egypt, and then J describes how they evade the pursuing Egyptians.

And it was told the king of Egypt that the people fled: . . . And he made ready his chariot, and took his people with him: . . . and he pursued after the children of Israel: . . . And . . . the children of Israel lifted up their eyes, and, behold, the Egyptians marched after them; and they were sore afraid: . . . And Moses said unto the people, Fear ye not, stand still, and see the salvation of the LORD, which he will shew to you today: for the Egyptians whom ye have seen today, ye shall see them again no more for ever. The LORD shall fight for you, and ye shall hold your peace . . . and the pillar of the cloud went from before their face, and stood behind them: . . . and it was a cloud and darkness to them, but it gave light by night to these: so that the one came not near the other all the night . . . and the LORD caused the sea to go back by a strong east wind all that night, and made the sea dry land . . . And it came to pass, that in the morning watch the LORD looked unto the host of the Egyptians through the pillar of fire and of the cloud, and troubled the host of the Egyptians, . . . so that the Egyptians said, Let us flee from the face of Israel; for the LORD fighteth for them against the Egyptians . . . and the sea returned to his strength when the morning appeared; and the Egyptians fled against it; and the LORD overthrew the Egyptians in the midst of the sea . . . Thus the LORD saved Israel that day out of the hand of the Egyptians; and Israel saw the Egyptians dead upon the sea shore. And Israel saw that great work which the LORD did upon the Egyptians: and the people feared the LORD, and believed the LORD, and his servant Moses.[10]

In this passage, the ellipses indicate where I have removed passages by other hands, leaving just the J account, which is the earliest of the four main sources for this story. What we have left here seems to be an entirely coherent account, but very different to the account of the sea miraculously parting with which we are familiar from Sunday School. In this version, the sea is just blown back by a strong east wind; there is no suggestion at all that the waves parted to create a corridor with walls of water on both sides, as so graphically shown in the film *The Ten Commandments*. We shall return to the subject when we examine other layers in this narrative.

The next J Source material comes in Chapter 15, where we are told how Yahweh solves the food and drink problem of the Israelite horde wandering in the Negev Desert. Moses, with Yahweh's help, turns the bitter lake of Marah into sweet water, and Yahweh rains down 'manna' from heaven every day. Both 'Marah' and 'manna' are obscure and disputed among scholars. But they reflect J's recognition that millions of people in the desert would need something miraculous and of this magnitude in order to survive. A lake of sweet water and food dropping from the skies on a daily basis would do the trick: I leave to the reader to judge the likelihood. Then, having got the Israelites miraculously fed and watered, some nineteen chapters later, J next tells the

---

10 Exodus 14: 5-31.

story of Moses receiving stone tablets containing the Ten Commandments. That ends the J narrative in Exodus.

The story according to J continues in the final section of Numbers Chapter 10. Moses announces that they are now setting off for Canaan and asks Hobab, who is Reuel's son (and therefore Moses' brother-in-law), to accompany them because he knows the desert well – presumably better than Moses? J next picks up in Chapter 13, at which point they have all arrived on the borders of Canaan, and Moses sends out scouts to check things out. True to form, the places they spy out in southerner J's version are all in the south – they never venture into the north at all. The scouts report back to confirm the attractions of Canaan, but also (in a passage we referred to earlier) about the powerful Canaanite peoples already there, including the Nephilim giants. This gives the Israelites pause which, in turn, infuriates Yahweh at their lack of trust in Him. The only exception among the scouts is Caleb, who exhorts the Israelites to have faith that Yahweh will protect them: Caleb is the patriarch of the Calebites – a family of the Judah tribe and another southern hero. Yahweh threatens to slaughter them all in his anger, but Moses talks him down by pointing out that it would not exactly be good PR for Him. Yahweh calms down but declares that the current generation must die out before he will allow their descendants to inherit the Promise; he tells Moses to lead them south again into the desert in the direction of the Red Sea.[11]

The Israelites reject this and attempt to conquer Canaan on their own without the support of Yahweh, and they are beaten back.[12] Moses now faces an insurrection from some who still refuse to turn south, but Yahweh causes them to be

---

11 Numbers 14:25.

12 Numbers 14:39-45.

swallowed up alive by the earth.[13] He then leads them as far south as Kadesh Barnea on the western border of the land of Edom and then, seeking to turn north again up the eastern side of the Dead Sea and the Jordan valley, asks permission to pass through Edom.[14] This is refused and, after a successful battle with Canaanites in the Negev,[15] the Israelites do travel north up the east side of the Jordan, but skirting to the east of Edom and Moab. The land north of Moab is occupied by Ammonites and Bashites who attack the Israelites. The latter win the battle and are then able themselves to occupy all the land bounded by the Dead Sea and Jordan to the west, the Ammonites to the east, and the rivers Arnon and Jabbok to the south and north respectively. They then extend their occupation further north still by defeating King Og of Bashan.[16] All this land covering the top half of Transjordan became known as Gilead and was, we are told, perfect for herding sheep, so, at this point the tribes of Reuben, Gad and half of the tribe of Manasseh ask for it for themselves. On condition that their fighting men continue to assist in the conquest of Canaan across the Jordan, Moses agrees to this and, that is where those tribes established themselves.[17]

The J Source then ends with a few verses that have found their way into Deuteronomy, recounting the death of Moses in Moab. The subsequent Conquest of Canaan on the west side of the Jordan thus takes place under Moses' successor, Joshua, and is recounted in the book that bears his name – the sixth in the Old Testament, coming immediately after the Pentateuch. But what seems clear thus far is that the J Source

---

13 Numbers 16:33.

14 Numbers 20:14-21.

15 Numbers 21:1-3.

16 Numbers 21:21-35.

17 Numbers 32:33.

is a much simpler, and in many ways believable, account of the Exodus than is presented in the finally redacted book of that name. Moses leads the Israelites out of Egypt and they evade capture. They avoid the warlike Philistines and fear the Canaanites; so skirt round to the east and establish a foothold in Transjordan from which to launch their Canaanite campaign. If we take the references to Yahweh out of the picture, the story J tells seems to accord with common sense, and of course, if Wellhausen, Friedman (and others) are correct in identifying J as the earliest source, then it is tempting to suppose that this is closer to what actually may have happened than the later elaborated versions. J does say that the Israelites cannot move into Canaan until a generation has passed, and this presumably equates to the forty years' delay familiar to us from other sources. It is not clear from J where they waited for the generation to die – Midian? Transjordan? – but there is no description of that period spent 'wandering' around the Negev aimlessly.

Let us now backtrack to the beginning of Exodus and review the story as narrated by E.

CHAPTER II

Moses according to E

E, in fact, provides the backstory to the Exodus, missing from J:

> Now there arose up a new king over Egypt, which knew not Joseph.[1]

We are still not told the new pharaoh's name, nor what period of time has passed. This pharaoh, apparently unaware of the history, but in any case not unreasonably concerned about the proliferation of aliens in any part of Egypt, enslaved Jacob's descendants. Pharaoh's specific worry was lest:

> when there falleth out any war, they join also unto our enemies, and fight against us, and so get them up out of the land.[2]

This motivation is understandable. Joseph and his family and presumably, therefore, their descendants, settled in

---

1 Exodus 1:8.

2 Exodus 1:10.

Goshen in the eastern Nile Delta, straddling the strategic route into Egypt from Canaan and beyond. For much of the history of Egypt, a series of pharaohs built and maintained forts across that route and sought to control the lands on its borders (like Canaan), from whence invasion might come. To have an alien population of potential defectors in an area of such strategic importance would worry any ruler. We shall see later that there is an Egyptian text that may well confirm that pharaoh's fear was entirely justified – that the Israelites in Goshen did indeed invite in Egypt's 'enemies' in the real events behind the Biblical Exodus.

The Israelites were set the task of building two 'treasure cities, Pithom and Pi-Ramesses'. The translation 'treasure cities' is uncertain. Our bibles are based on the Masoretic text – the authoritative Hebrew and Aramaic text for Rabbinic Judaism, copied, edited and distributed by a group of Jews known as the Masoretes between the 7th and 10th centuries AD. An earlier text is the Septuagint, the Greek translation of the Old Testament from the original Hebrew which goes back to the mid-3rd century BC. That version calls them 'fortified cities', which seems much more likely, given their strategic location between Egypt and potential enemies in Canaan and Asia Minor. In other words, Pharaoh was using the Israelites to build a defence against the very threat that they themselves represented. Pithom, also known as Per-Atum and Heroo[no]polis, was a major Egyptian city. Its precise location is a matter of debate, but it is generally agreed that it was somewhere along the Way of Shur, a main trade route from Egypt to Canaan, in the eastern Nile Delta, and therefore in the area of Goshen where the Israelites were settled. This was known to the Egyptians as the region (or 'None') of Tjeku or Sukkot/Succoth.

As we saw earlier, Pi-Ramesses was the new capital built by the 19th Dynasty, Ramesses II (1279–1213 BC), or possibly by his father, also in the eastern Nile Delta. We saw that both Ramesses I and Ramesses II ('the Great') have at times been identified as the Pharaoh of the Israelite Exodus from Egypt, placing that event sometime in the 13th century BC. In 1884, the pioneering Egyptologist and archaeologist Sir William Matthews Flinders Petrie (1853–1942) searched for Pi-Ramesses in the Delta, focusing on the modern, main branch of the Nile, but found what in the end turned out to be Tanis. The modern branch is known as 'Tanitic' for this reason. It was not until the 1960s that the Austrian archaeologist Manfred Bietak, who is probably the foremost Egyptologist of our day, realized that the Tanitic Branch of the Nile did not exist in the 13th century: the various branches of the Delta have shifted extensively over the millennia. Recognizing that Pi-Ramesses was known to have been located on the then-easternmost branch of the Nile, he painstakingly mapped all the branches of the ancient Delta and established another branch, now dried up, but was the main, eastern-most during the reign of the first two Ramesses. He struck gold – both the site of the Hyksos city of Avaris, and just 2 kilometres further north Pi-Ramesses, in modern Qantir. The ancient branch he traced is now known as the Pelusiac Branch because it empties into the Mediterranean at the site of an important Ancient Egyptian port called Pelusium. As we shall see, the identification of the Pelusiac Branch is of vital importance in the interpretation of the Exodus accounts but does little to pin down the date of that event, since Avaris of the Hyksos and Pi-Ramesses were both located on its banks.

When enslavement does not halt the proliferation of the Israelites in the Delta, Pharaoh plots genocide. E tells us that the agents of this are to be 'the Hebrew midwives . . . Shiphrah . . . and . . . Puah'. Just two of them: this gives us a clue as to just how numerous the Israelites in Egypt were at this time – perhaps an adult population of about 1,500 Israelites? Whatever the number, it certainly suggests a smaller population than the several million we are told participated in the Exodus, and it is a lot more than two midwives could cope with for sure! E does not tell us how much time elapses between the midwife incident and the Exodus. We are told that the midwives evaded Pharaoh's edict and that the Israelites continued to multiply, so it is just possible that the population grew from thousands to millions in the intervening period – but the implication of the midwife story is that perhaps the Exodus was a more modest, small-scale event than the narrative later would have us believe. It certainly would seem more likely.

E now jumps straight to the story of Moses and the Exodus. He not only gives no indication of timeframe but neglects also to give us any background story or genealogy for Moses. We are just told that Moses lives by tending the flocks of his father-in-law, Jethro. (This, of course, conflicts with J's version where he is called Reuel.) Jethro/Reuel is a Midianite priest and the action takes place on Mount Horeb. Subsequent events also take place there, most notably the creation of the tablets bearing the Ten Commandments. It is the holy mountain where God dwells and is always referred to by E (and by D) as Horeb. J and P, on the other hand, refer to a Mount Sinai in the same context. Some have tried to argue that they are different places, but it seems clear that they are two names for the same place. It seems that just as E and J had different traditions about the name of Moses' father-in-law, they also had different names for the mountain where he kept his sheep and where Yahweh dwelt. The precise location of Horeb/Sinai is disputed but presumably somewhere in the area occupied by the Midianite tribes – south of Edom and east of the Gulf of Aqaba.

The burning bush appears only in **J**; in **E**, God just calls to Moses, identifies himself as the God of Abraham, Isaac and Jacob, and of the Promise to Abraham, and tells Moses he has been chosen to lead the Israelites out of their bondage. Not unreasonably, Moses asks effectively, 'Why me?'. God does not answer directly but reassures Moses that he will support him. Moses then says:

> ... when I come unto the children of Israel, and shall say unto them, The God of your fathers hath sent me unto you; and they shall say to me, What is his name? what shall I say unto them?[3]

Note the 'your' fathers, not 'our' fathers – Moses here does not seem to regard himself as an Israelite. Does he regard himself as Midianite? Or, if we believe the **J** story, Egyptian? And note also that Moses does not seem to know God's name. For Moses at least, this is a new God – one he has not heard of before. Apparently, God's name is 'I am' or, in Hebrew, 'ehye'. This is a play on words, for this is the God Yahweh. It seems that Moses has never heard of him. From this point on, **E** refers to God by this name – Yahweh – rather than El. It seems that for **E** at least, the Canaanite God he had known as El was the same God as Yahweh – it is just that no one knew His real name until He revealed it to Moses.

Moses now asks Yahweh how he is going to convince Pharaoh of his mission. God offers him three proofs. First, he turns Moses' 'rod' or staff into a snake and back again; then he turns Moses' arm 'leprous as snow' and back again; and finally, he tells Moses that if he pours water on the ground it will turn to blood. In the event, Moses only uses the rod

---

3 Exodus 3:13.

trick and then, Pharaoh remaining famously intransigent, he invokes the seven plagues one by one. The first plague involves turning the Nile to blood, so is perhaps the equivalent of the third proof. But interestingly, no more is said of the leprosy trick. Why? First, we must be clear what is meant here by leprosy, because that disease never manifests itself as white like 'snow' as here described – 'raw, angry red' would have been more accurate. There is a body of evidence to suggest that the disease we now know as leprosy was not around in the Middle East (or perhaps even anywhere) at the time, and references throughout the Bible to leprosy refer to other diseases of the skin, such as psoriasis, which do manifest as white flakes. But again, why such a strange trick? This is an important matter to which we shall return. We shall see that it is a theme that recurs in Exodus, and in the later books of the Pentateuch which are concerned with the requirement of God's law for the Israelites. There really seems to be an unhealthy obsession with ritual purity generally, and diseases/complaints of the skin in particular. Why?

Moses tries one last ploy to shirk his mission – he complains:

> . . . O my Lord, I am not eloquent, neither heretofore, nor since thou hast spoken unto thy servant: but I am slow of speech, and of a slow tongue.[4]

Commentators on this passage often debate about Moses' speech defect, but the translation here hides the truth. The literal translation of the last few words would be 'heavy of tongue'. In Ezekiel,[5] the same phrase is used to describe foreigners:

---

4 Exodus 4:10.

5 Ezekiel 3:5-7.

people of a strange speech and of an hard language, whose words thou canst not understand.

Again, what the King James Version translates here as 'hard language' is literally 'heavy of tongue'. Moses, it seems, is a foreigner who cannot speak Hebrew – he comes from Egypt and now lives in Midian, where the language spoken would have been ancient Arabic of some variety. He needs not just someone more eloquent than him – he needs a Hebrew translator. And God (growing angry by now) gives him one – Aaron, who we are told is 'the Levite, thy brother'. As we shall see, the idea that Aaron is Moses' brother is not found in J or E. J introduces Aaron with no explanation at all, and even for E, Aaron is probably not related to Moses – he is a 'brother' because they are both Levites.

They travel to Egypt and Aaron tells the Israelites what Yahweh has said, whereupon they not only believe, they 'bowed their heads and worshipped'. Presumably this implies that they not only believed Moses to be their rescuer, but they also believed in the new God Yahweh. But Pharaoh is not so impressed:

Who is the Lord, that I should obey his voice to let Israel go?
I know not the Lord, neither will I let Israel go.[6]

'Lord' here should be translated as 'Yahweh'; Pharaoh is saying quite explicitly that, like Moses, and presumably like the Israelites themselves, he has never heard of a god called Yahweh. On God's instruction Moses and Aaron have told Pharaoh, not that the Israelites want permanent escape, but simply that:

---

6 Exodus 5:2.

. . . The God of the Hebrews hath met with us: let us go, we pray thee, three days' journey into the desert, and sacrifice unto the Lord our God; lest he fall upon us with pestilence, or with the sword.[7]

Why would God do that to His people – unless he was a new God, demanding an introductory act of obedience? And unless this was just a deception, why no reference here to slavery? The implication seems to be that the motivation was religious rather than sociopolitical. Was the idea that after placating Yahweh in the desert, the Israelites would return? Certainly, there is no mention here of a permanent Exodus, let alone a migration to Canaan.

Whatever the case, Pharaoh remains unimpressed and oppresses the Israelites even more, whereupon Moses returns to Yahweh and complains that his intervention has just made things worse. Yahweh tells Moses to return to Pharaoh, but Pharaoh remains obdurate through a sequence of ten plagues visited by Yahweh on Egypt – water into blood, frogs, lice, flies, murrain (death of cattle), hail and fire, locusts, darkness, and finally, the death of every firstborn. And Pharaoh at last lets the Israelites go – 600,000 men plus women and children, so presumably millions in total. The way to Canaan would then naturally take them up through Philistia, the land of the Philistines, which was in the south-west Levant. But crossing hostile Philistine territory would have been risky and, according to E's narrative, having to confront battle might have disheartened the Israelites into fleeing back to Egypt. So, Yahweh instructs Moses to lead them, armed for battle, 'through the way of the wilderness of the Red Sea' – that is, skirting south of Philistia and down into the Sinai

---

7 Exodus 5:3. Note that Yahweh is the 'God of the Hebrews' - as if the Israelites are not themselves 'Hebrews'.

Peninsula. Pharaoh then regrets the decision to let the Israelites go and takes after them with an army of 600 chariots – that is, one chariot per thousand Israelite fighting men. Those odds do not suggest that the Israelites would need much help from Yahweh to see the Egyptian army off. Yet the E narrative then refers to an intervention by an angel:

> And the angel of God, which went before the camp of Israel, removed and went behind them; . . . And it came between the camp of the Egyptians and the camp of Israel; . . . And took off their chariot wheels, that they drove them heavily.

And that's it – just an angel intervening to slow the Egyptians down. J's version had the wind blowing the sea back. But neither E nor J have the famous parting of the sea – that comes in later with P.

The E narrative now moves on to describe how the Israelites, having evaded pursuit, reached Mount Horeb (or Sinai) where Moses first met Yahweh, and they complain of thirst and blame Moses for leading them to die in the desert. Yahweh solves the problem by getting Moses to strike a rock with his staff and water springs forth. And we are to believe that this is sufficient for millions of people. At least J had a whole lake of fresh water. Having surmounted this problem, they come under attack from the Amalekites – inhabitants of Edom. Joshua now enters the narrative in E for the first time, although we are given no backstory. E features Joshua prominently because he is an Ephraimite and a northern hero. J does not mention him at all. Joshua leads the Israelites into battle with the Amalekites and prevails because the other northern hero Moses holds up his magic staff. It seems strange that although both J and E know of Moses – implying perhaps some common historical memory – only E knows of Joshua. According to the Deuteronomic Book of

Joshua, it is Joshua that leads the Conquest of Canaan. He seems to have been introduced into the story of the Exodus merely to set him up for his role in the subsequent Conquest.

Now Moses' Midianite family re-enter the story. Apparently, Moses' wife, Zipporah, and his sons, Gershom and Eliezer, had been staying with Jethro [Reuel] for safety and now they are all reunited again. Jethro recognizes the greatness of Yahweh, advises Moses to set up 'judges' to relieve him of personally handling everyday disputes, and then returns home and out of the story. All of which sounds gratuitous: one wonders if the only reason for his reintroduction to the story at this point is to provide an aetiological explanation for the later period when the theocratic Israelite nation eschewed earthly monarchical forms of government in favour of a more democratic system of law enforcement under a series of judges. Appropriately in that case, Yahweh now speaks with Moses from a cloud on Mount Horeb, frightens the life out of the Israelites, who ask Moses to always act as intermediary, and then delivers to Moses a range of such laws for the Israelites to follow and the judges to administer. These concern the treatment of servants, personal disputes, property rights, social responsibility, justice, and Sabbath observation. But while all this is happening on the mountain, the Israelites begin to wonder if Moses is ever going to come back down, and demand that Aaron make physical 'gods' for them. Aaron for some reason obliges, makes a golden calf, erects an altar before it, and the Israelites have a feast and cavort naked. Yahweh gets angry about this, but Moses talks Him down yet again and heads off down the mountain with two tablets of stone, inscribed in God's own handwriting.

This version is in reality a parallel story to the one given in J, except that these tablets are smashed by Moses in anger at the golden calf incident, and Yahweh's laws are much longer. J's version just gives the Ten Commandments; E's version constitutes a more detailed new 'Covenant' between Yahweh and the Israelites. The terms of the Covenant are quite explicit: if the Israelites follow Yahweh's detailed rules of behaviour, Yahweh in return will protect and bless them. RJE had the problem of reconciling E's long version with J's much shorter one: he solved the problem thus created by allowing two sets of tablets and inserting these words from Yahweh:

> I will write upon these tables the words that were in the first tables, which thou brakest.

The two versions presumably represent the different traditions in the north and the south. Perhaps RJE wanted to keep both versions to preserve their differences; and/or perhaps this is an indication that his usual method is to preserve both J and E accounts of things.

When Moses arrives at the scene of naked feasting, he shatters the stone tablets, destroys the calf and demands an explanation from Aaron, who really has none. Moses asks who is on Yahweh's side, and the 'sons of Levi' rally round him. He then instructs them to kill every man in the camp, resulting in the slaughter of three thousand men. One wonders how many 'sons of Levi' there must have been to achieve this slaughter. This passage points to the Levites as somehow differentiated from the other nascent tribes, and especially close to Moses. Yahweh then forgives the Israelites, sends them on to Canaan, but says He will not accompany them because he cannot trust Himself not to kill more of them, so angry is He about their unfaithfulness to Him. He promises to send an angel to go before them to drive out the existing Canaanites. As they travel, Moses communes daily with Yahweh in a 'tent of meeting' – the Tabernacle – and persuades Him to stay with them after all. And that concludes the E narrative in Exodus.

It is picked up again in Chapter 11 of Numbers, which describes more incidents of intransigence and rebellion by the Israelites against Moses' leadership and Yahweh's provision for them. Then, in Numbers Chapter 12, there is a curious incident that needs attention.

It involves Aaron and someone called Miriam. In J, Aaron is introduced with no explanation of who he is. And in E earlier, he is introduced as Moses' Levite brother, there being no indication of any familial tie beyond the tribal connection. But also in E, we are given the golden calf story, in which Aaron is implicated in idolatry, although his precise involvement is arguably ambiguous. Here, a little later in E's narrative, we are again given a negative story about Aaron. It also involves Miriam, who does not appear at all in J and appears unannounced for the first time here in E. Together, Aaron and Miriam object to Moses' 'Cushite wife'. Some scholars regard this as a second wife, others that she is identical with Zipporah, the Midianite. I lean to the latter view: Cushites were originally Arabian as well as African peoples. In any case, Yahweh gets very upset about this. He says that Moses is unique: Yahweh may speak to others in visions and dreams but only Moses gets to talk to Him face to face. As we shall see elsewhere, Miriam is depicted as a prophetess, so this is aimed at her in particular, and Yahweh renders her 'leprous, white as snow', as he had done previously to Moses on Mount Horeb. Moses pleads her case and Yahweh relents.

There are two things to note here. First is the relative roles of Moses and Aaron. For E, Moses is the main hero and Aaron gets a bad press. In both the golden calf incident and the Cushite wife incident, Aaron is seen in opposition to Moses. In both cases he escapes censure but is clearly culpable. These incidents do not appear in J, who presents Aaron in a more positive light. I referred earlier to the later historic rivalry between the Mushite priests descended from Moses and the Aaronide priests descended from Aaron. The former were strong in the north/Israel; the latter were strong in the south/Judah and Jerusalem. It is not surprising, therefore, that the northern writer E denigrates Aaron and the southern writer J approves of him. But the second point to note here is harder to explain. Why insert this strange story here at all? The references to leprosy here and in the earlier story of Moses' arm seem entirely arbitrary; they lead nowhere and yet surely hint at something. But what?

Another fragment from E follows in Chapter 21. As usual, the Israelites are complaining about the lack of food and drink. Yahweh sends a plague of snakes and Moses intercedes again. Yahweh tells him to make a bronze snake and put it on a pole: the sight of this totem will heal snake bites. The story is told to provide an aetiological explanation for a snake totem that seems to have been used in the north at later times. Then in Chapters 22–24 the strange and obviously ancient Canaanite fable of Balaam and his talking ass is inserted. Balaam was some sort of prophet, probably dwelling in Ammonite country, who is asked by the King of Moab to put a curse on the invading Israelites, who were settling in Gilead to their north and therefore represented a threat. Balaam consults Yahweh, and on his instruction blesses rather than curses the Israelites and prophesies the triumph of Israel over their Transjordan enemies. Part of this long, repetitive tale involves Balaam's ass talking to him to warn him of an invisible angel – another example of E's obsession with angelic beings. And with that piece of prophecy, made with the 20/20 vision of hindsight and combined with animal fable, E's contribution to Numbers comes to an end. The only other passage that seems to have come from E is found in Deuteronomy Chapter 31, where E, true to form, describes Yahweh's appointment of the northern hero Joshua as Moses' successor.

CHAPTER 12

Moses according to P

Unlike Genesis, the **P** Source is important in Exodus, so we must now deal with its version of the same events. **P** tells in just three verses[1] how the Israelites grew in numbers in Egypt and were oppressed. God hears them[2] and calls Moses.[3] He is given no introduction or backstory, but the narrative is coherent. God introduces himself as Yahweh and, as in **E**, indicates that:

> . . . I appeared unto Abraham, unto Isaac, and unto Jacob, by the name of God Almighty, but by my name Jehovah was I not known to them.

The Hebrew phrase translated here as 'God Almighty' is 'El Shaddai'. It appears a handful of times before this, usually in connection with fruitfulness. 'El' of course is the Canaanite word for God, but the etymology of 'Shaddai' is obscure and much debated by scholars, with potential associations as diverse as wilderness, mountains, destruction and female

---

1 Exodus 1:7, 13-14.

2 Exodus 2:23-25.

3 Exodus 6.

breasts. The point here is that this is the time in the history of the Israelites when God entrusts his 'real' name to them. The implication again is that Yahweh worship was an innovation introduced at the time of Moses.

Moses carries the message to the Israelites, who are too oppressed to listen, so Yahweh tells Moses to go direct to Pharaoh with the message to let them go. At this point, the **P** narrative is interrupted by another passage of unknown authorship, but almost certainly dating from the same period as **P**, sandwiched between Chapter 6:12 and Chapter 7:30, which are repeats of each other. The passage lists the 'heads of the[ir] fathers' houses' that came out from Egypt. The house/tribe of Reuben, Jacob's firstborn, is listed first. We are given the names of his four sons. Next comes Jacob's second son, Simeon, and we are given the names of his six sons. Third comes the third son, Levi. Here we are given much more detail: the names of three sons, eight grandsons, seven great-grandsons, and a great-great-grandson. The remaining nine sons of Jacob and their tribes are not listed at all, or even referred to. Three possible explanations spring to mind: either the other nine patriarchs were fictional in some way; or the writer stopped at Levi because he was the most important; or both are true. Whatever the case, the importance of the priestly Levites, already apparent from their attachment to Moses and their violence in his name, is indicated not only by the extra detail, but by the fact that both Moses and Aaron are listed among the grandsons of Levi – both the sons of Amram and Jochebed. Amram is Levi's grandson and Jochebed is his (Amram's) aunt!

A key point to note here is the number of generations between Jacob and Moses: four. It will be recalled that God promised Abraham that the Exodus would be after four generations, so there is a potential concordance of information here. If the Israelite Sojourn in Egypt was indeed about four generations, and each generation is about 30 years as we would calculate in modern times, we arrive at a figure of about 120 years. The earlier reference in Genesis gives 400 years for the Sojourn, and we earlier noted the disparity. The other conclusion we might draw from this passage is one that we have addressed before – that the number of people involved in the Exodus would have been in the hundreds rather than millions – a fact we began to suspect on the basis of the number of Hebrew midwives. Moses is only three generations down from Jacob's son Levi. Twelve sons over three generations would suggest a number of Israelites in the low thousands – a number that two midwives could handle, but falling far short of the millions suggested by E. It really seems on this evidence that if the Exodus happened, it was a low-key event, that were it not for the Biblical record, would have left little or no mark at all on history.

Returning now to the main narrative, Moses complains that he is of 'uncircumcised lips'.[4] This is usually interpreted as referring either to impurity or to defect in speech. My own view is that it means that like the rest of him, Moses is not circumcised, and that he is not therefore an Israelite, and as argued above, he does not speak Hebrew. This is important if we are later to identify the historical truth behind the identity of Moses. There is a strange incident recorded at around this time only by J; Moses is on his way from Yahweh to tell the Israelites of their potential rescue:

At a lodging place on the way, the LORD met Moses and was about to kill him. But Zipporah took a flint knife, cut off her son's foreskin and touched Moses' feet with it. "Surely you are a bridegroom of blood to me," she said. So the LORD let

---

4 Exodus 6:30.

him alone. (At that time she said "bridegroom of blood", referring to circumcision.)[5]

Commentators, not surprisingly, have always had a problem with this passage – it just seems weird, and unless you believe that Scripture cannot be in error, it surely indicates that a text has got scrambled here at some point. Even the final redactor seems to have found it strange and obscure, hence the 'explanation' offered at the end in brackets. Taken at face value it seems to refer to a reluctance on the part of Moses to circumcise his son, as required by Yahweh. This in itself must surely point to a non-Israelite origin for Moses.

I do have another interpretation – but it requires a slight modification. I think this passage originally described the circumcision of Moses himself. A later redactor, uncomfortable with the idea that an uncircumcised Moses implies a non-Israelite Moses, has replaced 'his' foreskin with 'her son's'. In the immediately preceding passage, which is by **E**, Yahweh has told Moses to say to Pharaoh:

'This is what the LORD says: Israel is my firstborn son, and I told you, "Let my son go, so he may worship me." But you refused to let him go; so I will kill your firstborn son.'[6]

I would suggest that the redactor has sought to use this passage to 'explain' the circumcision passage. In the original narrative, perhaps there was a now deleted passage in which Yahweh required Moses' circumcision – a painful procedure for an adult – and Moses declined. This would explain Yahweh's anger and desire to 'kill' Moses – we have often seen Him do more for less in these books. We saw that when

5 Exodus 4:24-6.

6 Exodus 4:22-3.

Yahweh commissions Moses to go to Pharaoh, Moses'
unwillingness to accept the job enrages Yahweh. Perhaps
part of this unwillingness was reluctance to accept adult
genital mutilation. To defuse the confrontation, Zipporah
takes things into her own hands (literally), circumcises her
husband and throws the foreskin at his feet declaring, in
effect, now you are a proper Israelite husband. This interpretation is of course unprovable, but it is consonant with the
case I am gradually building about the identity of Moses,
and in reality only requires a change of two small words.
Either way – father or son – the reluctance here to circumcise betrays a non-Israelite origin, and the garbled nature of
the passage betrays embarrassment about it.

P's narrative now continues with *his* version of the
plagues: water to blood, frogs, boils and then the killing of
the firstborn. The list is shorter than E's and boils only
appear in P. Then P tells us that:

> Now the sojourning of the children of Israel, who dwelt in
> Egypt, was four hundred and thirty years.[7]

This is always regarded as a key text for interpreting the
historicity and dating of the Exodus account, and Jewish
history generally. The problem is that it conflicts with the
other statements elsewhere in these books; we now have four
hundred years, four generations, one hundred and twenty
years, and now four hundred and thirty years. Theologians
divide into two camps on this – those who argue for a 'long
Sojourn' of about 400–430 years and those who prefer a
'short Sojourn' of about 120 years. We shall see later that
both are probably correct – if you interpret the meaning of
'Sojourn' correctly. P now exhibits his priestly concerns

---

7 Exodus 12:40.

by setting out the rules for observing Passover – the Jewish celebration of their Exodus from Egypt – before turning to the famous 'miracle' of the parting of the Red Sea, allowing the Israelites through and drowning Pharaoh and his army.

More nonsense has been talked about this miracle than almost any other part of this narrative. The miracle and the ten plagues that precede it, like all miracles in the Bible, tempt rationalistic commentators to find natural causes for what are described as supernatural events. I see no need and, in any case, the explanations rarely if ever properly fit with the Biblical description. We saw that the other two sources describe mundane victories involving wheels getting bogged down and strong winds. It is the later P Source that gives us the full-blown parting of the sea:

> And the LORD spake unto Moses, saying, Speak unto the children of Israel, that they turn and encamp before Pi-hahiroth, between Migdol and the sea, over against Baalzephon: before it shall ye encamp by the sea. For Pharaoh will say of the children of Israel, They are entangled in the land, the wilderness hath shut them in. And I will harden Pharaoh's heart, that he shall follow after them; and I will be honoured upon Pharaoh, and upon all his host; that the Egyptians may know that I am the LORD. And they did so. . . .
>
> And the LORD hardened the heart of Pharaoh king of Egypt, and he pursued after the children of Israel: and the children of Israel went out with an high hand. But the Egyptians pursued after them, all the horses and chariots of Pharaoh, and his horsemen, and his army, and overtook them encamping by the sea, beside Pi-Hahiroth, before Baalzephon. And when Pharaoh drew nigh, the children of Israel lifted up their eyes, and, behold, the Egyptians marched after them; and they were sore afraid: and the children of Israel cried out unto the LORD. . . .

And the LORD said unto Moses, Wherefore criest thou unto me? speak unto the children of Israel, that they go forward: But lift thou up thy rod, and stretch out thine hand over the sea, and divide it: and the children of Israel shall go on dry ground through the midst of the sea. And I, behold, I will harden the hearts of the Egyptians, and they shall follow them: and I will get me honour upon Pharaoh, and upon all his host, upon his chariots, and upon his horsemen. And the Egyptians shall know that I am the LORD, when I have gotten me honour upon Pharaoh, upon his chariots, and upon his horsemen. . . .

And Moses stretched out his hand over the sea; . . . and the waters were divided. And the children of Israel went into the midst of the sea upon the dry ground: and the waters were a wall unto them on their right hand, and on their left. And the Egyptians pursued, and went in after them to the midst of the sea, even all Pharaoh's horses, his chariots, and his horsemen. . . .

And the LORD said unto Moses, Stretch out thine hand over the sea, that the waters may come again upon the Egyptians, upon their chariots, and upon their horsemen. And Moses stretched forth his hand over the sea, and the sea returned to his strength when the morning appeared; . . .

And the waters returned, and covered the chariots, and the horsemen, and all the host of Pharaoh that came into the sea after them; there remained not so much as one of them. But the children of Israel walked upon dry land in the midst of the sea; and the waters were a wall unto them on their right hand, and on their left.[8]

P here also gives more detail of the route taken by the fleeing

---

8 Exodus 14:1-29.

Israelites. They start out from the eastern Delta fortress of Pi-Ramesses, which it will be recalled was where **P** had Joseph and his family finally settled. The natural route from there would be to follow the Pelusiac Branch of the Nile north-east to Pelusium on the coast, then take the coast road east and then turn north into Philistia. The problem with this route, apart from the Philistines themselves, was that the coast road was narrow, bounded by the desert to the south and the marshes, bogs and sand dunes of the Mediterranean coast to the north. The region was legendarily treacherous in antiquity. The worst area was modern day Lake Bardawil, which is one of the major lakes of the Sinai, running for 30km along the coast eastwards from Pelusium and stretching up to 14km south towards the desert. It is shallow, reaching a depth of only about 3 metres. In antiquity, it was called Lake Serbonis, and Herodotus, writing in the 5th century BC, referred to it as the 'Serbonian Bog': because sand blew onto it, the 'bog' had a deceptive appearance of being solid land but was a notorious quagmire in which, according to Herodotus, whole armies were fabled to be swallowed up and lost.[9] The coastal road ran east–west between the bog and the desert, and on the western extremity was the major port city and Egyptian stronghold Pelusium, now silted up but originally built upon the Pelusiac Branch of the Nile where it opens into the Mediterranean. As Bietak showed, the Pelusiac Branch was the main branch of the Nile at the time. So, the Israelites would have followed the Pelusiac Branch up to Pelusium and then turned east to follow the coast road with the Serbonian Bog to their left and the desert to their right.

---

9 The term 'Serbonian Bog' became, and still is, a metaphor for a convoluted situation from which extrication is difficult.

Fig. 8: Map of the Nile Delta Area 1

E told us that Yahweh prevented the Israelites taking the coast road to Philistia and diverted them south towards the Red Sea. **P** says that Yahweh told them to 'turn [back]' and:

> encamp before Pi-Hahiroth, between Migdol and the sea, over against Baal-zephon.

The locations of these three places are obscure. However, a much later (Hellenistic) text now in the Cairo Museum[10] lists four border fortresses in the eastern Delta, the third being 'Midgol and Ba'al Zaphon'. In the context of the text, this fortress appears to have been located on the route down to the Red Sea coast. But how far down? The location of the

---

10 *Cairo Papyrus 31169.*

parting of the sea is usually located at the Red Sea, far to the south. But it has been recognized for centuries that 'Red' is a mistranslation of 'Reed' and 'Reed Sea' could describe any of the major Sinai lakes, or the marshy hinterland of the Red Sea, or indeed the similar terrain bordering the Mediterranean. All these have been identified as the location of the miracle.

The location Pi-Hahiroth is much disputed, although a Hebrew etymology meaning 'mouth of the gorges' is possible, so therefore a river mouth seems indicated. Migdol is more straightforward. It means simply 'watchtower', consonant with a fortress location, and there was one such on the Pelusiac Branch, just south of Pelusium itself, on the western edge of the Serbonian Bog. Baal was the Canaanite storm god – he appears often in the Old Testament as the antithesis of Yahweh. Baal-zephon was an avatar of Baal, associated specifically with storms at sea; appeasing him was necessary for the protection of ships at sea, so cultic shrines to this deity were scattered all round the Mediterranean. Zephon is Mount Zaphon where Baal was worshipped. Unfortunately, Mt. Zaphon is confidently identified as the modern Jebel Aqra much further north on the Syrian–Turkish border. However, wherever that god was worshipped, there appear to have been other places known as Baal-Zephon so one such may have been in the Pelusium area. Jebel Aqra was known as Mons Casius, and a sanctuary of Zeus Casius is known of from the 5th century BC onwards in the vicinity of the Serbonian Bog. The sanctuary is identified with a hillock on the *western* extremity of the lake. If these various identifications are right, and if Pi-Hahiroth is 'between Migdol and the sea' and 'over against Baal-Zephon', this surely points to it being the name for Pelusium. Surely this area is where we should look for the location and the explanation of the 'miracle'.

I would argue that the Israelites (whoever they were, and however many of them there were) left Pi-Ramesses and quite naturally headed up the eastern bank of the Pelusiac Branch of the Nile towards Pelusium and the coast road towards Philistia and Canaan beyond. Pharaoh, based further south on the Nile in Thebes, would have been several days behind them. It is a peculiarly modern assumption that travel by road is quickest and easiest. In ancient times, before tarmac and the ball bearing were invented, road transport was slow, uncomfortable and uncertain. If there was a sea or river route available, it would have been far preferable. This was particularly true in Egypt, where the Nile was the main transport artery. There is no suggestion of it in the Bible, but I would suggest that any Egyptian looking to travel fast towards Pelusium would have done so by ship up the Pelusiac arm. What we need to determine is what happened then.

We have so far examined three sources of the story. E says that the Egyptians just got bogged down, so entirely consistent with the Serbonian Bog. J says that an east wind blew the sea back and then dropped so that the water swept back and drowned the Egyptian army – again, consistent with something like the Serbonian Bog, where wind and sand can dramatically change the landscape very quickly. P gives us the story of a real miracle: the sea actually parting to create a path between two walls of water – consistent with no known laws of physics. There is, however, one more source for the story. It is in the form of two songs – the Songs of Moses and Miriam – that seem not to have been the original work of J, E or P. They purport to be the words of Moses and Miriam in celebration of the Egyptian defeat. Both are regarded by many scholars as among the oldest texts in the Bible, on the evidence of the archaic Hebrew employed in them. Both describe how Pharaoh's army is drowned by wind and waves in the sea:

Then sang Moses and the children of Israel this song unto the LORD, and spake, saying, I will sing unto the LORD, for he hath triumphed gloriously: the horse and his rider hath he thrown into the sea. The LORD is my strength and song, and he is become my salvation: he is my God, and I will prepare him an habitation; my father's God, and I will exalt him. The LORD is a man of war: the LORD is his name. Pharaoh's chariots and his host hath he cast into the sea: his chosen captains also are drowned in the Red Sea. The depths have covered them: they sank into the bottom as a stone. Thy right hand, O LORD, is become glorious in power: thy right hand, O LORD, hath dashed in pieces the enemy. And in the greatness of thine excellency thou hast overthrown them that rose up against thee: thou sentest forth thy wrath, which consumed them as stubble. And with the blast of thy nostrils the waters were gathered together, the floods stood upright as an heap, and the depths were congealed in the heart of the sea. The enemy said, I will pursue, I will overtake, I will divide the spoil; my lust shall be satisfied upon them; I will draw my sword, my hand shall destroy them. Thou didst blow with thy wind, the sea covered them: they sank as lead in the mighty waters. Who is like unto thee, O LORD, among the gods? who is like thee, glorious in holiness, fearful in praises, doing wonders? Thou stretchedst out thy right hand, the earth swallowed them. Thou in thy mercy hast led forth the people which thou hast redeemed: thou hast guided them in thy strength unto thy holy habitation. The people shall hear, and be afraid: sorrow shall take hold on the inhabitants of Palestina. Then the dukes of Edom shall be amazed; the mighty men of Moab, trembling shall take hold upon them; all the inhabitants of Canaan shall melt away. Fear and dread shall fall upon them; by the greatness of thine arm they shall be as still as a stone; till thy people pass over, O LORD, till the people pass over, which thou hast purchased. Thou shalt

bring them in, and plant them in the mountain of thine inheritance, in the place, O LORD, which thou hast made for
thee to dwell in, in the Sanctuary, O LORD, which thy hands
have established The LORD shall reign for ever and ever. And
Miriam the prophetess, the sister of Aaron, took a timbrel in
her hand; and all the women went out after her with timbrels
and with dances. And Miriam answered them, Sing ye to the
LORD, for he hath triumphed gloriously; the horse and his
rider hath he thrown into the sea.[11]

Note a couple of things here. First, the language: God
'throws' or 'casts' them into the sea; they 'sink to the bottom
like a stone' or 'as lead'. Second, there is no mention of the
Israelites passing through the sea – just the Egyptians drowning. The description is closest to the J Source but it is also
entirely consistent with a pursuing army embarked on ships,
getting caught in a storm and being wrecked.

So, we have four sources and four versions, only one of
which involves the full-blown miracle of the parting of the
waters. If the two Songs are indeed the oldest versions, then
things would be simpler. But although they appear to be
ancient songs, some scholars argue that writing in archaic
Hebrew was a much later poetic fashion (rather like the
archaic poetic language of 19th-century English poets) and
these Songs are not as old as they seem. Given that there is
no consensus about the dating of the other sources either, it
seems you can take your pick. Perhaps the Egyptian army
got bogged down, perhaps they were drowned in the
marshes, perhaps their ships were sunk in a storm. What I
think we can be sure of is that there was never a parting of
the seas as described by P. Most scholars do believe that P is
the latest of the sources – it is a minority that argue other-

---

11 Exodus 15: 1-21.

wise – and in my own view, some combination of the other sources reflect the racial myth that the Egyptian force, like many others in history, got bogged down and/or drowned in the notoriously treacherous marshy bogs of the seacoast to the east of the Nile Delta, and left the Israelites free to continue their flight.

P then gives *his* version of how the Israelites were fed and watered in the desert and, typically, his main concern is that no gathering of food should take place on the Sabbath – Yahweh thoughtfully provides double helpings on the preceding day! The section concludes with the statement that the wandering in the desert was to take forty years. Chapters 25–31 are then all the work of **P**. They are solely concerned again with priestly obsessions: the construction of the Ark of the Covenant (of *Indiana Jones* fame) and the Tabernacle, rules about sacrifices and offerings, priestly garments and rituals and finally, again, Sabbath observation. These are picked up again at the end of the book. There is one passage worth noting in these final chapters – Chapter 34:29-35 – which relates how when Moses came down from Mount Sinai/Horeb, the 'skin of his face shone'. This seems then to have been permanent – Moses would keep his face veiled at all times except when he went into the Tabernacle to converse with Yahweh. One can well understand the theological meaning of this – Moses has been marked out as unique: only he actually meets and converses with Yahweh. But one must wonder if there is a rational explanation. Perhaps that might also explain why God speaks to Moses from a burning bush. Presumably the fire didn't burn his face, but his face looked radiantly red and the story of the fire reflects this. It is surely possible that Moses hid his face with a veil because he had a skin disease of some kind. The same disease that led to the previous stories about leprosy. By definition, Moses could not be ritually unclean in this way, so his 'leprosy' was explained away as transfiguration of some sort.[12] I am not making a derogatory comment here. I believe that the stories of the burning bush, Moses' transfiguration and his veil are all aetiological explanations for a real folk memory about something in Moses' appearance. And the stories about Moses' leprous arm and Miriam's leprosy stem from the same embarrassing memory. The reason that this is important will become clear later.

Exodus is followed by Leviticus, which is entirely the work of **P**. Most of it concerns priestly preoccupations: Yahweh's rules, delivered through Moses to the Israelites after they arrive at the holy mountain. The rules concern what is required for holiness and how to make offerings to Yahweh. But sandwiched between them are some passages that we should not pass by. The first of these is in Chapter 8, where the priesthood for the new religion of Yahweh is instituted. This makes clear that the priesthood is to be the sole birthright of Aaron and his descendants. At this point we must pause to consider who exactly Aaron was and why he received this honour. Jewish and Christian tradition regard Moses, Aaron and Miriam to be siblings but there is nothing in **J** or **E** to bear this out. **J** tells the story of Moses in the Bullrushes. According to him, Moses had an elder sister who watched over the Ark. We are not told her name and the word translated here as 'sister' can mean simply 'kinswoman', so this is no firm evidence of a sister called Miriam or anything else. **J** also introduces us to Aaron, calling him 'Aaron the Levite thy brother'.[13] But again, this probably means simply that Moses and Aaron are from the same tribe: there is no firm indication that they are siblings. Later, **J**

---

12 Jesus underwent a similar transfiguration on a mountain, but that narrative is just a deliberate reworking of the Moses story.

13 Exodus 4:14.

introduces Miriam as 'the sister of Aaron';[14] this too could just mean kinswoman and, in any case, does not mention Moses as it surely would in this account of Moses' leadership. It is the undoubtedly later **P** Source that makes the sibling claim [in Numbers 26:59] and the unknown writer of Exodus Chapter 6, writing in the same period as **P**, also tells us that Moses and Aaron are the sons of Levites called Amram and Jochebed. We have seen how, for **J** and **E**, Yahweh's will outweighs genealogical descent and birthright every time. It is **P** that is obsessed with genealogy generally, and here specifically because the priesthood of his time was concerned to establish the legitimacy of their inheritable priestly status, descended from Aaron. How much more powerful if Aaron was Moses' brother.? So according to **P**, in Leviticus, Yahweh declares that Aaron *and his descendants* are to be His priests – not all members of the Levite tribe, but only those that can trace their genealogy to Aaron.

The second narrative worth noting in **P**'s Leviticus is found in Chapters 11-15 inclusive, which constitute nearly a fifth of the entire book, devoted entirely to uncleanliness and its treatment. And within those five chapters, two whole chapters are devoted to diseases of the skin and their treatment. Is there not something somewhat obsessive about this? Yahweh clearly worries about what his people eat and drink, who they have sex with and how, and how they should worship him. But right at the top of the list seems to be skin infections. Why? Particularly because we read this in the light of the other evidence of the same obsession detailed above. The Bible clearly identifies leprosy with sin: it seems to be Yahweh's favourite way of punishing sin. And perhaps that is all there is to it – just a strange quirk of religious belief. But I *do* think there is more to it than that. Animals

---

14 Exodus 15:20.

to be sacrificed are to be unmarked and unblemished and there is even a passage in Leviticus about the need for homes and clothing to be free of mildew: a not unreasonable ambition, but surely not worthy of extensive religious rules.[15] It appears that a large chunk of the Aaronide priesthood is to be taken up with such matters. Was there a particular problem with the Israelites – a genetic disposition, or an endemic disease of some sort – to provoke such keen interest? Or perhaps something in the very roots of the religion itself that was the cause for embarrassment and concern? We shall seek to answer this in a later chapter.

Leviticus is followed by Numbers, and much of that book too is the work of **P**. In the early chapters, the Israelites are still encamped at the holy mountain and receiving their instructions from Yahweh via Moses. The first instruction involves taking a census of adult males by tribe to determine the strength of the fighting force in preparation for the invasion of Canaan. Once again, **P**'s obsession with birthright and genealogy is to the fore. The total comes to a very exact 603,550. As I have noted above, just do the math and this implies a total population of several million people. So, something like the modern population of Wales is pictured wandering in the Negev Desert! I think we can confidently reject these numbers; perhaps they are the result of a census undertaken centuries later. But there are some curious things in this account. First, we can note that even at the outset, according to **P**, the descendants of Joseph are split into those of his two sons, creating a list of twelve tribes: the Levites are specifically excluded from the twelve.

The Levite tribe is dealt with separately. **P** repeats the designation of Aaron's descendants as Yahweh's priests, and says that Yahweh designated the Levites to be only assistants to them. The Levites basically were to do all the menial work

---

15 Leviticus 13: 47-59.

involved in a sacrificial cult, always under the direction of the Aaronides, and only the latter could approach the holiest places and conduct the holy rites. As noted before, this inherited Aaronide birthright is entirely the innovation of **P** and runs directly counter to the main force of **J** and **E** narratives, which are at pains to establish over and over again that Yahweh is not influenced by accidents of birth: indeed, Yahweh seems intent at all turns to ride roughshod over any such genealogical claims. **P** lists the descendants of both Aaron and Levi – the Levite Patriarch. Yet, strangely for a source so obsessed with genealogies, **P** nowhere here provides the ancestry of Moses and Aaron – his principal characters. Furthermore, among Aaron's sons is one Eliezar and among Levi's sons is one Gershon; according to E, Gershom and Eliezer are the names of the only sons of Moses by Zipporah.[16] These might be just family names handed down, but it does look as if we have garbled tales here.

The fact is that nowhere in the Pentateuch outside of the comparatively late **P** Source and the writer of Exodus 6, are Moses or Aaron identified either as brothers, or in fact, even as Levites. Outside the Pentateuch, in Chronicles I,[17] which is also a late text, Aaron and Moses are both described as Levites and it is made clear that Moses' descendants are *only* that – they are not part of the Aaronide priesthood. Surely all this is very strange. Moses was chosen by Yahweh for the unique distinction, not only of introducing Him to the Israelites, but of being the only human ever to be granted direct communing with Yahweh. Yet Yahweh's priesthood is assigned to Aaron, who may or may not have been Moses' brother. And Aaron is surely a strange choice. **P** tells the convoluted story of the Ark and the Egyptian princess to explain

---

16 Exodus 18:3.

17 23:14.

how an Egyptian could also be a Levite, but for the other sources, he seems to come from a Midianite priestly family and is not an Israelite at all: he does not even speak Hebrew. Aaron *does* speak Hebrew so may well have been an Israelite. But was he a Levite? In the tale of the golden calf he is somehow implicated, and although he escapes retribution, it is exacted on all the others involved in the blasphemy by the Levite tribe who Moses recruits for the purpose. The status of Moses, Aaron and the Levites, and their relationship with the twelve tribes of Israelites, seems to have been not at all as the finally redacted narrative would have us believe.

Having established exactly who is authorized to do what, P returns again to the subject of purity and yet again deals with the issue of skin diseases[18] before then covering a number of ritual requirements, paying particular attention to how much money the Aaronide priesthood should receive for their exclusive services. All the above is recorded in the first ten chapters of Numbers, which constitute a single chunk of text from the hand of P. The next fifteen chapters revert to the narrative of the Israelites, wanderings in the desert and have been redacted from J, E and P. The last's contributions all betray his priestly interests: more ancestries, priestly responsibilities, reiteration of the Aaronide birthright and heavenly retribution rained down on those who oppose Moses and Aaron. It is P, in fact, who records Yahweh's decision that the Israelites should wander in the desert for forty years:[19] it will be recalled that outside of P, the judgement was that a generation should pass. We also learn from P of the death of Aaron, preceding that of Moses. Then from Chapter 26 to the end of the book (Chapter 36) comes another solid chunk of P. He tells of a second census that

18 Numbers 5:1-4.
19 Numbers 14:34.

lists all the various clans of the twelve tribes, the appointment of Joshua as Moses' successor, and a bunch of more
ritual observances.

Then Yahweh sends the Israelites off to slaughter the Midianites. This is apparently in revenge for an incident recorded
earlier, when an Israelite man sinned with a Midianite
woman, provoking Yahweh to send a plague on the Israelites, but it is linked to a similar story about the neighbouring
Moabites and is part of the narrative of Israelites gaining dominance in the Arabian Peninsula south of Moab, before moving
north into the Transjordan region. We noted earlier that
Midian is a place unknown outside the Bible and many
scholars believe it represented a loose league of tribes, connected perhaps by a common religion. But all this is puzzling,
since E tells us that not only was Moses married to the daughter of a Midianite priest – Reuel/Jethro – but that the priest
was present with Moses in the Negev and offered him sound
advice which he took. So, E seems to have regarded Midianites
as good guys, but P writing centuries later presents them not
just as an enemy, but one that is to be slaughtered. The puzzle
parallels that concerning Aaron – again, good guy and founder
of the priestly birthright according to P, but antagonist of
Moses on at least two occasions according to E. All will
become clear when we discover later exactly where the worship of Yahweh originates, and who brought that religion to
the Israelites; in other words, who was Moses in reality? And
what is so important about Midian that P seems to want to
play it down?

The final chapters of Numbers contain two more P texts
that need attention. First, in Chapter 35, Yahweh tells Moses
that the Levites, now no longer regarded as one of the twelve
tribes, but who are to act as a priestly caste, are to be scattered among the tribes, given land of their own on which to
dwell in the tribal lands, and in particular, to be given 48

towns of their own, including six 'cities of refuge'. These last are to provide protection to anyone accused of murder, ensuring that they receive a fair trial. And second, Yahweh rules that not only must Israelites not marry 'out' with surrounding nations – they must marry within their tribe to maintain each tribe's birthright. Once again, for **P**, birthright overrides everything else. And finally, **P** records the death of Moses in a short passage now in Deuteronomy.[20]

---

20 Deuteronomy 34: 8-9.

CHAPTER 13

Moses according to D

Because the D Source is late – dating to the 6th or 7th century BC, depending what scholar you want to follow – we shall not spend much time on it here. It repeats material in Numbers and Leviticus, the differences betraying the interests of the writers. Identifying the writer or writers of Deuteronomy is, however, more problematical than for the other sources. One thing we can say with some confidence is that it originates in the north because, like E, it refers to Yahweh's holy mountain as Horeb: J and P always refer to it as Sinai. It seems highly likely, therefore, that the writers of Deuteronomy brought their version of Yahweh worship down to the southern kingdom after the northern Israel was destroyed by the Assyrians. The clash then between northern beliefs, rituals, holy objects and narratives with those of the south, is the essential background to the way in which these Books of Moses get finally redacted. Deuteronomy is not only the final book of the Pentateuch – it is the first book of the Deuteronomic History narrated by the books that follow. That history reinterprets the original narratives in the light of subsequent events, so it would be as well to rehearse those here briefly.

The Book of Joshua follows Deuteronomy in the Deuteronomic History. It supposedly relates the Conquest of Canaan by the Israelites, now led by Joshua following the death of Moses and Aaron. In fact, it is more a collection of individual tales about conflicts, battles and sieges in different tribal areas. There may or may not be historical truth behind some or all of these, but they do not tell a coherent story, and they are clearly based on old, oral tales. The obvious parallel is to Homer's tales of the Trojan War: disparate stories about heroes and their exploits, handed down over the generations, from an era far removed from that in which they were finally written down. In both cases, that era was just before the Bronze Age Collapse, at the tail end of the 2nd millennium BC. The dark age that followed separated event from redacted narrative, so it is difficult to be sure of anything. Perhaps there was a Trojan War, perhaps there was a siege of Jericho: but we can be certain that neither event happened in the way described. Homer tells us that Troy was eventually taken through the unlikely stratagem of the wooden horse. Joshua tells us that the walls of Jericho tumbled down at the sound of the Israelites' trumpets. Unlikely, but it could be argued so was the parting of the Red Sea. If you want to believe in miracles, the likelihood increases. But the rational mind recognizes that in the case of the Red Sea parting, the story has developed over the years from a much simpler, mundane event (an army lost in a notorious bog) and we can trace that development because we have four different versions of it, written at different times. In the case of the Deuteronomic History from Joshua onwards, we have only one record so we cannot see the myth developing. But myth it surely is.

As the Deuteronomic History progresses through subsequent books, the likelihood of events gradually increases as the time between event and book gradually decreases. We are told that the Israelite tribes settled in Canaan and were ruled for a period by 'judges' rather than kings. We cannot be sure how long this period lasted, but there is nothing inherently unlikely in the story, given the theological implications of Yahweh's intimate relationship with His people: there seems little room for royalty in tribes who believe their priests have a direct hotline to the deity who, through those intermediaries, directs day to day life right down to the smallest detail. For this reason, priests would have been relatively powerful, alongside the judges. The priesthood, as well as the judges, were scattered across the tribes and their lands. Worship and sacrifice were performed at local shrines, although some were clearly regarded as more important than others – Shiloh and Shechem in the north, for example, Hebron and Nob in the south, and Bethel straddling the two. Jerusalem in the south remained in Canaanite hands until King David united all the tribes in a single monarchy. His son, Solomon, built a grand central temple to Yahweh in Jerusalem and this led to a centralization of worship and sacrifice there for the united country. After Solomon, however, the country split in two on north–south lines. Jerusalem became Yahweh's centre for the southern kingdom of Judah, and Samaria for the northern kingdom of Israel. Israel disappeared when invaded by Assyria in the 8th century BC; Judah became an Assyrian vassal state and then, as the power of Assyria dwindled in the region, later in the 6th century BC, Judah was subdued by the new kids on the block: the Babylonians. The ruling elites of Judah were taken into captivity in Babylon but later returned to rebuild the temple in Jerusalem and, over subsequent centuries, evolved the Judaism with which we are familiar.

Around the seventh century BC, so after the fall of Israel but before the fall of Judah, according to the Deuteronomic History, there was a king in Judah called Josiah, who was a strong follower of Yahweh. This had not always been the case with his predecessors, who had worshipped other

Canaanite gods. During his reign, an old scroll was rediscovered in the Jerusalem Temple that was called 'the book of the Law of the Lord given by Moses'.[1] This book astonished the king because it set out a clear Covenant between Yahweh and the Israelites under which, provided they kept their side of things by following the 'law', Yahweh would reciprocate by protecting them from their enemies. This put history into a new light for Josiah. Israel had been scattered to the four winds and although Judah had survived, it too had been under the heel of Assyria ever since. This 'Book of the Law', if true, clearly implied that these disasters must be the direct result of the Israelites reneging on the Mosaic Covenant (as it is now called). Josiah was devastated by this bolt from the blue and instigated a rigorous national programme of religious renewal.

This story, of course, betrays the entire myth that Yahweh had been the sole God of the Israelites since at least the time of Moses and that worship of other gods was always frowned upon and put down. The truth is much more believable and much less black and white. Worship of Yahweh had always been a cult. It may have been widespread throughout Canaan since the time of Moses, but it sat alongside other cults and competed with them. Ironically, the reason we know this is because Moses and the priests and prophets that followed him all fulminated against worship of these other gods – not because they were 'false' but because, in the battle between the gods for men's hearts and sacrifices, and in the concomitant battle between different priesthoods for worshippers' money, the priests of Yahweh championed their own cause. The belief they held was that *for the Israelites*, and not necessarily for other nations, Yahweh was the most important of the gods. He wanted to be *their* god. This is not

---

1 2 Kings 22:8-11; 2 Chronicles 34:14.

monotheism, and the idea that ever since Moses the Israelites had been monotheistic just isn't true. It became true, of course, after the return from the Babylonian exile, when Judaism gradually took on its distinctive monotheistic form, but in the period of the Exodus and long after, it would have been regarded as crazy. It was self-evident that there were many gods, and who was Yahweh to suggest otherwise? And, of course, we didn't need the story of Josiah to explode this myth. El never disappeared, but just over time became identified with Yahweh. Even as Yahweh was supposed to be leading the Israelites through the desert, they would still worship golden calves, Baal and other Canaanite gods. The document discovered in Josiah's reign was the first step on the road to monotheism: it said that Yahweh, already known and worshipped in Judah, was special. He was not even just the most important of the gods, but the only god who should be served.

So, what was this 'Book of the Law' and why was it unknown before – or at the very least, somehow lost for centuries before being rediscovered in Josiah's reign? Most scholars now believe that it was the original text from which the book of Deuteronomy grew to its final redacted form. Unfortunately (and as is usual) scholars are deeply divided about the detail of what was the original text and the stages by which it reached its final form as part of the total Deuteronomic History. But most are agreed how the original text found its way into Josiah's hands. We saw above that Deuteronomy bears the hallmarks of a northern origin, so it seems virtually certain that the 'Book of the Law' was a northern version of the laws of Moses, different from the versions preserved in J and P, and it found its way to Judah with refugees heading south after the Assyrian invasion of Israel. Further evidence for this is provided by the books of two prophets. The southern prophet Isaiah, who was active in Jerusalem about a century before Josiah, makes no mention at all of the Exodus, or the Mosaic Covenant. However, the northern prophet Hosea does makes frequent reference to those things.

Most scholars would subscribe to the same broad understanding of how the Book of Deuteronomy grew out of the original Book of the Law that came down from the north. That original book was probably the origin of Chapters 12–26, which is a fully blown code of law – in effect a constitution for a Yahwist theocracy – covering everyday religious observance; the duties of judges, kings, priests and prophets; civil law; and criminal law. Some but not all of this can be found elsewhere in the Pentateuch, but nowhere as rigorously codified as here. The hands of redactors can easily be identified at places in the code where amendments have been made to take account of later events, such as the transition from judges to kings that took place long after the Exodus events, or the centralization of worship that became a feature when Jerusalem became the capital of a united kingdom. Before Chapter 12 is a recapitulation of the whole Exodus story, couched as an address by Moses to the Israelites after their forty-year wanderings in the desert. After Chapter 26 come dire threats as to the fate of the nation if it fails to uphold its side of the Covenant by obeying the code, followed by a narrative of the death of Moses and his succession by Joshua. These introductory and closing chapters were added to the original code chapters at the end of the Babylonian Exile. Based very much on northern traditions, they are, at the same time, of contemporary relevance to a people who, like the Israelites of the Exodus, are returning to the promised land to build a new nation.

There are just a few passages that we should note here as indicative of our concerns in this book. First, is a curious passage concerning bigamous marriages; these are not condemned, but the Code is concerned about the birthright consequences:

> If a man have two wives, one beloved, and another hated, and they have born him children, both the beloved and the hated; and if the firstborn son be hers that was hated: Then it shall be, when he maketh his sons to inherit that which he hath, that he may not make the son of the beloved firstborn before the son of the hated, which is indeed the firstborn: But he shall acknowledge the son of the hated for the firstborn, by giving him a double portion of all that he hath: for he is the beginning of his strength; the right of the firstborn is his.[2]

One wonders how any priest or judge could enforce this given the impossibility of knowing another man's heart. But, of course, there is a subtext here. There can be no question that this refers directly to the tale of Jacob, Rachel and Leah in which, despite Leah giving Jacob his firstborn sons, it is Rachel's son Joseph who receives the birthright. Even the language is the same.[3] The story in Genesis is quite explicit that Jacob loves Rachel, the wife of his choice, and not Leah, who he is tricked by Laban into marrying. The injunction of the code that birthright overrides other considerations is directly counter to the tenor of this and other Genesis birthright tales in which God's will overrides accidents of birth. I argued that this was to provide justification for the Conquest of Canaan, to which its original Hamite occupants had the prior claim. It could be argued that God's will is one thing and marital preference another, but the parallel between the Genesis tale and the code injunction is so specific that

2 Deuteronomy 21:15-17.

3 Deuteronomy 21:17 and Genesis 49:3 both have 'the beginning of his strength'.

something particular must be intended, over and above a concern for neglected wives.

In fact, what we have here is evidence of the protracted ongoing struggle between the northern and southern tribes for supremacy in the region, and particularly between the pre-eminent tribes in the north and south – Ephraim and Judah respectively. The rivalry between their respective matriarchs – Rachel and Leah – became its archetype. As we saw, the plot by Leah's sons to remove Rachel's son Joseph carried the feud into the next generation. Then the first king of the united monarchy, Saul, was descended from Rachel via her second son, Benjamin, but he is deposed by David, who is a descendant of Leah via her son Judah. And when David's son Solomon dies and the nation splits into two again, the founder of the breakaway northern kingdom is Jeroboam from the tribe of Ephraim – descended from Rachel via Joseph. The subtext of this passage in Deuteronomy, therefore, written after Israel has disappeared but the northern survivors are integrating into southern Judah, is to reinforce the legitimacy of Judah and the descent from Leah, contrary to Jacob's reported preferences.

Chapters 18 and 23 are part of the original code and deal with the role of priests. Compared with the **P** narrative this is slender indeed. And unlike **P**, there is no mention of Aaron and his descendants and no consequent division between their exalted role and the more menial role of the Levite tribe as a whole. Indeed, the book makes clear that all priests are Levites and all Levites are priests, in complete opposition to **P**, indicating that the Aaronide priesthood was a southern innovation, unknown in the north, and that priests were only one element of the ruling class. Second, the emphasis on ritual purity that we find in **P** is missing here. There are one or two references to the need for cleanliness and a single reference to leprosy,[4] but compared with **P**, very little emphasis. So both the priesthood, generally, and its traditional concern for ritual purity, that are an obsession with **P**, are passed over lightly in **D**, almost certainly indicating an origin for the latter outside the priesthood. There is, however, one last small passage worth pointing out in this regard:

> And the LORD will take away from thee all sickness, and will put none of the evil diseases of Egypt, which thou knowest, upon thee; but will lay them upon all *them* that hate thee. [5]

What on earth does this mean? Was Egypt specifically felt to be a medically dangerous place? More so than Canaan? The word 'evil' here often gets translated as 'horrible' or 'bad'. But 'evil diseases' I think hints at something more. As we saw, skin diseases like leprosy seem to have had a particular interest for the writers of the Pentateuch, and they were certainly regarded as 'evil' because they were linked in the Israelite mind with sinfulness: Yahweh punished sin with angry red, or snow white, skin afflictions. Was there a tradition, vaguely remembered here and in similar passages elsewhere by the other Pentateuch writers, of a particular problem with skin complaints affecting the Israelites in Egypt?

So, what have we learned so far about Moses and the Exodus?

CHRONOLOGY
There is no real indication of the length of the period between the death of Jacob at the end of Genesis and the enslavement of the Israelites at the beginning of Exodus; or

---

4 Deuteronomy 24:8.

5 Deuteronomy 7:15.

between the enslavement and Moses leading the Israelites out. As we have seen, various figures are given in different places for these periods, but they conflict.

SCALE

There are problems with the numbers of Israelites involved in the Exodus. Specific references to numbers seem to indicate several million people. It is just not credible that such a large number of people could have wandered in the desert for forty years – even with miraculous delivery of food and water. On the other hand, there are suggestions that the number was actually much smaller – thousands, perhaps even just hundreds, rather than millions.

LEVITES

The tribe of Levi is given a prominence in Exodus that it does not receive in Genesis. According to P at least, Moses is a Levite and it is the Levites who take the lead after the golden calf incident. The tribe of Levi are not allotted land of their own, making way for the two sons of Joseph and thus preserving the idea of twelve tribes.

MOSES

The Israelite genealogy of Moses seems suspect – he was uncircumcised, married to a Gentile and did not speak Hebrew; he was raised in Egypt but then lived in Midian. The different sources reveal how embarrassment over this led to elaboration of the story of his roots.

AARON

The familial relationship between Moses, Aaron and Miriam is contentious. Large sections of Exodus derive from the P Source and reflect later justification of priestly rules and rituals, rather than any historical reality.

YAHWEH

Moses seems to have been the first to understand the name of God as Yahweh and to introduce that to the Israelites. We are told this was a revelation from God, but a rational question would be where he got the concept from.

MIRACLES

The stories of the plagues of Egypt differ from source to source and are inconsistent with each other. The same is true of the miracle of the parting of the Red Sea, which almost certainly was a less dramatic event that took place on the shores of the Mediterranean Sea in an area notorious in antiquity for such losses and disappearances.

The big questions that remain unanswered so far and need to be carried over into the next chapters are:

1. Was there an Exodus? If so, who led it, how many were involved and when did it take place?
2. Was there a Conquest? If not, what differentiated Israelites from Canaanites and how did the former come to think of themselves as different from the tribes around them?
3. Where did the Yahweh cult originate, how and when was it introduced to Canaan, and how did it supplant Canaanite deities, notably El?

We have begun to suggest some answers. But we still have a long way to go, and we need now to look outside of the Bible to get to the truth. In the next chapter we shall move on to look at Egyptian sources for events described in the Pentateuch.

CHAPTER 14

Contemporary Egyptian Sources

The story of the Israelites is inseparable from that of Egypt. As I stressed previously, the histories of Canaan and Egypt intertwine continuously in the first millennium BC. Egypt needed to control Canaan as a buffer between itself and the mighty empires of Asia, who themselves sought to extend their influence south and west. Always based on trade, but often resulting in war, relationships between the two lands thus ebbed and flowed as Egypt sought to control its northern borders.[1] The Sunday School version of events speaks of a single Sojourn and a single Exodus, but we have already seen that Abraham was in Egypt long before Joseph got there; that Jacob and his descendants were there for a period in which they prospered; and that the Exodus took place at a third time. So, any attempt to determine the history of the Exodus must inevitably have to come to terms with events and personalities in Egypt. Egyptian references in the Bible are generalized and influenced by the time they were written, rather than the time in which the events are supposed to have occurred, so cross reference is notoriously complex. To

---

1 The same is true, of course, of the relationship with the African peoples to its west and south.

take one obvious example: the Bible often refers to kings and pharaohs without specifying which, and when it does so specify, the names given have gone through so much cross-translation that they end up unrecognizable from their Egyptian origin. Nevertheless, scholars – and we – must make the attempt. In doing so, I shall be using what is known as the Conventional Chronology: that is, the 'standard' version that represents the current consensus view.

We have a variety of sources for contemporary Egyptian history, and the light those sources sheds opens up the way to a more balanced perspective on the Biblical narratives. The latter are without a doubt hampered as reliable sources by their parochial, aetiological and partisan roots. But we have also seen that aspects of them are not at all irreconcilable with historical truth, not least the recognition that Canaan, Asia and Egypt were intimately intertwined. My contention here will be that properly understood, and in a broad sense, the narratives of the Biblical sources and of the Egyptian sources can indeed be reconciled with each other, and with the archaeological record. Unfortunately, the period with which we are here concerned – the Bronze Age – is particularly problematical when you get down to fine detail.

Egyptologists divide the three millennia of Ancient Egyptian history into just over thirty dynasties. Basically, as long as Egypt was a united country and rule was handed down from pharaoh to pharaoh, often from father to son, all is relatively plain sailing. Occasional problems arise due to co-regencies, unexpected deaths, palace coups and the like, but by and large, the dynastic story proceeds clearly. When a dynasty comes to an end, however, the transition to a new one is, by definition, a period of some turbulence, and the records can be unclear about exactly what happened to bring about the demise of one dynasty and the rise of another. The transition between Dynasties 19 and 20 at the end of the 13th century

BC is one such period when things get very muddled. It will be recalled that, for those not enamoured of a 16th century BC Hyksos dating for the Exodus, or a mid-15th BC century dating as suggested by Biblical calculations, a 13th century BC Exodus has archaeological and other attractions. As we shall now see, there is evidence from Egyptian sources that also points to the 13th century BC as a fruitful period to explore in this context, and the transition between the 19th and 20th Dynasties will be where we need to focus our attention.

In addition to the breaks between dynasties, there are three other periods that span groups of dynasties, in which the transition from one dynasty to another is particularly problematical, because the dynastic struggles and turbulence continues over an extended time frame. These are three periods in Egyptian history where the fine detail is a particular riddle: Egyptologists call them the First, Second and Third Intermediate Periods. They are intermediate in the sense that they are the muddled periods that sit between the long periods of time in which matters are more straightforward. The intermediate periods occur when there are more fundamental breakdowns in the order of things. The First Intermediate Period falls at the end of the third millennium BC, and is therefore too early for consideration here. But the Second Intermediate Period does fall right in the era that is the subject of this book. It lasted nearly four times as long as the First Intermediate Period – some 450 years – when Upper and Lower Egypt were ruled as separate lands, and it includes the period when Canaanite invaders, including the Hyksos, were dominant in Lower Egypt. The Third Intermediate Period lasted 400 years. It started with the 21st Dynasty in 1069 BC and did not end until the advent of the 26th Dynasty in 664 BC. That whole period is the long dark age between the Bronze Age Collapse and the emergence of new Iron Age civilizations. All this will require untangling before we can begin to answer the questions raised in this book.

Before we begin the untangling, however, it would be as well, as we did with Israelite history, to begin with a brief overview of Ancient Egyptian geography and history to provide a high-level orientation.

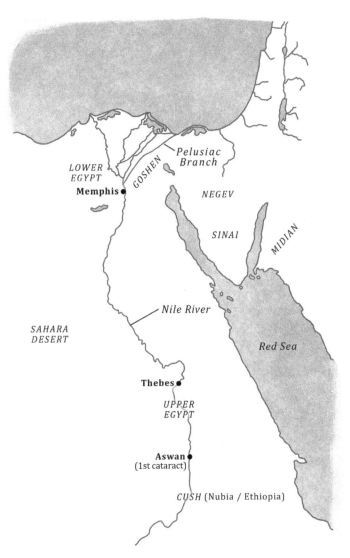

Fig. 9: Map of Egypt

When we speak of Egypt we think of the whole area between the Nile Delta and the first cataract of the Nile, where the modern Aswan Dam marks the southern boundary. The Nile Delta was, as we have seen, a triangular area of marshland about 150–200 miles wide and stretching about 150 miles from the Mediterranean in the north to Memphis in the south. This area was known as Lower Egypt. From Memphis down to Aswan is another 600 miles or so and was known as Upper Egypt. The famous modern Aswan Dam is built at what was known as the first Nile cataract, a turbulent stretch of rocks and rapids that in ancient times made navigation further south problematical. The area between that first cataract and the second cataract (now submerged under Lake Nasser) was known to the Egyptians as Nubia; to the Greeks and Romans as Ethiopia; and to the Israelites as Cush. Like Canaan to the north, this area was a vital buffer zone for Egypt and control of it a strategic necessity. During much of the Bronze Age, it was ruled by an Egyptian viceroy, but as with Canaan, this was always precarious and under constant threat from without. The 'Lower' Delta area and the 'Upper' southern area were always known as the Two Lands, and at times of internal strife or external threat had a tendency to revert to separate rule. But the history of Ancient Egypt as we know it is regarded as starting with the first unification of the Two Lands under the 1st Dynasty of pharaohs.

Ancient Egyptian civilisation began at the outset of the Bronze Age. The first two dynasties – known as the **Early Dynasties** – date from the late 4th millennium BC (so, over 5,000 years ago) and endured for nearly half a millennium. They were followed by what is known as the **Old Kingdom** of a united Egypt, which had a further four dynasties and lasted another half a millennium. Together these six dynasties constitute a remarkable millennium of stability and prosperity.

The greatest symbols of Ancient Egyptian civilization – the pyramids and Sphinx of the Giza plain near modern Cairo – date to this early period. When this amazing civilization finally faltered in around 2180 BC, it was followed by the **First Intermediate Period,** which lasted about 125 years at the end of the third millennium BC, and saw four dynasties – the 7th, 8th, 9th and 10th – come and go in quick succession. It was a dark age in which the united Old Kingdom split back into the original two lands – Upper and Lower Egypt – and chaos and disorder reigned. Order was restored again in 2060 BC with the 11th and 12th Dynasties – which together constitute what is now known as the **Middle Kingdom.** Egyptologists are on firmer ground with this period and its sixteen (or thereabouts) pharaohs are fairly well documented. They reigned for about 260 years from 2060 BC to 1802 BC before the kingdom broke into two again with the advent of the **Second Intermediate Period.** That lasted for another 250 years or so between 1802 BC and 1550 BC, and saw five dynasties – the 13th, 14th, 15th, 16th and 17th – which often ran concurrently. As noted above, it is of particular interest because the 15th Dynasty was ruled by the Hyksos kings in the Delta and Lower Egypt. The Hyksos were finally evicted after about 140 years, and the kingdom was reunited once more, by Ahmose I, the founder of the 18th Dynasty and what is now known as the **New Kingdom.** The 18th Dynasty is best remembered today for the reigns of Akhenaten, who introduced a religious revolution in Egypt, and his son, Tutankhamun, who restored the old religion. After 260 years and 13 pharaohs, the 18th Dynasty came to an end and was replaced in 1290 BC by the 19th Dynasty. This in turn lasted 100 years and New Kingdom power and influence peaked under its third pharaoh, Ramesses II ('The Great') who reigned for two-thirds of the century. As noted above, the end of the 19th Dynasty descended into chaos again, before order was re-established in 1190 BC by Setnakhte and his son, Ramesses III, the first two pharaohs of the new 20th Dynasty. This dynasty lasted for 125 years or so before everything fell apart again in the **Third Intermediate Period.** This was catastrophic. It lasted for over four centuries and its five dynasties – the 21st, 22nd, 23rd, 24th and 25th – followed the great Bronze Age Collapse throughout the Mediterranean world. Then, as we move into the Iron Age, in 664 BC, the **Late Period** began with the 26th Dynasty and continued until the 31st Dynasty saw Egypt absorbed into the Roman Empire.

So, that is three thousand years of Egyptian history in a single paragraph. It is a lot to take in. For the purposes of this book, the really important period is the 500 years or so from about 1675 BC when the Hyksos came to power, down to the re-establishment of the united kingdom by Setnakhte and Ramesses III of the 20th Dynasty. Figure 10 shows the dynasties and pharaohs of those 500 years. Clearly, half a millennium of ancient history will be the subject of much controversy and disagreement among scholars about fine detail. In the chart, I have tried to avoid getting caught up in any of that. It is, therefore, much simplified by me to focus on the matters of concern to this book and most dates are approximate. Where I have skated over controversial areas, I do not believe my simplification has any impact on the conclusions I reach in this book. The main/usual candidates for the pharaoh of the Exodus are indicated in bold type. I should perhaps trail my coat a little here and warn the reader that in my view none of these are correct.

I will provide further charts to elucidate detail as we progress, but the intention in Figure 10 is to provide a basic orientation and introduce the key figures.

Fig. 10: Chart of the 13th to 20th Dynasties

Date From (BC)	Date To (BC)	Dynasty	Pharaohs	Comments
				Start of Second Intermediate Period
1803	1649	13th		Middle and Upper Egypt
1805	1650	14th		Lower Egypt
1650	1550	15th		Hyksos in Lower Egypt
1650	1580	16th		Thebes area only
1650	1550	17th		Upper Egypt
				Start of New Kingdom
1550	1524	18th	**Ahmose I**	**Drove out the Hyksos. A candidate for Exodus Pharaoh**
1524	1503		Amenhotep I	
1503	1493		Thutmose I	
1493	1479		Thutmose II	
1479	1458		Hatshepsut	
1458	1425		**Thutmose III**	**A Candidate for Exodus Pharaoh**
1425	1397		Amenhotep II	
1397	1388		Thutmose IV	
1388	1351		Amenhotep III	Also, Vizier Amenhotep
1351	1334		Akhenaten	Previously, Amenhotep IV
1335	1334		Smenkhkare	
1334	1332		Neferneferuaton	
1332	1323		Tutankhamun	Previously, Tutankhaten
1323	1319		Ay	

1319	1292		Horemheb	
1292	1290	19th	Ramesses I	A candidate for Exodus Pharaoh
1290	1279		Seti I	
1279	1213		Ramesses II	'The Great'. A candidate for Exodus Pharaoh
1213	1203		Merneptah	
1203	1197		Seti II	
1201	1198		Amenmesse	Usurper
1197	1191		Siptah	
1191	1189		Twosret	
1190	1186	20th	Setnakhte	Reunited the Two Lands
1186	1155		Ramesses III	

With this orientation in place, let us now review the relevant period of Ancient Egyptian history in more detail, focusing particularly on the connection with Canaan and Israelite history.

Following the period of dynastic confusion and political division known as the First Intermediate Period, the establishment of the Middle Kingdom by the 11th Dynasty in around 2060 BC ushered in two centuries of central control again, with relative unity, stability and prosperity. This seems to have been based partly on climatic changes that created high water levels in the Nile, fertilizing wider tracts of the Nile Valley and creating agricultural surpluses that in turn led to increased export trade, especially in grain. For much of the period this was accompanied by strong dynasties, presumably built upon economic expansion. Military activity was almost all focused southwards into Cush/Ethiopia/Nubia. Expansion north and east was limited to a reoccupation of the Sinai Peninsula, which had been lost in the previous period, and the consequent establishment of

considerable mining enterprise. In the whole Middle Kingdom period there is only one isolated record of military cam-
paigning beyond the Sinai – an expedition of some sort to
Shechem, which was established long before Abraham and
his descendants arrived there. Otherwise, relations with
Canaan seem to have been peaceful and based on mutual
trade, underpinned by a series of peace treaties with the
major Canaanite tribes. The treaties were enforced by the
series of walls and forts that were built across the Eastern
Delta at this time and that feature in the Exodus story.

But the Middle Kingdom declined gradually and ended at
the dawn of the 19th century BC as national unity fell apart
again and we enter the Second Intermediate Period. This was
a time – around 1800 to 1550 BC, so 250 years long – when
unified rule in Egypt fragmented and different pharaohs ruled
concurrently in Upper (i.e. southern) and Lower (i.e. northern)
Egypt. The pharaohs of the 14th and 15th Dynasties ruled in
Lower Egypt from their capital in the Delta, called Avaris. In
parallel, the 16th and 17th Dynasty pharaohs ruled from
Thebes in Upper Egypt. The latter were native Egyptians, but
the pharaohs ruling from Avaris were alien invaders, known
as the Hyksos. The precise origin of the Hyksos is debated,
but they were clearly Asian and, more specifically, Levantine.
As noted above, in the context of the Exodus stories this is
clearly intriguing, and we shall return to the subject of the
Hyksos presently.

The whole Second Intermediate Period is a relative dark
age in Egyptian history. Scholars are divided about order and
overlaps; evidence is often scarce and ambiguous, but here is
a summary of the current state of play. The Middle Kingdom
ended when the 12th Dynasty pharaoh, Queen Sobekneferu,
died leaving no heir. The 13th Dynasty was characterized by
a series of often unrelated pharaohs ruling for short periods,
who gradually lost control of the Delta area. At this point

there is a sharp division between scholars about when this happened. The traditional view has been that the 13th Dynasty ruled for a century or more before they lost control of the north around the mid-17th century BC. More recently, however, a Danish scholar – Kim Ryholt[2] – has argued that a 14th Dynasty of Canaanite pharaohs controlled the north from the outset of the 13th Dynasty and the two dynasties ran in parallel. The issue remains unresolved. What all are agreed upon, however, is that the Hyksos reign in the north *proper* began around 1650 BC and lasted for a little over 100 years up to the mid-1500s BC, at which point they were ejected from Egypt and united rule was re-established as what we now call the New Kingdom. We need not be concerned here with all the other intricacies of the Second Intermediate Period which had (arguably) five different dynasties overlapping with each other to an extent that we may never finally disentangle it all.

Greater certainty returns to the record with the arrival of the pharaoh Ahmose, I who ascended to the throne in Upper Egypt in about 1550 BC, drove the Hyksos out, united the two lands and established the 18th Dynasty – the first of what is known as the New Kingdom in Egypt, at which point the story gets tidier again for a while. If the Hyksos period is to be associated in some way with the Exodus story, then Ahmose I is a good candidate for the unnamed pharaoh who finally allowed the Israelites to leave. But military ejection of a foreign army is, of course, a very different thing from the Biblical account, and, it hardly needs saying, there is nothing in the Egyptian account of the Hyksos departure that sounds anything like the plagues or the parting of

---

2 Kim Steven Bardrum Ryholt (b.1970) is Professor of Egyptology at the University of Copenhagen and has made a special study of the Second Intermediate Period.

the sea. On the other hand, it seems entirely reasonable that the stories of Abraham, Joseph and their descendants of the Sojourn in Egypt, as opposed to the Exodus, could be reflected in the Hyksos story somehow. After Ahmose I came seven more pharaohs, most if not all of whom have been implicated one way or another in the Exodus story with little or no real evidence other than wishful thinking. But the 18th Dynasty also bears on our concerns in this book because of what happened after those seven pharaohs, and about a century after the exit of the Hyksos. At this point, the interest of the story shifts from political affairs to religious ones.

The ninth pharaoh of the 18th Dynasty was Amenhotep III, who reigned for about forty years in the first half of the 14th century BC. He introduced a new god to the Egyptian pantheon: the Aten, or the Sun Disc. The Aten was at this point understood to be merely one aspect of the primary Egyptian sun god, Ra. Amenhotep III may have been influenced in this religious innovation by his namesake, Amenhotep, the son of Hapu, who was a priest that served in several senior capacities at the pharaoh's court. I suspect this 'other' Amenhotep may have been involved in the Aten introduction because after his death, perhaps for that reason, he became a religious cult figure, initially revered for his religious and philosophical teachings, and eventually over the next few centuries, coming to be worshipped as a god in his own right. Pharaohs were regarded as incarnations of the gods, but it is exceedingly rare for a non-royal figure like this to be so honoured. There is little if anything in what we know of his official duties during his working life to justify his later cult status; he seems to have acted as an architect and then as a royal property manager, hence my suspicion that it was the religious innovation of the Aten that lies behind his elevated status. And the more so, because in the reign of the next pharaoh, Amenhotep IV (the son of Amenhotep III), the Aten was to become the major

defining issue of his reign. The coincidence of two Amen-
hoteps – pharaoh and adviser/vizier – is something we shall
return to later because it becomes very important to our story.

Amenhotep IV is better known to posterity as the Pharaoh
Akhenaten, a name change that reflected his defection from
the god Amun to the Aten. Akhenaten famously sought to
break the power of the predominant priesthood of Amun by
declaring himself the human manifestation of the Aten. He
deserted the capital, Thebes, and created a new capital city in
the Delta called Amarna, dedicated to a 'monotheistic' Aten
worship. Scholars debate about the true extent of this monotheism; as with Israelite monotheism, it is very hard to tell
from language alone the difference between full-blooded
monotheism, in which the god is regarded as the only god,
and racist monotheism, in which the existence of other gods
is recognized, but worship is reserved exclusively to the chief
god of the people He protects. Either way, it has been argued
many times, most notably by Sigmund Freud,[3] that this
emergence of monotheism in Egypt at a period often associated with the Exodus would suggest that the Israelites
derived their own monotheism from Akhenaten, some even
going so far as to suggest that Akhenaten was the origin of
the Hebrew 'Moses' figure. Given that the ancestors of the
Israelites had been in the Delta region themselves for centuries by this time, one could equally argue the reverse: that
Akhenaten derived his monotheism from them and he established Amarna in the Delta precisely because that was where
the Israelites were located. All depends on when the Israelites
themselves adopted monotheism, and scholars debate that
one endlessly as well. For now, let us just note that, like his
father, Akhenaten will play a role in our story later on.

Akhenaten's religious reform was hugely controversial and

---

3 *Und Die Monotheistische*, 1939.

divisive. His son, the famous Tutankhamun, was originally called Tutankhaten, but changed his name as he gradually rolled back his father's reforms, and by the time we get to the 19th Dynasty, just four decades after Akhenaten's death, it was as if those reforms had never happened. Indeed, the pharaohs of the 19th Dynasty rewrote history as far as they could, to exclude any memory of the Amarna era, and it has only really been rediscovered in detail by scholars and archaeologists in the twentieth century.[4] Those pharaohs also had to rebuild Egyptian dominance north and south that had slipped in the Amarna period, arguably either through neglect or through a mistaken belief that diplomacy and appeasement would be more effective than military might. During the reign of the 19th Dynasty's third pharaoh, Ramesses II, known as 'The Great' (1279–1213 BC), that reimposition of Egyptian control in Canaan and Nubia was complete. He built Egyptian power and prestige to its greatest height. He is another pharaoh favoured by many as the pharaoh of the Exodus on no other basis in reality than his celebrity. He ruled for sixty-six years and in the first half of his reign, by military might rather than negotiation, he consolidated the borders of the Egyptian Empire. Only then did he sign treaties to preserve the peace during the second half of his reign. To do this he needed to confront threats from Asia to the north-east and Africa to the west and south. By the middle of his reign, he had secured Canaan as a buffer to the north; a lasting peace treaty with the Hittite Empire in Asia; a secure border with Libya; and reinforced Egyptian rule between the first and second cataracts of the Nile. On the religious front, Ramesses particularly favoured the god Set: he had red hair and red was the colour associated with

---

4 Although, as we shall see, it was known to the 3rd/4th century Egyptian historian, Manetho.

Set. He probably passed that trait down to his sons and all the pharaohs descended from him seem to have revered that god above others. It will be remembered that red was also the colour of Esau and the nation he founded, Edom. Set was particularly associated with the Negev Desert in the Sinai, and Edom was just to the east of that. Once again, Egyptian and Israelite myths converge.

Ramesses died in around 1213 BC aged about ninety, so we now enter the last hundred years of the Bronze Age before its collapse. His earliest military success was against sea pirates, known as Sherden, Lukka and Shekelesh. These and other 'Sea Peoples' were to trouble his successors over the next century and play a key role in scholarly theories about the causes and effects of the Late Bronze Age Collapse. As we have seen, until now, all military activity by Egyptian pharaohs has been directed towards the 'buffer zones' of Nubia in the south and Canaan [and Syria] in the north. Yet as we shall see, scholars identify these Sea Peoples as something entirely new and different. Insofar as they attack by sea, rather than overland through Canaan and Nubia, there seems some logic to this, although even adherents to that theory accept that this was not exclusively the case. In the case of this first incursion, however, there certainly was a seaborne attack. Pirates were harassing Egyptian shipping along the Delta coast. Ramesses deployed his navy in ambush and defeated them at one blow. The Sherden seem to have been the main protagonists of this action, and Ramesses took many of them prisoner and redeployed them in his own army later.

Ramesses had a very long reign; he lived into his nineties, outlasting most of his sons and even some of his grandsons. He had about a hundred children by his wives and concubines and about half of those were therefore sons and a good few of those would have had hopes of succession. His first chief queen was Nefertari, who is remembered as one of the great queens of Egypt. She married Ramesses before he ascended the throne and gave him four sons. The second main queen was Isetnofret who became the chief queen after Nefertari died. She had at least three sons, the last of whom was Merneptah who, although 13th in line of succession, succeeded to the throne because the previous 12 had all died by then. Before moving on to Merneptah's reign, we need to look at Isetnofret's second, and Ramesses' fourth, son because he will be important to our story.

Prince Khaemweset died a decade before his father, but for the last five years of his life was Crown Prince and in line to succeed. Although uncrowned, he was remembered far more than most actual pharaohs for his life, and by the Roman period his exploits – real and fictional – had become the stuff of legend. In his early life, from the age of only four, he accompanied his father on his military exploits in Nubia and Syria. But after this military training, he turned to the priesthood of Ptah in Memphis, rising to become Chief Priest. He became closely associated with the Apis Bull cult, designing and building a major extension to the Serapeum, where the divine Bulls were buried in state. A coffin in the Serapeum was found in the nineteenth century with his insignia and a mask of his face. The mask survives, but there are confused accounts of what was actually found in the coffin. The contents have not survived and no mummy has ever been found, but on one account at least, the coffin contained the bones of an Apis Bull, arranged to resemble a human figure. This coffin connects his Apis association with another aspect of his life that was remembered and revered: his devotion to the restoration of ancient tombs and monuments of previous pharaohs, promoting the veneration of those dead divinities. In the centuries after his death, this interest in tombs and cultic veneration led to stories of him as an occult magician, able to communicate with the dead and travel to the 'other side'. Reflecting his father's veneration of Set, he had another name: Setne Khamwas. In classical times, he was remembered as Prince **Setna** and in this guise, as I shall show later, he can be associated in some way with the first pharaoh of the 20th Dynasty, **Setna**khte.

Returning now to the main dynastic line, Merneptah inherited the throne from his father Ramesses II in 1213 BC and was without doubt Ramesses' eldest surviving son and the rightful heir, but he was seventy years old or so when he ascended the throne and he ruled for only ten years. They were very eventful years. According to an inscription on a pylon at Karnak, about halfway through his short reign Egypt was attacked by the King of Libya – the North African land to the west of the Nile Delta. It will be recalled that Ramesses II had secured a peaceful border with Libya and at the start of his reign had quashed incursions by the Sherden, Shekelesh and Lukka. Now, it seems, the two enemy forces combined: the Libyan forces were reinforced by soldiers – especially bowmen apparently – from the Sherden, Shekelesh and Lukka. And in addition, these were joined by more so-called Sea Peoples – the Teresh and Ekwesh, characterized as 'northerners from all lands'. We shall deal with them – who they were and where they came from – in the next chapter, but apparently at this time they were mercenaries in the pay of Libya. The attack was successfully beaten off by Merneptah and the Egyptian forces at a place called Perira, on the western border of the Delta.

The pylon inscription does not reveal the motive for the attack, but we can probably guess. This was a time of unprecedented famine across the whole of the eastern Mediterranean and Asia. As we saw earlier, Egypt was not immune from famine, but tended to be less affected because its agriculture, and indeed its whole economy, was based upon the regular annual inundation of the Nile Valley by river waters swollen from mountain rainfall near its source in the south. A great deal of work has been done to establish the reality of this famine, by historians, archaeologists and scientists from a range of disciplines. It began during the 19th Dynasty, lasted for many decades, and was a major component in the Late Bronze Age Collapse. We have documents surviving from Asian and other civilizations of the time, describing grain shipments from Egypt going to various lands to relieve this famine. This was not 'famine aid' as we would understand it today – the Egyptian economy was boosted by selling grain abroad throughout Egyptian history and they did not just give it away in times of famine. We also have, of course, a very detailed description of such a famine, and such relief, in the story of Joseph in Genesis. In that narrative, a famine in Canaan forces Jacob's family to seek grain from Egypt – a parallel to which we shall return presently. We cannot be sure that the Libyan/Sea Peoples attack was motivated by the famine, but I think it is a not unreasonable hypothesis.

Another inscription dating from the time of Merneptah has become even more famous – the Merneptah Stele, also known as the Israel Stele, discovered by the accomplished archaeologist Sir William Matthew Flinders Petrie, more commonly known as Flinders Petrie (1853–1942), in Thebes in 1896, and now in the Egyptian Museum in Cairo. The stele dates originally from the reign of Ramesses II and one side of it is taken up with a rehearsal of, and praise for, the temple and building programme that characterized the second, peaceful half of Ramesses' reign. The other side, however, was inscribed in the reign of Merneptah and its 28-line inscription mostly contains another account of the Libyan invasion and defeat, but as we noted earlier, it ends with a few lines that contain the earliest reference to 'Israel' that has yet been found outside of the Bible:

The princes are prostrate, saying, "Peace!"
Not one is raising his head among the Nine Bows.
Now that Tehenu has come to ruin,
Hatti is pacified;
The Canaan has been plundered into every sort of woe:
Ashkelon has been overcome;
Gezer has been captured;
Yano'am is made non-existent.
Israel is laid waste and his seed is not;
Hurru is become a widow because of Egypt.

First some clarification of people and places mentioned: 'Nine Bows' is a traditional Egyptian descriptive term for their northern enemies; 'Tehunu' is Libya; 'Hatti' is the Hittites; 'Ashkelon', 'Gezer' and 'Yano'am' are Canaanite cities; and 'Hurru' is a reference to the Hurrians. But who or what is meant by 'Israel' at this time? When Petrie first discovered this inscription, his comment was: 'Won't the reverends be pleased?' And indeed they (and the rabbis) were and are. But over a century later, scholars are still wholly divided about this. The majority consensus is probably that it refers to a 'people' rather than a 'place': Egyptian hieroglyphics have symbols to distinguish the two, and the 'people' symbol is used here (although presumably the two are not mutually exclusive, so the evidence is not exhaustive). And those 'people' are clearly Canaanite. The list of three Canaanite cities that precede the Israel reference perhaps suggests that the 'Israel' people are Canaanites that did not live in cities – so, pastoral nomads. Or the reference here could imply that there were indeed a people in Canaan at the time who called themselves 'Israel' and the three cities were part of their culture, which of course would be the 'reverends' favoured reading.

Most scholars seem to assume that the key, last five lines

refer to entirely separate and different events to the Libyan/ Sea Peoples invasion in the reign of Merneptah, but there is nothing on the stele to confirm, or indeed suggest, this. Ashkelon was (and is) an ancient Levantine seaport, 50 km south of modern Tel Aviv. Gezer was a major fortified Canaanite city midway between Tel Aviv and Jerusalem – a strategic position at the crossroads of the ancient coastal trade route linking Egypt with Syria, Anatolia and Mesopotamia. Yanoam has yet to be positively identified but must from the context be Canaanite. There is nothing in principle to prevent all these places and peoples being part and parcel of the Libyan invasion. Alternatively, some scholars have argued that the final section is indeed separate from what goes before, but that it is, in fact, a final coda to the whole stele, front and back. In this interpretation, in these final lines, Merneptah is reviewing the achievements of his dynasty rather than just his reign; the references to Canaan and Israel in this interpretation, therefore, would be reflections on the achievements of his father, creating a predominance of Egyptian interest in Canaan that still existed in Merneptah's time.

Certainly, there is no surviving reference to a major incursion in Merneptah's reign other than the Libyan one. If that indicates that 'Israel' and the three cities did not attack Egypt, there seems no reason why Egypt should have initiated hostilities. One clue that this might be the case is the reference to Israel's 'seed'. This could of course refer to descendants – such hyperbole was commonplace on inscriptions such as this. Or it could mean grain seed. This was a time of famine and I suggested that the Libyan invasion was motivated by access to Egypt's grain. The destruction of an enemy's grain store at such a time would reduce their future ability to wage war. But why would Egypt destroy Israel's grain rather than sell them some? And if 'Israel' had a grain store, they could surely not have been pastoralists after all.

Perhaps the 'reverends' were right; perhaps Israel referred to a *tribal* grouping that embraced cities *and* nomads. We saw earlier in relation to Midian that this was precisely the sort of political model that operated in Canaan at the time. Primary allegiance was given to family, village and city but either for cultic purposes, or at times of war, or both, tribal affiliations came to bear. The Bible portrays the early Israelites as a tribal grouping. Could that be what we see here? And was that grouping gathered at a time of famine, allied itself with Libya and attacked Egypt for its grain? In that case, we might conclude that the mysterious Sea Peoples were at least in part of Canaanite origin. The resolution of this will be the subject of the next chapter.

Merneptah was probably succeeded by his son Seti II who reigned from 1203–1197 BC. The sources are silent about the circumstances but what is certain is that the succession did not go without challenge, and we now enter a period of dynastic intrigue and short reigns. Scholars are divided about the details because the surviving evidence is far from clear. Seti's mother was Queen Isetnofret II, but Merneptah had another wife called Queen Takhat and her son, Amenmesse, seems to have challenged Seti for the throne. For a long time, the standard chronology has shown their reigns as sequential, with no certainty about who preceded whom. But many scholars now argue that their reigns in fact overlapped, and for a period of a few years Upper and Lower Egypt were ruled separately again – Seti in the north and Amenmesse in the south. The story of these two brothers was clearly one well remembered in ancient Egypt. A papyrus has survived from the time of Seti II, known as the *Tale of Two Brothers*, which is probably a political satire on Seti and Amenmesse.[5]

---

5 The story is preserved on the *Papyrus D'Orbiney* in the British Museum.

Scholars have also noted parallels between the story of the two historical brother kings and the Moses/Aaron narrative in Exodus, and between the *Two Brothers* satire and the story of Joseph and Potiphar's wife. I would not wish to overplay these parallels but they do yet again point to both the Egyptian origins of many of these Biblical stories and the way in which the same stories get told and retold about different characters and fitted into narratives in various different ways to suit the writer.

Seti II seems eventually to have gained the upper hand but the ultimate fate of Amenmesse is obscure. Around that time, there was an Egyptian viceroy in Nubia called Messuy, and this could have been Amenmesse either before or after his attempt to usurp the throne, but chronologies throughout this period are blurred and no one can as yet say for sure. The problem is exacerbated because, following his defeat of Amenmesse's ambitions, Seti II had his memorial inscriptions removed or defaced – much as had been done to Akhenaten. What we can be sure of is that these were turbulent times and struggles for power, internal and external, were to be a feature of the last years of the 19th Dynasty.

Seti II reigned in some way or another for only about six years before he died, at which point the internecine struggle for power that had dominated his reign continued. There were candidate offspring from Merneptah and from his two sons, all of whom had wives and concubines with whom they had children. A Syrian or Canaanite known as Chancellor Bay, already a prominent court official, seems to have seized the opportunity to act as a power broker among the various claimants to the throne, and on the evidence of several inscriptions inspired by himself was instrumental in securing the succession for a pharaoh known as Siptah, who was still a child at the time. There is no consensus at all among modern scholars as to Siptah's parentage, although he was clearly one of the family contenders. Siptah was succeeded by Queen Twosret. She seems to have been co-regent with Bay from the start of Siptah's reign and continued for a couple of years after his death. But for the roughly seven years of Siptah's reign, the real power behind the throne was undoubtedly Bay, who effectively became Pharaoh in all but name – holding the offices of, according to different inscriptions, vizier, treasurer and major general. He is depicted in inscriptions alongside and the same size as, the two pharaohs, and he even had his name inscribed on a Mnevis Bull[6] statue, a prerogative usually reserved for divine pharaohs. Bay's boasted power and influence is unparalleled, particularly for a foreigner. He was deposed at the end of Siptah's reign, either by Siptah or by Twosret, and buried in his tomb, built in the Valley of the Kings alongside Siptah and Twosret. The tomb has been excavated and is immense and elaborate, with wall carvings depicting him with the funerary gods – again, the prerogative of pharaohs.

If the story of Bay is ringing bells with you, it should: it uncannily mirrors the Biblical story of Joseph. The story of Bay and the story of Joseph both involve northerners who win a pharaoh's approval in a time of famine and win pharaoh-like responsibilities. There is also a clue to the truth in a neglected passage in Genesis, when Joseph describes his position at court to his brothers:

> God . . . hath made me a father to Pharaoh, and lord of all
> his house, and a ruler throughout all the land of Egypt.[7]

There seems no reason not to take this literally; Joseph's 'Pharaoh' seems to have been underage, and Joseph acted as

---

6 Of which, more later.

7 Genesis 45:8.

regent during his minority. Indeed, it is hard to think of any other circumstances in which a pharaoh would assign such sweeping powers to anyone. As Joseph is depicted here as regent, so with Bay and the child pharaoh, Siptah. Of course there are differences in the detail, but then we do not have all the detail of Bay's reign. He may well have built grain stores like Joseph, for example – we just don't know. Perhaps not a coincidence, Siptah's reign of seven years reflects the length of the famine prophesied by Joseph. But the key elements of both stories are so similar, one has to wonder why the connection has not been acknowledged.[8] There are two answers, I think. One is the issue of chronology. Bay is obviously centuries too late for Joseph if you accept the Genesis account. But as soon as you accept that this is an old story with Egyptian origins that has somehow found its way incongruously into the Biblical narrative, that objection vanishes. The other issue is that the two names are different. Bay is not obviously an Egyptian name, but 'Beyah' appears a couple of times in the Old Testament as an epithet or name of Yahweh, so Bay(a) may well be Semitic. And I think it is germane to note here that a small statue of Bay has been found at Heliopolis in the Delta. Heliopolis was also called On and Joseph is said to have married the daughter of a priest of On.[9]

In my analysis of Genesis, I suggested that there is something odd about the story of Joseph, that it just doesn't seem to fit. The line of genealogical narrative runs from Abraham through Jacob, not Joseph, and his intrusion into the story

---

8 Long after I made the connection, I discovered a couple of articles by Professor Israel Knohl, Professor of Bible at the Hebrew University of Jerusalem, published online in The Torah.com that reach similar conclusions to myself on this and other related matters that follow below. I am happy to acknowledge this here, and provide more details in my Bibliography.

9 Genesis 41:45.

creates all sorts of problems to do with the twelve sons/tribes that have to be resolved in tortuous ways. In my view, Joseph's story is in reality, the story of Chancellor (or Vizier) Bay. He was a Canaanite who achieved unique dominance in Egypt as regent for the child pharaoh Siptah. The story of his rise to power was passed down throughout Israel, north and south, and was co-opted into the Israelite racial myth in a way that displaced him in time but preserved his memory as a Canaanite who, for a time, was pharaoh in all but name. There was no Israelite tribe called Joseph – his place was taken by his sons, Ephraim and Manasseh. But we shall see in a later chapter, that there may well have been a tribe called Joseph among the nomadic tribes of the Sinai area. History does not record the precise origin of Bay: perhaps he came from that Joseph tribe? It was in any case a great source of Israelite pride that their race had not always been in slavery in Egypt – that Yahweh had prospered earlier generations in a way that he would do again at the time of the Exodus. If I am right about this, it is an important first step in connecting the Israelite racial myth with recorded Egyptian history. And as we shall see in chapters to come, other connections can be discerned if we are prepared to be guided by parallels of person and incident rather than preconceived ideas about a mass Exodus and a single campaign of Conquest.

Returning to the fortunes of the 19th Dynasty, following the death of Bay, Twosret reined for only a couple of years before she too died. The turmoil of the 19th Dynasty then finally came to an end with the accession to the throne in 1189 BC of the first pharaoh of the 20th Dynasty – Setnakhte. He arrives on the scene unannounced and unheard of until then, and he seems not to have descended from Seti II, Siptah or Twosret. However, most scholars believe he was descended in some way from Ramesses II: his son and all the other 20th Dynasty pharaohs were called Ramesses. Setnakhte did not just walk into power – he had opposition and had to fight for the throne at a time when Egyptian politics were still in turmoil. We have two contemporary sources for this. The first is a stele from the city of Elephantine in Upper Egypt, only discovered about fifty years ago in 1971 but vital to an understanding of how Setnakhte came to power. Set up by Setnakhte, the stele describes a country in political and religious turmoil. This certainly accords with scholarly opinion that following the civil war of the two brothers, Seti II and Amenmesse, there was a period of short reigns and strife bringing the 19th Dynasty to a messy end. According to the stele, this was caused by 'troublemakers' who Setnakhte drove off in the first year of his reign. But it also provides some detail about who were behind the turmoil: apparently, unnamed Egyptian rulers had imported Canaanite mercenaries to assist them. They were to be paid in gold and silver, but they abandoned this when they fled. By the second year of Setnakhte's reign, the stele asserts that all his enemies had been defeated and religious order had also been restored: apparently, during the years of unrest, temples had been closed and traditional offerings to the gods had ceased. The overall impression is that Setnakhte's mission had been inspired by religion as well as politics.

Setnakhte is usually assigned a reign of only about three years before he died of natural causes and was succeeded by his son, Ramesses III. It seems likely, therefore, that he was already of advanced years when, with his son, he retook the Egyptian throne. Ramesses III went on to have a reign of around three decades, from 1186 BC to 1155 BC. Eric H. Cline,[10] in his bestselling book on the Late Bronze Age Collapse,[11] dates that event

---

10 Eric H. Cline (1960–) Professor of Ancient History and Archaeology at the George Washington University, in Washington, D.C.

11 See Bibliography.

to an over-precise 1177. He explains that this was a marketing ploy rather than an academic judgement, but he chose that date because it was exactly then that the Sea Peoples made their final and most ambitious appearance on the scene. It was Ramesses III's defeat of them that seems to have ended their incursions, but the Collapse happened with remarkable rapidity after 1177. Egypt certainly suffered from the Collapse and, although it was less severe there than elsewhere, Egypt never again recovered the power and prestige it had enjoyed during the Middle Kingdom period. Ramesses III was, in effect, the last really great pharaoh of Egypt. The Middle Kingdom finally fell apart a century after him, and the succeeding 400 years were a dark age in Egypt – as everywhere else in the Eastern Mediterranean – known in Egyptian chronology as the Third Intermediate Period.

The second source we have for the reigns of Setnakhte and Ramesses III is known as the Great Harris Papyrus, so called because it is the largest papyrus to have survived from ancient Egypt. It documents the reign of Setnakhte's son, Ramesses III, but begins in the preceding period. Here is the traditional translation of 1906, by James Henry Breasted, a pioneering American archaeologist and Egyptologist:

> The land of Egypt *was overthrown from without*, and every man was thrown out of his right; they had no "chief mouth" for many years formerly until other times. The land of Egypt was in the hands of chiefs and of rulers of towns; one slew his neighbour, great and small. Other times having come after it, with empty years, . . . [12] [author's emphasis]

This account of course parallels the Elephantine Stele, but provides more detail, particularly of exactly who was

---

12 Translated in 1906 by James Henry Breasted (1865–1935). See Bibliography.

responsible for the turmoil of the period. In particular, it seems to bear out the stele account that the troublemakers were assisted by Canaanite/Syrian outsiders. Unfortunately, the section of the papyrus we are dealing with here is notoriously difficult to translate.

More recently, in 1979, another scholar – Hans Goedicke[13] – published a different translation, suggesting that the turmoil was wholly internal:

> The land *belonging to Egypt was abandoned abroad* and every man in his loyalty, he did not have a chief-spokesman for many years first until the times of others when the land belonging to Egypt was among chiefs and city-rulers — one was killed, his replacement was a dignitary of wretches. Another of the family happened after him in the empty years, . . . [author's emphasis]

So was Egypt overthrown from without (Breasted), which suggests invasion of some sort or, at the very least, the use of mercenaries, or did Egypt just abandon its territorial possessions abroad (Goedicke)?[14] There can be no doubt at all that the stele and the papyrus are descriptions of the same events, and since the key phrase here can be interpreted in two ways, and since the stele is quite explicit about the

---

13 Hans Goedicke was Professor Emeritus in the Department of Near Eastern Studies at Johns Hopkins University. He was perhaps most famous for proposing that the parting of the Red Sea could be associated with the volcanic explosion on Santorini in *c.* 1600 BC, neatly coinciding with the Hyksos era. The idea has never really caught on. And, of course, it would be incompatible with the suggestion that the Elephantine Stele describes events associated with a later Exodus.

14 Israel Knohl, who we noted above as identifying Bay with Joseph, translates the key phrase as 'The land of Egypt had been cast aside' which is neatly ambiguous. He does, however, go on to accept the Elephantine Stele version that does speak of 'Levantine' outsiders.

involvement of outsiders, motivated by 'gold and silver', I am not inclined here to follow Goedicke's translation. But Goedicke's translation does, I think, clarify the next lines that in Breasted's translation are indeed obscure. Under Goedicke's interpretation, those lines can clearly be seen to refer to the two brother pharaohs (Seti II and Amenmesse) and the Bay/Siptah regency period that followed. In this case, I do not think Breasted and Goedicke are at odds; Goedicke merely expresses better the underlying intention of the passage.

The papyrus continues thus immediately after the quotation above:

Irsu ('a self-made man'), a certain Syrian (Kharu) was with them as chief (wr). He set plundering their (i.e. the people's) possessions. They made gods like men, and no offerings were presented in the temples. But when the gods inclined themselves to peace, to set the land in its rights according to its accustomed manner, they established their son, who came forth from their limbs, to be ruler, LPH, of every land, upon their great throne, Userkhaure-setepenre-meryamun, LPH, the son of Re, Setnakht-merire-meryamun, LPH. He was Khepri-Set, when he is enraged; he set in order the entire land which had been rebellious; he slew the rebels who were in the land of Egypt; he cleansed the great throne of Egypt; he was ruler of the Two Lands, on the throne of Atum. He gave ready faces to those who had been turned away. Every man knew his brother who had been walled in. He established the temples in possession of divine offerings, to offer to the gods according to their customary stipulations.[15]

---

15 I follow Breasted here; I do not believe Goedicke's version differs significantly, except that he has 'Su' instead of 'Irsu'.

Again, the Papyrus account bears out the Stele – that Setnakhte defeated the rebels, united Egypt under his rule and re-established the traditional worship of the Egyptian gods. And again, the emphasis seems as much religious as political: Setnakhte is sent by the gods themselves to re-establish divine authority. What is new, of course, is the name of the leader of the rebels – one *Irsu* (or, according to Goedicke, *Su*). This seems not to have been his actual name, but an epithet meaning 'self-made man', or in other words, a common upstart with no royal blood in his veins.

Can we identify this Irsu? For some years, scholars were confidant of his identity – they believed him to be Chancellor Bay. It seemed plausible and could be made to fit with some elements of the story. But this was based on the belief that Bay lived throughout this period – before it was discovered (by a new translation of an old inscription) that Bay was executed in Siptah's fifth year, so was not alive in the 'empty years' described here. So, if not Bay, then who? I believe we can answer this question by moving on from contemporary accounts to that provided by an Egyptian historian of a later age, Manetho. But before we do so, we need to examine one more piece of background. The Sea Peoples have inserted themselves into our story from the time of Merneptah. So who were they exactly, and can the accounts of their incursions help understand events in these years?

CHAPTER 15

The Sea Peoples

The Sea Peoples are a scholarly construct, by which I mean that no tribe, nation, land or confederation in history ever called themselves that. The term was invented to account for the Egyptian incursions over a period of a century or so that we have noted above and is bound up with the history of our understanding of the Late Bronze Age Collapse in the half-century between *c.*1200 BC and 1150 BC. This saw, among others, the cultural collapse of the Mycenaean kingdoms of ancient Greece, of the Kassite rulers of Babylonia and of the Hittite Empire in the Levant and Asia Minor, as well as the demise of the New Kingdom in Egypt and its descent into the turmoil and obscurity of the Third Intermediate Period, and similar chaos throughout Canaan. Almost every city of any size at all was destroyed one way or another, many never to rise again. The collapse of governments and law and order throughout the eastern Mediterranean and the deterioration of these governments disrupted the complex network of trade routes, which had underpinned the prosperity of these Bronze Age civilisations, and virtually eliminated literacy throughout the region, making historical reconstruction a thankless task.

It was, without a doubt, the worst disaster of the ancient

world – even more so than the fall of the Roman Empire a millennium and a half later, yet while the latter is taught in schools from primary years onwards, the former is virtually unknown today.[1] That Collapse, as we have seen, is not a modern discovery: the Greeks and Romans knew of a golden age before their own and knew that it was separated from their own time by catastrophe of some sort. Hesiod, the Greek poet who lived around the time of Homer, in the 7th or 8th century BC, spoke of heroic Ages of Gold, Silver and Bronze, separated from the mundane modern Iron Age by catastrophe. The Third Intermediate Period in Egypt did not destroy stone inscriptions or the literacy needed to read them, and the Iron Age Egyptians were very proud of the continuity of their civilisation and their records of the distant past. In his *Timaeus* and *Critias*, Plato recorded the story of Atlantis, as told (allegedly) to the 6th/7th century BC Greek statesman, Solon, by priests from the Egyptian Delta. Much nonsense is written about Atlantis, but there can be little doubt in my view that the story reflects traditions surviving from before the Bronze Age Collapse. Plato/Solon quotes an Egyptian priest thus:

> . . . you Greeks are always children . . . You are young in soul, every one of you . . . you possess not a single belief that is ancient . . . And this is the cause thereof . . . There have been and there will be many and diverse destructions of mankind . . . At such times . . . the Nile . . . saves us . . . Hence it is . . . that what is here preserved is reckoned to be the most ancient.[2]

---

1 The parallel is superficially attractive. Both collapses can be seen to have resulted from similar causes – invasions by 'sea peoples' on the one hand, and by Huns and Goths on the other. But just as the causes of the Fall of the Roman Empire were many and complex, so too were the causes of the earlier Collapse, as we shall now see.

2 *Timaeus*, 22. trans. by E.V. Rieu, Penguin Classics.

We shall see this Egyptian pride in the continuity of their records again when we come to examine the writings of the Egyptian historian Manetho.

Various causes for the Collapse have been identified over the years.

Natural Catastrophes: These were the 'destructions' that Solon's Egyptian priest had in mind. He maintained that, contrary to Greek (and we might add, Jewish) belief, there had not been one Great Deluge but many, and he also described earthquakes that were, and still are, common in the Mediterranean. It is not hard to find evidence for natural disasters like these across the region, and many have proposed one or more of these as responsible for the Collapse.

Climate Change: Related to these natural catastrophes is the idea that dramatic changes in climate could have caused prolonged famine, leading to mass migrations and invasions in search of food. Famine was, of course, a fact of life as we have seen, and there is some evidence that drought in particular was a problem in the region at the time, but no conclusive evidence that this alone was a pivotal cause.

Internal Rebellions: Revolts by the poor and/or slaves against the rich is also sometimes cited as a cause, but in the absence of surviving records, socio-political causes leave no discernible traces that can be distinguished from other causes. For example, the destruction of Hazor has been attributed to this cause by those (among others) who would identify the Exodus as an earlier event.

Invasions: The invasions of the Sea Peoples are the prime candidates under this heading, either through incursions from overseas, or through later uprisings by defeated pirates, now slaves or mercenaries.

Disruption of Diplomatic and Trade Networks: This certainly happened but it is hard to see how this could have been a cause of the Collapse, rather than a consequence of it. Which brings us to the central issue of cause and effect: all the above factors no doubt played their part in the Collapse, but is there a discernible order to these events?

The traditional model for the Bronze Age Collapse involved all the above factors in a set sequence, a domino effect: earthquakes brought down cities, and poor harvests caused famine, which led to social and political instability, resulting in internal rebellions; at the same time, large populations uprooted from their own lands by the same difficulties migrated to the Mediterranean and, in their quest for a new home, disrupted existing populations; and all of these pressures finally resulted in the loss of diplomatic and trade relations and the fall of civilization in the Mediterranean. Neat though this linear model is, it is just too good to be true. All of these civilizations had survived all of these factors before. One factor does not necessarily lead to another, and certainly not across a number of civilizations at the same time. The odds against are like an 'accumulator' bet in horse racing – astronomical – and for the same reasons. Scholars were trying to fit the facts to a theory rather than allowing a theory to evolve from the facts.

For many years, and for many scholars, the invasions of the Sea Peoples were, if not the 'prime' cause of the Collapse, then the 'pivotal' cause that cut the odds against a linear, domino-effect model. Quite simply, it was too convenient a scapegoat to ignore. The theory was first propounded in 1855 by the French Egyptologist Emmanuel de Rougé,[3] who coined the phrase *peuples de la mer* and until relatively recently the idea has never looked back. In essence, the theory is that the Sea Peoples were a warlike confederation that at the end of

---

3 The Vicomte Olivier Charles Camille Emmanuel de Rougé (1811–1872).

the Bronze Age sailed around the Eastern Mediterranean wreaking havoc throughout Greece, Asia Minor, Syria, Phoenicia, Canaan, Cyprus and Egypt. But given that our knowledge of these peoples derives primarily from Egyptian accounts of Egyptian attacks, it seems in retrospect to have been rather a large leap to identify them as the cause of so much destruction and upheaval elsewhere in the region. Ideas about where they came from and who they were could differ, but there seemed no doubt that in their marauding about the place they triggered the end of Bronze Age civilization.

Common sense might have given some pause for thought. Theories of origins were developed that involved peoples throughout the Mediterranean from west to east, but no one sought to ask just how these varied peoples came to club together and organize themselves into a single entity. We fall into the trap of assuming such possibilities because we are used to modern communications. But this was the Bronze Age. There were certainly highly evolved trading routes across the Mediterranean, using the sea as the main highway. But the exchange of goods across great distances is very different to an agreement to create a confederacy for war. Such confederacies were not unknown – the Midianites and the Israelites being examples. But these were peoples living adjacent to each other and in daily communication by land. The only viable possibility would surely be one people displacing another in a catastrophic, unplanned chain reaction, but then we are back to domino effects again, and the argument becomes circular – what was the cause of the chain reaction in the first place? Such theories that seek to identify the 'Sea Peoples as cause', end up seeing them as only 'effect' after all.

Theories of the Sea Peoples as 'effect' rather than 'cause' have gradually come to replace the simpler original concept. But there is no scholarly consensus about this either.

One prominent school of thought sees the Sea Peoples as western opportunists, taking advantage of a pre-existing collapse in the east to resettle there with minimum effective resistance. But this then begs the question of what caused the eastern decline and weakness in the first place. As with the 'cause' theories, the 'effect' theories turn out to provide no answer to anything. I have referred above to Cline's book on the subject. Having surveyed all the evidence, his conclusion (which is supported by a majority of scholars today) is that the Collapse was not the result of a chain reaction, but the result of what he calls a 'perfect storm' of catastrophes:

> ... the Sea Peoples may well have been responsible for some of the destruction ... but it is much more likely that a concatenation of events, both human and natural – including climate change and drought, seismic disasters ... , internal rebellions, and 'systems collapse' – coalesced to create a 'perfect storm' that brought this age to an end.[4]

I am sure he is right. But he does not then go back to basics and re-examine the traditional identifications of the Sea Peoples. Those identifications arose from the traditional 'cause' and 'domino' theories. In my view, even in that original context they looked decidedly unlikely for various reasons, and given a new paradigm along the lines suggested by Cline, I think it is high time they were re-examined.

---

4 Eric H. Cline *1177 B.C.: The Year Civilization Collapsed*, p.11.

Fig.11: Map of the Sea Peoples' Origins

We first encountered the Sea Peoples in the reign of Ramesses II, when they are described as sea pirates. The most prominent in that encounter seem to have been the **Shardana**, (also known as the **Sherden**). The inscription describes them as coming from 'the midst of the sea', 'unruly' and 'irresistible'. Yet resist them Ramesses did, and consequently he incorporated some of them into his own armies. We know what they looked like from the inscriptions: they are uniquely dressed in helmets surmounted by a disc and horns. This has resulted in some truly weird and wonderful identifications, most notably the proposition that these were Vikings, despite the fact that those redoubtable Scandinavian warriors wore horned helmets only in Hollywood, and although they just might have 'discovered' North America, it seems unlikely to say the least that they would have landed up on the shores of Egypt in enough numbers to cause trouble.

Putting the lunatic fringe to one side, the most usual identification of a home country for the Shardana by scholars is Sardinia, the second-largest island in the Mediterranean Sea. This idea is based initially on linguistic parallels. For the non-linguists among us, the simplest way to view etymological parallels like this is to omit the vowels on the basis that ancient scripts did not recognize them and compare the consonants. The result is never proof of anything and can result in outlandish theories, but it can be a starting point. In this case, it is easy to see how Shardana/Sherden [SRDN] becomes Sardinia [SRDN]. So, case proved? Certainly, Bronze Age Sardinia boasted an extraordinary and enigmatic culture that has scholars foxed even today. Known as the Nuragic culture, named after the 'nuraghes' or towers that litter the Sardinian plains in huge numbers, it lends itself to many romantic theories. It has been linked with both Atlantis and Troy in one way or another, but the archaeological basis for such theories is tenuous. Trading of goods throughout the Mediterranean reached a peak before the Bronze Age Collapse, and it would be surprising indeed if pottery and armour from Sardinia were not to be found in the eastern Mediterranean and vice versa. The various theories about the Sardinian/Shardana connection reflect this, with some scholars arguing migration west to east and some the reverse. The truth is that the Sardinian/Shardana connection is largely based on the kind of etymological parallels noted above, and all the rest is pure conjecture.

My starting point in these identifications is very different. I ask myself: why does all the evidence for the Sea Peoples comes from Egypt?[5] It may be because, as noted earlier, they

---

5 There are, of course, records of incursions into other areas during the Collapse, and these are often attributed to the Sea Peoples as part of the theory concerning their role in the Collapse. But the attribution is hypothetical: only in the Egyptian records do we find the specific references to the tribes/peoples we are now seeking to identify.

are the only surviving civilization with records of the period. But equally, it could be hypothesised that this was a local Egyptian problem with no wider implications for the Bronze Age Collapse. Certainly, if we accept the 'perfect storm' explanation for the Collapse there is no need for any such wider implications. And if the local hypothesis is correct, then we should be able to locate the Shardana and the other Sea Peoples among the traditional foes of the Egyptians. There is, in fact, an equally convincing etymological parallel much closer to home than Sardinia. It will be recalled that one of Jacob's sons by Leah was Zebulun, who founded the Israelite tribe that bears his name. In Jacob's prophetic blessing of his sons, he says of Zebulun that his tribe will be seafarers:

Zebulun shall dwell at the haven of the sea; and he shall be for an haven of ships[6]

The tribe of Zebulun were located between the Sea of Galilee and the Gulf of Haifa on the Mediterranean. The modern seaport of Haifa was founded in the Late Bronze Age and is no doubt the haven referred to by Jacob. The southern border of Zebulun was marked by the town of Sarid (now a kibbutz) and the chief clan of Zebulun were descended from a man called Sered and were known as Sardites. If one is looking for an SRD root nearer Egypt, this cannot be bettered. The Sardites were clearly a people of the sea, but they were also fierce warriors like the Shardana. They feature several times in the battles of the Conquest and are described as 'expert in war, with all instruments of war'.[7]

The clinching evidence is, in fact, the distinctive helmets they wore with disc and horns.

---

6 Genesis 49:13.

7 I Chronicles 12:34.

Fig. 12: Illustrations of Shardana Warriors and the Goddess Hathor

The illustrations in Figure 12 do not show Viking headgear. The picture on the left is by Breasted, taken from Egyptian reliefs showing the Shardana. The picture on the right depicts the goddess Hathor. Helmets were worn, then as now, to protect the head in battle. Cumbersome projections from the helmet as shown on the left could have been no assistance in protection and could even have been a disadvantage. The only possible reason for adorning a helmet in this way would be to secure the protection of a deity – in this case, Hathor. The disc is the sun disc and the horns are those of Hathor, a cow goddess associated with the Mnevis Bull, who in turn was regarded as the physical embodiment of the syncretic sun god, Atum-Ra.[8] The cult of Hathor was spread widely in the lands around Egypt, but was particularly prevalent in the

8 A fuller description of the Mnevis cult will come in a later chapter.

Sinai/Edom area, and further north in the Levant, especially in Phoenicia, where the city of Byblos became regarded as her home. The Canaanite land of Zebulun and the Sardites bordered the south of Phoenicia, and before the introduction of Yahweh would very probably have incorporated Hathor worship. What seems more likely: that the Shardana came from Sardinia, some 2,500 kilometres distant, or that they were the Sardites, a Canaanite people worshipping Hathor, right on Egypt's borders? Let us now look at the other so-called Sea Peoples to see if we can make similar identifications.

Accompanying the Shardana in the pirate raids on Egypt in the time of Ramesses II were two other of the Sea Peoples – the Shekelesh and the Lukka. The **Shekelesh** are traditionally associated by scholars with the ancient tribes of Sicily. The archaeological arguments for this identification are no more solid than those for Sardinia/Shardana, and insofar as the identification rests on etymology, even less convincing. I would suggest that there are much better possibilities in the Levant. To begin with, the name sounds Semitic: Jews then and now have the shekel as their currency, deriving from the Hebrew for 'to weigh' and we have already come across the cultic centre of Shechem and the tribe of Issachar. But I would suggest the Shekelesh came, like the Shardana, from a Canaanite sea port – Ashkelon. It will be recalled that the Merneptah Stele, recording Ramesside conquests in Canaan, included a statement that 'Ashkelon has been overcome'. We noted the uncertainty about whether this was related to the Libyan/Sea Peoples incursion, or something different and separate. If Ashkelon and Shekelesh are one and the same, we have the answer to that question. The etymological parallel is strong: Ashkelon/Shekelesh. Ashkelon had been an important Levantine seaport since Neolithic times. In the Bronze Age it was relatively large, with as many as 15,000 people, covering more than 150 acres and with walls measured 2.4 km long, 15 m high and 46 m thick. What better candidate?

The **Lukka** are usually associated with the Lycians from Asia Minor, and I think the link in this case is pretty unassailable. The borders of Lycia varied over time, but at its centre was the Teke Peninsula of south-western Turkey, which juts southward into the Mediterranean, facing Cyprus to the south. The Lycians have left no written records of themselves at all from this period, but late Bronze Age Hittite and Egyptian records describe Lycia and the Lycians as rebels, pirates and raiders, often allied to the Hittites.

So, in Egypt's first recorded encounter with these 'Sea Peoples' at the time of Ramesses II, the raiders came from either the Levantine coast or a peninsula in Asia Minor close by. The next time we encounter them is a couple of decades later, in the time of Ramesses' successor, Merneptah, who defeated an incursion from Libya aided by mercenaries from the Lukka, Shekelesh and Shardana, but also two new ones – the Ekwesh and the Teresh, both described as coming from the sea. The **Teresh** are traditionally associated with either the Etruscans of Italy or with Troy in Asia Minor. The two associations are linked by the idea that, assuming that the Trojan War was historical rather than just mythical, then fugitives from Troy might have made their way westwards to Italy and Sardinia: Taruisa, a Hittite name for Troy, and the Tyrrhenians, a Greek term for the Etruscans, are clearly etymologically possible. But if no one had identified the Shardana with Sardinia, or the Shekelesh with Sicily, would anyone have gone looking for the Teresh in that part of the world? Particularly when there is an obvious Levantine candidate – Tyre – with equal if not better etymological credibility. I can see two objections to this association.

First that Tyre, along with Canaan and Phoenicia was under Egyptian governance of some sort throughout the first millennium. But that is precisely the point: at the end of the Bronze Age, that Egyptian control had vanished. And second, the Phoenicians are associated with peaceful trade rather than war. But that was an Iron Age development. In the 12th century BC, with Egypt in turmoil and losing its grip; with the possibilities of trade sharply curtailed by the collapse of civilizations all round; and drought and famine raging across the eastern Mediterranean, it is not hard to imagine the Tyrian Teresh throwing in their lot with a Libyan/Levantine alliance seeking salvation in Egypt's grain stores.

The identity of the **Ekwesh** really gives the game away, however. The traditional association for this Sea People is the Achaeans – the pre-classical, Mycenaean Greeks celebrated in Homer. This has always been an important identification because it purports to give non-Homeric clues about these people. Yet scholars have maintained this identification despite, and in the face of, one very inconvenient fact that makes it highly unlikely, if not (and certainly in my view) impossible. The Ekwesh are described by the Egyptians unequivocally as being circumcised and no scholar has ever seriously suggested that circumcision was practised outside of Egypt and the Levant, let alone in Greece. And yet again, as with all the foregoing peoples, there is an equally etymologically valid candidate to be found on Egypt's Levantine doorstep – the Philistine city of Ekron. As we saw above, the Philistines were a Pentapolis made up of the five cities of Ashkelon, Ashdod, Gath, Gaza and Ekron. The last had been a thriving city from before the Bronze Age and had expanded during the Middle Kingdom (2040 BC to 1782 BC). During the Bronze Age Collapse it shrunk in size, consistent with the possibility that Philistines from Ekron joined with their cousins from Ashkelon in raids on Egypt. And, of course, people from Ekron would have been circumcised.

The return of the Sea Peoples in the reign of Ramesses III

saw the appearance of the last four names we must identify. The first – the **Peleset** – is easy: this has always been identified as the Philistines and I see no reason to disagree. We have already identified two of the Philistine Pentapolis – Ashkelon/Shekelesh and Ekron/Ekwesh. Were the Peleset from Gath, Gaza or Ashdod – or just Philistines with no city allegiance? What matters is that three out of five of the Philistine Pentapolis took part in the Sea Peoples raids. The Philistines were, of course, famous in the Bible, and in the Egyptian record, for their ferocity and predilection for conflict; Moses led the Exodus southwards precisely to avoid them.

The **Denyen** then fall simply into place. For those enamoured of the Ekwesh/Achaean hypothesis, a Denyen/ Danaan identification seems obvious: Homer refers to his 'Greeks' by both these descriptors. But if the Ekwesh were from Ekron we do not have to search very far afield to find the Denyen – and certainly not to ancient Greece. The Israelite tribe of Dan were (in the Biblical account) allocated coastal land including the harbour now known as Jaffa (perhaps the Yanoam mentioned on the Merneptah Stele?). The Song of Deborah describes them on ships, and in Jacob's blessing of the twelve tribes they are described as like a snake that bites a horse's heel, bringing down the rider – so presumably warlike. Once again, in Denyen/Dan we find an etymologically viable identification with close connection to seagoing in the Levant.

The last two peoples, both mentioned in the Great Harris Papyrus, are the Tjeker and the Weshesh. The **Tjeker** have been associated with the Teucrians, who were located at or near Troy, so if the Teresh were Trojans that might make sense. But if the Teresh were from much further south in Tyre, then we need to look there for the Tjeker also. And the hunt yet again is not difficult. About 30 km south of Haifa

– the port of the Shardana/Sardites – was the Canaanite port of Dor, and in the 12th century BC (i.e. the Late Bronze Age), it was taken by force by a people called the Tjeker and turned into a large, fortified city. There is no consensus about where they came from, but the Egyptians called the eastern Delta area Tjeku. This was the land of Goshen – the very area where the Hyksos kings built Avaris and where the Israelites were in captivity according to the Bible. Does this then reflect some historical truth behind the Exodus story? Whatever the case, the Tjeker surely came originally from Tjeku on Egypt's very doorstep, and their subsequent occupation of Dor to the north reflects both their itinerancy and their warring capabilities.

And finally, the **Weshesh**, (not to be confused with the Meshwesh, who were a Libyan tribe). Scholars have had particular difficulty identifying this tribe. Some have suggested Greek or Cretan origins on not very convincing etymological grounds. But with all the foregoing evidence, it becomes relatively straightforward to locate them just a short distance up the Mediterranean coast from Dor. The name **Weshesh** is surely a version of **Ueshesh**, which means 'men of Uash' in Hebrew, and hence a corruption of the Israelite tribe of Asher, who held land on the coast north of Dor and Haifa.

I would be the first to accept that all of the above Levantine associations are based largely on consonantal equivalences. But, in my view, so are all the other identifications that have been offered. In Volume II of this trilogy, I shall use the philosophical tool of Occam's Razor extensively: in simple terms, it says that all other things being equal, the simplest explanation of a problem is usually the right one. In my view, we should look here too for the simplest explanation. Is it likely that peoples from right across the Mediterranean, thousands of kilometres apart should have come together as a war confederacy and plunge a range of civilizations into a dark age? Or is it more likely that a collapse of those civilizations, caused by (among other things) drought and famine, should as one relatively small by-product have impelled a range of Levantine coastal cities and ports to join together to raid Egypt for its grain stores? And if that was the case, given that this took place at precisely the time that we have found there to be a period of turmoil in Egypt, when the Bible describes Joseph/Bay preparing against famine, perhaps associated with the Exodus, we should regard the Sea Peoples as important in understanding the Exodus.

In this regard, it is to be noted that the coastal Israelite tribes of Zebulun, Asher and Dan all seem to have been involved. How could this be if the Exodus only occurred at around this time? It would surely suggest that not only 'Israel' itself predates the Exodus (as evidenced by the Merneptah Stele), but that at least three of the twelve tribes of Israel also predate the Exodus.[9] And if those tribes were 'Canaanite' long before they were 'Israelite', what exactly could the 'Exodus' have been? As the next step in answering those questions, let us leave the Sea Peoples to one side for a moment, and turn to a documentary source from Egypt that postdates all these events – the history of Egypt written by Manetho and preserved (in part) for us by the Jewish historian Josephus.

---

9 We also saw earlier that Benjamin may have ancient Amorite roots.

CHAPTER 16

The Sojourn

Josephus can help us, not because his Jewish sources were any different from ours, but because he was able to consult an Egyptian source that is now lost to us – Manetho's *History of Egypt*. Josephus wrote two books of Jewish history in Greek for a Roman audience. He based one – his account of the first century AD wars between Rome and the Jews – on personal experience, having lived through the period and having been a prominent participant. The other – his *History of the Jews* – however, was a retelling of the Old Testament, as interpreted and redacted by the Jewish religious authorities of his time.[1] He seems to have written this book to show the Roman world that his people, the Jews, were of great antiquity and that their religion, in particular, had been sanctified by time and experience. Unfortunately, there were some at the time who, like many today, were sceptical that any race could trace its history back as far as Josephus and the Jewish Scriptures claimed to do; and they remained sceptical on the matter even after the 'publication' of his History. So Josephus wrote a third

---

1 We shall return to these two books by Josephus in Volume II of this trilogy – *Mistaken Messiahs* – where they will be central to our understanding of the real Jesus Christ.

book, *Contra Apion*, setting out the intrinsic reasons why Jewish Scripture could be trusted as genuine history and also the extrinsic corroboration provided by the writings of other cultures. In the latter regard, Egypt was of prime importance, for it too claimed to have a record of its history extending back thousands of years and, given the stable longevity of Egyptian culture, this was more likely to be believed.

Among the extrinsic evidence offered by Josephus is the *Egyptiaca* or *History of Egypt* by Manetho. We know very little about Manetho. He probably lived in the late fourth to early third century BC, born in Egypt but writing in Greek for an educated Greek audience. The *Egyptiaca* was his most substantial and important work, providing king lists for Egypt from earliest times, elaborated by 'historical' accounts that have a substantial admixture of myth and legend. In that respect he is, of course, no different from the writers of the Pentateuch, or indeed any other classical historian, and that fact does not stop Egyptologists from relying on him heavily in their work. That work, however, is hampered by other problems. Only fragments of the *Egyptiaca* have survived, preserved by other historians (like Josephus) who *did* have access either to the whole text or to excerpts from it and/or to Josephus's version. We cannot be sure that they have preserved Manetho's words faithfully or have not been tempted to redact in line with their own prejudices and perspectives. So, in judging Manetho we have to judge his redactors as well. Another problem relates to the names of the kings and pharaohs. First, Manetho rendered them into Greek and his redactors may have found it particularly tempting to revise those translations. But even more fundamentally, Egyptian pharaohs had no less than five different names, and each of these could vary several times over their lifetimes. Manetho exercised no consistency at all in his use of these names and, worse still, seems even at times to have invented his own. Egyptologists have somehow to reconcile these names with those provided by other sources[2] – a riddle that has and will continue to be a fertile hunting ground for doctoral theses for many years to come.

We shall return to all this in more detail presently, as we examine Manetho's record of these times. But, before doing so, we must look at Josephus because most of what we have of Manetho's account of these times is filtered through him. Josephus does not seem to have had a complete copy of Manetho; as we shall discover, he has gaps that infuriatingly occur at precisely the points in which we are interested. He was probably working from an 'epitome' (essentially, a summary) of the complete work. Other sources for Manetho do survive, notably later Christian writers who, like Josephus, were looking for external evidence of the historicity of the Bible: Theophilus (second century AD), Africanus (second to third century AD), and Eusebius (third to fourth century AD).[3] These seem to draw upon both Josephus himself and a now lost epitome of Manetho, but most of them just provide king lists and regnal periods. These often differ from Josephus's version, and with each other, in the spelling of names, the order of kings and the regnal lengths. I shall follow Josephus as the main and earliest text, but I shall bring in the other versions when appropriate. Unfortunately, all the sources betray their Christian viewpoint, and Josephus himself, writing from a Jewish standpoint, also has some views about Manetho's account that can obtrude themselves into the text, so we need to be careful at times to distinguish between Manetho's original and Josephus' gloss.

Josephus' *Against Apion* is, as the title suggests, a book written specifically to counter the arguments of a contemporary scholar and writer called Apion, who was a 'Hellenized'

---

2 Notably the *Turin Royal Canon*, the *Old Kingdom Annals* and a plethora of inscriptions on stone monuments and buildings of all kinds.

3 Surviving in two versions, known as *Eusebius* and *Armenian Eusebius*.

Egyptian – that is, an Egyptian who participated fully in the culture of the Roman Empire, based as it was on the more ancient civilization of the Greeks. In this respect, he mirrored Josephus himself, who was a Hellenized Jew, but importantly for understanding the background to Josephus's book, Apion was a notorious anti-Semite. Famous in his time, nevertheless, none of his writings have survived, but we know that he wrote a work attacking the Jews and this was the occasion of Josephus's work written to refute that attack. It is written in two sections. The second section contains the specific refutation of Apion and need not concern us here. But in the first section, Josephus sets out his case for the great antiquity of the Jewish nation and religion and it is here that we find his quotations from Manetho. Unfortunately, those quotations form part of a refutation of some part of Manetho's account, and Josephus even at one point refers to Manetho as an 'enemy', so we need to tread carefully.

Having outlined his intention to refute anti-Semitism, Josephus addresses the common prejudice of his time among Hellenized intellectuals that if something does not appear in the writings of Greek historians, it cannot be true. He points out that, irrespective of the claimed antiquity of the Jewish race, there are others, such as the Egyptians, the Chaldeans and the Phoenicians, whose records go back much further than the Greeks, who are themselves, in comparative terms, a young civilization:

> . . . almost all these nations inhabit such countries as are least subject to destruction from the world about them; . . . but as for the place where the Grecians inhabit, ten thousand destructions have overtaken it, and blotted out the memory of former actions . . .[4]

---

4 *Against Apion* I:9-10.

This whole section, and there is much more than I have quoted here, has, I believe, been lifted from Plato's story of Atlantis that we noticed earlier. Both Plato and Manetho go on to make exactly the same point: that following such destructions, most civilizations have to learn once more to write things down and start again, but the ancient established Egyptian civilization has records going back thousands of years. Indeed, Josephus makes the same claim for the Jews as Solon's priest did for Egypt: that their records are made, maintained and preserved by a hereditary priesthood. The similarities cannot be coincidental and are germane to the method adopted in this book: if we seek to understand the late Bronze Age Collapse, we need to consult the writings of the two civilizations that alone preserved records of those times – Israel and Egypt.

Following further preliminary arguments, Josephus moves into the heart of his argument – the evidence produced by Manetho. He states at the outset his intention to be faithful to the original:

> I will set down his very words, as if I were to bring the very man himself into a court for a witness: . . .[5]

This is a strong statement. And Josephus in the following passages is careful to indicate when he is actually *quoting* from Manetho and when he is *commenting* on Manetho's words. This is important. Too many commentators on Manetho fail to discriminate between quotation and paraphrase: as we shall see, Josephus sometimes tries to reconcile perceived shortcomings in Manetho and succeeds only in muddying the waters still further. However, when he is actually quoting, it does seem to me inconceivable in a polemic

---

5 *Against Apion* I:74.

document like this, attacking another writer who would have had every opportunity and capability to answer back, that Josephus would have taken the risk to alter his sources. Indeed,[6] in all his historical writings Josephus does seem to care very much to set things down the way they happened insofar as he has knowledge of them. My own view is that we can rely on his faithfulness precisely *because* Josephus finds some parts of Manetho's account to be offensive: when he quotes him in order to rebut him there would be no point in toning Manetho down; and when he quotes him approvingly there would be nothing to gain from altering anything.

At first, Josephus seems to have nothing to quarrel with. Manetho describes in some detail the period of Egyptian history in which the Hyksos ruled over northern Egypt. It will be recalled that this was the 15th Dynasty, ruling the Delta during the Second Intermediate Period. For ease of reference, Figure 13 shows *my* chart of that period.

Fig. 13: Chart of the Second Intermediate Period

Date From	Date To	Dynasty	Pharaohs	Comments
				Start of Second Intermediate Period
1803	1649	13th		Middle and Upper Egypt
1805	1650	14th		Lower Egypt
1650	1550	15th		Hyksos in Lower Egypt
1650	1580	16th		Thebes Area Only
1650	1550	17th		Upper Egypt
				Start of New Kingdom
1550	1524	18th	Ahmose I	Drove out the Hyksos

---

6 As we shall see in Volume II.

Josephus translates Hyksos as 'Shepherd Kings', lists six kings – 'the first rulers among them' – and describes them founding Jerusalem after their eventual expulsion from Egypt. Josephus (not Manetho) then makes the specific connection between the Hyksos and the Exodus:

> . . . these shepherds, as they are here called, . . . were none other than our [i.e. Jewish] forefathers [who] were delivered out of Egypt . . .[7]

That connection has been made many times since, but as we have seen, constructing a chronology based on it is problematical. Most scholars just accept that the Exodus narrative preserves ancient oral memories of the Hyksos era and leave it at that; and Josephus takes pretty much the same view. He is not interested in chronologies – just in showing that the Jews are an ancient people – so from his point of view, the more ancient the better.

Why then does Josephus elsewhere in *Contra Apion* refer to Manetho as an 'enemy'? The reason is to be found in a second narrative that Manetho recounts and which Josephus obviously regards as in conflict with the Hyksos account, and in any case scurrilous in its portrayal of the Jewish people. Most modern scholars take the same view. That narrative does indeed seem to parallel the Hyksos account, but it is placed by Manetho at an unspecified time after the Hyksos period, involves a Pharaoh difficult to identify and, crucially for us, involves a character called Moses. Josephus tears into this narrative almost line by line and calls it in bald terms 'a lie'. He concludes that in the case of the Hyksos narrative, Manetho was working from ancient records but that the Moses narrative was based on 'fabulous stories',

---

7 *Against Apion* I:103.

either of Manetho's own invention, or adopted by him from some other anti-Semitic author.

The problem is that there is nothing at all in the narratives themselves to substantiate the claim that one story is any more likely than the other. And if one puts aside the preconceptions of modern interpretation, the same can still be said. We know the Hyksos were a Canaanite/Asian dynasty whose story in some broad sense can be aligned with the Exodus narrative – but only in the broadest sense: to reiterate, there is a world of difference between a story of slaves escaping Egypt and a dynasty of northern pharaohs being ousted by their southern counterparts. And all in the 'wrong' time period. On the other hand, the later narrative is exactly that – later – so perhaps reconcilable with other history, and it does, in fact, tell a story about slaves in the Nile Delta being led out to freedom by a man called Moses. A modern reader might, like Josephus, be repelled by the scurrilous elements of the story, but there must be a *prima facie* case for regarding it to be at least as likely as the other. Let us proceed with an open mind.

Josephus's record of Manetho is thus divided into two sections, reflecting two different time periods separated by a length of time not made explicit by Josephus. Essentially, the two sections provide two very different narratives that could be taken to relate to the Biblical Exodus. In the next two chapters we shall deal with these in order. But first, with this background in mind, we can now turn to what Manetho has to say about the Hyksos era of the 15th Dynasty, spanning the 17th and 16th centuries BC. The first quotation from Manetho concerns a pharaoh called Timaus.

There was a king of ours whose name was Timaus. Under him it came to pass, I know not how, that God was averse to us, and there came, after a surprising manner, men of ignoble birth out of the eastern parts, and had boldness enough to make an expedition into our country, and with ease subdued it by force, yet without our hazarding a battle with them. So when they had gotten those that governed us under their power, they afterwards burnt down our cities, and demolished the temples of the gods, and used all the inhabitants after a most barbarous manner; nay, some they slew, and led their children and their wives into slavery. At length they made one of themselves king, whose name was Salatis; he also lived at Memphis, and made both the upper and lower regions pay tribute, and left garrisons in places that were the most proper for them. He chiefly aimed to secure the eastern parts, as fore-seeing that the Assyrians, who had then the greatest power, would be desirous of that kingdom, and invade them; and as he found in the Saite Nomos, [Sethroite,] a city very proper for this purpose, and which lay upon the Bubastic channel, but with regard to a certain theologic notion was called *Avaris*, this he rebuilt, and made very strong by the walls he built about it, and by a most numerous garrison of two hundred and forty thousand armed men whom he put into it to keep it. Thither Salatis came in summer time, partly to gather his corn, and pay his soldiers their wages, and partly to exercise his armed men, and thereby to terrify foreigners.[8]

Most scholars conclude that 'Timaus' is a corruption of the Egyptian name Dudimose or Dedimose. There are a number of different ways in which the Greek Timaus could have resulted from the Egyptian Dudimose but most seem agreed that, one way or another, the equivalence is valid. There were two pharaohs with this name, both ruling during the Second Intermediate Period, and there is some evidence that they

---

8 *Contra Apion*, I:75-9.

were father and son. Unfortunately, there is no scholarly consensus about exactly which dynasty they belonged to.[9] The story Manetho tells here is undoubtedly that of the Hyksos invasion, so presumably Timaus is either Dudimose I or Dudimose II and Manetho's sources at least suggest that the Hyksos incursion took place on their watch.[10] Manetho speaks of 'ignoble' invaders from the east who subdue Egypt by force without a battle. They then burn cities and temples and enslave populations. They locate themselves in the Old Kingdom capital of Memphis in the southern Nile Delta, from where they extract tribute from Upper and Lower Egypt. Their first King is called Salitis. He recognizes the need to protect his territory from further invasion from Asia, particularly the Assyrians, so he rebuilds an existing city, Avaris, further north and east in the Delta as a massive, fortified stronghold. He does not rule from there but visits it from Memphis every summer.

Avaris is often regarded as the 'capital' of the Hyksos kings, but that is not, in fact, what Manetho says: the capital was Memphis and Avaris was a fortress city. Manetho also seems to think that the name Avaris has a religious ['theologic'] origin, although modern scholarly opinion is that it derives from the Egyptian 'Hatwaret', which means 'house of the department' and denotes the capital of an administrative division of the land. Both t's in the word were silent, and it was therefore vocalized something like 'Hawara' which it is argued equates to 'Avaris' in Greek. In fact, Avaris had been a population centre for Canaanite immigrants to the Delta since the Middle Bronze Age. They would have brought their own gods with them – El, Baal, etc. – so perhaps the etymology is Semitic and reflects that, as Manetho asserts? In

---

9 Some scholars argue for the thirteenth, and some for the sixteenth.

10 The most likely is Dudimose II, but it hardly matters for our purposes.

linguistics, the consonants 'v' and 'b' are often interchangeable so Avaris could have been pronounced Abaris. And, of course, in Hebrew this would derive from the same root as Abraham, meaning Father.[11]

So, we can conclude that Manetho's account is clearly related to the Canaanite/Hyksos period. There are very deep scholarly divisions about the Second Intermediate Period of which these Hyksos were part. Standard chronologies recognize five different dynasties that overlap in time and ruled over different parts of Egypt at different times. So exactly where in this sea of contention and confusion does Manetho's account sit? So far, we have learnt that the Egyptian pharaoh defeated by the Canaanite/Hyksos invaders was one Timaus, and that the first Hyksos king was one Salitis. Manetho next goes on to list the Hyksos kings that followed Salitis and the lengths of their reigns:

Salitis	19 years
Beon	44 years
Apachnas	36 years 7 months
Apophis	61 years
Jonias	50 years 1 month
Assis	49 years 2 months

Manetho then goes on to say, quite explicitly:

And these six were the first rulers among them, who were all along making war with the Egyptians, and were very desirous gradually to destroy them to the very roots. This whole nation was styled Hycsos – that is, *Shepherd-kings*: for the

---

11 Abaris is also the name of an ancient Hyperborean sage who was a priest of Apollo, the Greek Sun god – equivalent to the Egyptian god Ra, creator of the cosmos. Probably a coincidence.

first syllable, *Hyc*, according to the sacred dialect, denotes *a
king*, as is *Sos a shepherd*; but this according to the ordinary
dialect; and of these is compounded Hycsos: but some say
that these people were Arabians.[12]

The etymological interpretation of Hyksos as 'shepherd
kings' suits Josephus well, because, of course, the Bible says
that Jacob and his sons were originally shepherds. This may
be evidence therefore of Josephus's redaction of the original
Manetho text. The correct etymology is almost certainly
from an Egyptian phrase meaning 'rulers from foreign lands'.
But, given that we cannot pin down with any certainly the
Timaus/Dudimose connection, can we nevertheless identify
Manetho's Hyksos rulers with dynasties and pharaohs that
we know of from other sources? I think we can. One name
stands out clearly in the above list – Apophis. This is the
Greek version of the well-attested pharaoh Apepi. Other
sources tell us he was indeed a Hyksos king ruling over
Lower Egypt but, reigning for 40 years (not 61 years, as
Manetho suggests in the table on page 218), also had considerable power and influence across the whole country. He is
clearly attributed to the Hyksos 15th Dynasty and lived in
the early half of the 16th century BC. The Hyksos were probably driven out finally only a couple of decades after his
death. Manetho says that he was preceded by Apachnas. I
think this was Aperanat, who Kim Ryholt has argued also
belongs to the 15th Dynasty. But if this is, therefore, a king
list of the Hyksos 15th Dynasty, Manetho's reign lengths
cannot be right.

Manetho says that the Hyksos kings he lists are the 'first
rulers among them'. His list adds up to 260 years or so. He
then goes on to say that the Hyksos 'kept possession of

---

12 *Against Apion* I:81-2.

Egypt five hundred and eleven years',[13] so presumably he believed that there were many others. The mistake he seems to have made is to assume that all the five dynasties of the Second Intermediate Period followed one another, rather than overlap as we now know. But even then, his Hyksos period is far too long. The five overlapping dynasties of the Second Intermediate Period constitute a period of about 250 years – from around 1800 BC to 1550 BC. The Hyksos 15th Dynasty lasted for a little over 100 years. I think what we have here is Manetho seeking to make sense of the entire Second Intermediate Period. If scholars today have trouble working it out, we shouldn't blame Manetho for having the same difficulty. Knowing just five names, and having five centuries to fill, he extended reign lengths and just alluded vaguely to many more. Perhaps his list is based on the most prominent and powerful pharaohs of the period; perhaps it is based solely on the half dozen or so 15th Dynasty pharaohs. From the point of view of the concerns of this book, what is important is that, as Manetho attests, the events he is describing in this passage are those of the Second Intermediate Period which ended in the mid-16th century BC.

Salitis,[14] the first of Manetho's Hyksos kings, has yet to be firmly identified. One theory intriguingly suggests that it was not the name of a king, but the title given to a chief administrator of a region. The evidence for this comes from the Bible. It will be recalled that Joseph was, according to Genesis, a pharaoh in all but name. He, Jacob, and his other sons, came to live in the Delta, like the Hyksos, and the word used to describe Joseph's office is 'Shallit'. Perhaps Salitis is a corruption of that office title. There are no 'Josephs' or anything like it in the lists of the 120 or so Second Intermediate

---

13 *Against Apion* I:84.

14 Alternatively, Salatis or Saiitis, in some other sources.

Period kings and pharaohs. But also, intriguingly, there are a couple that sound very like Jacob. One is Yakbim Sekhaenre, who Ryholt has proposed to be the first king of the Canaanite 14th Dynasty, and who others have equated with Salitis himself. Of course, the Genesis narrative puts Joseph in this sort of position as a pharaoh-equivalent. For the writers of Genesis, Joseph's father Jacob may be the patriarch of the Israelites, but, for some reason, this particular son of Jacob gets more prominence. I suggested earlier that the Joseph story does not 'fit' well in the genealogical narrative of Genesis and probably belongs elsewhere in the chronology. If I am right about that, then the way is open to recognize Jacob as the founder, not just of the Israelites, but of the Canaanite/Hyksos rule in Egypt. Yakov/Jacob was a common Canaanite name at the time: a ring with that name has been unearthed at Avaris. Another Canaanite/Hyksos ruler was Yaqub-Har: here the equivalence to Jacob is even stronger. There is considerable disagreement about where he fits in the chronology, but his name would suggest again that Yakov/Jacob was a favoured regnal name among the Hyksos. Perhaps in some sense, therefore, we can conclude that, just as the Joseph story reflects the historical Chancellor Bay, the Biblical story of Jacob, the patriarch of the Twelve Tribes, reflects memories of real Canaanite rulers of Egypt.

But Manetho gives us much more information of relevance, preserved by Josephus, to which we now turn. He next describes the ejection of the Hyksos from Egypt under a pharaoh he calls Misphragmuthosis. This pharaoh drove the Hyksos north to their fortress city of Avaris where they made a stand. There the son of Misphragmuthosis, called Thummosis by Manetho, laid siege to them, resulting in an armistice allowing the Hyksos to leave Egypt peaceably. We are told there were 240,000 men, women and children who thus made their way to Canaan and there established the

City of Jerusalem. This last assertion is part of the quotation from Manetho, not overtly at least, an addition by Josephus, seeking to make a Hyksos/Exodus connection, but as stated in Manetho it cannot be true. The site of Jerusalem was occupied from the third millennium BC and there is some evidence that it was known by that name as early as the start of the second millennium BC; it was heavily fortified a couple of hundred years later in the 18th century BC. The Hyksos would have arrived there in the mid-16th century BC. If Manetho is correct in outline at least, it is perhaps just conceivable that the Hyksos enlarged the existing urban area to accommodate an influx of a quarter of a million people. Unfortunately, there is currently no archaeological evidence to confirm or deny this, and in my view, this part of the story is just an elaboration of the Hyksos/Exodus identification. Manetho/Josephus had no idea when Jerusalem was established, but, regarding it as the eternal home of the Jewish people, assumed it must have been founded following the Exodus.

Can we identify the gloriously named Misphragmuthosis and his son Thummosis? The latter is easy: a little later, Manetho uses another name for him:

> When this people . . . were gone out of Egypt to Jerusalem, Tethmosis the king of Egypt, who drove them out, reigned afterward twenty-five years and four months, and then died . . .[15]

Surely, Thummosis/Tethmosis has to be the pharaoh who we know from other sources was responsible for finally ejecting the Hyksos from Egypt – Ahmose I, founder of the 18th

---

15 *Against Apion* I:94.

Dynasty and the New Kingdom.[16] This means that his father, Misphragmuthosis, was the father of Ahmose I – Seqenenre Tao – who ruled over Upper Egypt at the end of the 17th Dynasty. What we know of these events from other sources broadly bears out Manetho's account. The revolt by the south against the Hyksos north was begun by Seqenenre Tao, who had relatively little success and seems from the evidence of his mummy to have been captured and executed by the Hyksos. He was succeeded by his eldest son, Kamose, who does not figure at all in Manetho's account, presumably because he reigned for only about five years before his death from unknown causes. In the last couple of years of his reign, he renewed the attack on the north by sailing his forces up the Nile and had some success in pushing the border northwards, but he never attacked the key stronghold of Avaris. He seems to have appointed his younger brother Ahmose as co-regent while he was engaged in these military excursions, and when he died, Ahmose I became pharaoh and founder of the new 18th Dynasty – the first of the New Kingdom. Ahmose seems to have defeated the Hyksos exactly as Manetho describes. Instead of a full, frontal attack on Avaris, he circled round it, cut it off from either retreat or relief from Hyksos allies in the east, and then successfully laid siege to it. Other records do not say what became of the Hyksos, but there is no evidence to contradict Manetho's assertion that, following the siege, they were allowed to retreat east into Canaan.

I believe that the Hyksos period, as described by Manetho, and recorded by Josephus, is broadly in accord with the historical record and, more than that, is reflected in the Biblical story of the Sojourn – but not the Exodus, which

---

16 This is confirmed by the Africanus version of Manetho which identifies this king as 'Amos'.

was a different event at a different time. Whether or not one chooses to see Jacob's name reflected in one or two of the earliest Hyksos kings (and I don't think we will ever know definitively one way or the other), the Biblical account recalls both a period when the founders of the Israelites lived in Egypt, but also, in the story of Jacob's family, a period when those same Canaanites held positions of power in the Delta area of Lower Egypt for several hundred years. The story of Joseph's quasi-pharaonic status would seem to bear this out, but, for all the reasons given above, that story does not belong to this period at all. If any personality in the historical record 'fits' with Joseph it is Chancellor Bay who lived, not in the 15th Dynasty Hyksos period (1674–1535 BC), but in the late 19th Dynasty (1292–1189 BC). The Hyksos period reflects the Sojourn but, even though the Hyksos did indeed depart eventually from Egypt and presumably went back to Canaan from whence they came, it does not reflect the story of the Exodus. That will be found, as the next chapter will show, around the time of Chancellor Bay, right at the end of the 19th Dynasty and the beginning of the 20th Dynasty.

CHAPTER 17

The Exodus

Following Manetho's description of the ejection of the Hyksos, Josephus next reasserts his own argument that the Hyksos are to be equated with the Israelites and the Exodus, following which he again quotes Manetho at length, listing the pharaohs of the 18th Dynasty from Ahmose I onwards and their regnal lengths. In Figure 14, I have listed these following Manetho, alongside the current scholarly understanding of the same period. The date column gives the current best estimate of the starting year for each pharaoh's reign. The regnal lengths are all rounded in the case of Manetho and approximate in the case of the other sources. It will be seen that there is a reasonable match between the two lists. Manetho's Greek names, of course, do not match very often with the Egyptian names, and there are some real discrepancies: Manetho has clearly missed a few pharaohs with the same name and added a few with similar names where he knows there is a gap in his chronology. But I have highlighted in bold the pharaohs where I think we can be confident that the match is good, and these predominate substantially. As described in Chapter 14, the 18th Dynasty was notable particularly for the Amarna period when, building on his father's legacy, Akhenaten introduced his religious revolution. Arguably,

Fig. 14: Pharaohs of the 18th Dynasty

Date (BC)	Manetho	Reign (years)	Other Sources	Reign (years)
c.1560	Alis[Mis]phragmuthosis		Seqenenre Tao	5
c.1555			Kamose	5
18th Dynasty				
c.1550	Thummosis/Tethmosis/Amose	25	Ahmose I	25
	Chebron	13		
c.1525	Amenophis	21	Amenhotep I	21
c.1506			Thutmose I	13
c.1493			Thutmose II	13
c.1480	Amesses (female)	21	Hatshepsut (female)	21
c.1459	Memphres	13	Thutmose III	34
c.1425	Mephramuthosis	26	Amenhotep II	26
c.1400	Tethmosis	10	Thutmose IV	10
c.1390	Amenophis	37	Amenhotep III (The Magnificent)	37
c.1353	Orus	36	Akhenaten	17
c.1335	Acenchres (female)	12	Neferneferuaten (female)	2
c.1334	Rathotis	9	Tutankhamun	9
	Acencheres	12		
	Asencheres	12		
c.1323			Ay	4
c.1319	Armais	4	Horemheb	27

that revolution contributed to the demise of the 18th Dynasty and the pharaohs of the 19th Dynasty turned their backs on it completely. Manetho calls Akhenaten 'Orus'. 'Orus' is Horus, the divine son of the Egyptian gods Osiris and Isis. He is often depicted as a baby in the arms of Isis, very like a Madonna and Child. For the ancient Greeks he was regarded as the Egyptian equivalent to their sun god, Apollo, and that is presumably why Manetho names Akhenaten (who worshipped the Aten sun disc) 'Orus'. We shall see further evidence that this identification is correct presently. Manetho lists the 19th Dynasty pharaohs immediately following on from the previous list of the 18th Dynasty pharaohs. Figure 15 is on the same basis as Figure 14.

Fig. 15: Pharaohs of the 19th Dynasty

Date BC	Manetho	Reign (years)	Other Sources	Reign (years)
*c.*1292	Ramesses	1	Ramesses I	1
*c.*1290			Seti I	11
*c.*1279	Armesses Miammoun	66	Ramesses II (the Great)	66
*c.*1213	Amenophis	19	Merneptah	10
*c.*1203	Sethos		Seti II	6

Again, the key correspondences (in bold) seem straightforward. Manetho knows of only one Seti that he calls Sethos, and thus misses out Seti I. He calls Ramesses II 'Armesses Miamoun'.[1] He calls Merneptah 'Amenophis' and he doubles the length of his reign. Despite these confusions, it does seem clear from Figure 15 that 'Sethos' has to be Seti II, not Seti I. At this point, Josephus stops quoting Manetho's king list, but we know that following Seti II the last two pharaohs of the 19th Dynasty were Siptah and Twosret. Manetho seems, in fact, to have referred to the last of these at least, because some of the other sources for Manetho's text list a 'Thuoris', who is almost certainly Twosret. Figure 16 sets out all the Manetho sources for this period at the end of the 19th Dynasty for comparison.

---

1 'Ramesses, Beloved of Amun'.

Fig. 16: Pharaohs of the 19th Dynasty, (All Sources)

Josephus		Theophilus		Africanus		Eusebius		Armenian Eusebius	
Ramesses	1	Ramesses	1	Ramesses	1				
Armesses Miammoun	66	Ramesses Miammun	66			Ramesses	68	Ramesses	68
Amenophis	19	Amenophis	19	Amenophath	19	Ammenophis	40	Amenophis	40
Sethos	59	Sethos / Ramesses	10	Sethos	51	Sethos	55	Sethos	55
Rhampses	66			Rapsaces	61	Rhampses	66	Rampses	66
Amenophis				Amenophthes	5	Ammenephthis	40	Amenephthis	8
Ramesses						Ammenemes	26	Ammenemes	26
				Thuoris	7		7		7

At first glance this looks a horrendous muddle, as indeed it is. All the Manetho sources are having difficulty with this period. But the muddle can be unpicked if you look for patterns in the information, and particularly for places where the same information has been duplicated. The horizontal alignment of the different lists with each other is mine and is based on the following reasoning. First, look at the Josephus column and compare the two groups of three pharaohs: I have accentuated these by separating them out with shaded partitions. The first group derives from Manetho's list and directly reflects the list in the previous table. The following three pharaohs are derived not from Manetho, but from Josephus's commentary, which we shall examine below. It is broadly reflected in the other sources, although the names differ. Josephus at no point mentions Thuoris (Twosret) so the other sources must have got this direct from Manetho. It will be evident that trying to identify the degree to which the other sources rely on Josephus and the degree to which they reflect the other versions of Manetho available to them is extremely difficult, if not impossible, to discern. However, I would suggest that the sixty-six years attributed by Josephus to both Rhampses and Armesses Miammoun is the clue that unlocks the confusion: both refer to the same pharaoh – the strongly attested sixty-six years of the famous Ramesses II (the Great). Josephus has got confused here and has listed the same three pharaohs twice. Africanus, Eusebius and Armenian Eusebius all fall into this trap and broadly do the same thing.

Why does any of this matter? Because it means that the second Amenophis listed in bold in Figure 16 is a mistaken repetition of the first one also in bold, and disentangling different pharaohs called Amenophis will be crucial to our argument. There were two pharaohs called Amenophis by Manetho in the previous 18th Dynasty. Amenophis is Greek for Amenhotep, so these are without any doubt Amenhotep I and III, as I have identified in Figure 14. Manetho gets their regnal lengths right. Amenhotep II is called Mephramuthosis by Manetho, but he gets the regnal length right so, again, I believe this identification is also secure. To clarify, we shall give them numbers as follows:

Amenophis 1[2] is **Amenhotep I**, who reigned at the beginning of the 18th Dynasty, from about 1525 to 1506 BC.
Mephramuthosis is **Amenhotep II**, who reigned at the end of the 15th century BC, from about 1425 to 1397 BC.
Amenophis 2 is **Amenhotep III** (The Magnificent), who reigned from about 1390 to 1353 BC. From our point of

---

2 I will use Arabic numerals to avoid confusion with the convention of using Roman numerals for Egyptian pharaoh names.

view, he is the most important as we seek to unravel things. Most notably, it will be recalled that Egypt reached one of its pinnacles under this pharaoh, partly through the efforts of his vizier and namesake, **Amenhotep, Son of Hapu**, who was later regarded and worshipped as a god.

Following these three, there is a third pharaoh Amenophis here in the 19th Dynasty – listed twice but, I would argue, in error.

Amenophis 3. This must have been the 19th Dynasty pharaoh **Merneptah** (c.1213–1203 BC). Although Manetho gets his name and regnal length wrong, he is sandwiched between Armesses Miammoun (Ramesses II) and Sethos (Seti II) so, referring back to Figure 14, this identification must be correct.

Confusion by Josephus about different pharaohs called Amenophis creates huge problems with Josephus's account of this period as we shall now explore, so it would be as well at this point to state where I am going with all this. In addition to the confusion explored above where Josephus records the same Amenophis twice in his account of the 19th Dynasty, I shall demonstrate that Josephus confuses Amenophis 2 (Amenhotep III) of the 18th Dynasty with yet another Amenophis of the 19th Dynasty, who we will encounter later in this chapter and whom he declares to be fictional and so, on that basis, rejects much of Manetho's account. Once one separates *these* two pharaohs and identifies the time period between them, all falls into place as we shall see.

So, turning back now to Josephus: he abandons Manetho's king list at Sethos/Seti II. He does not give a regnal length for the latter but, for the first time since he began listing the

pharaohs from the beginning of the 18th Dynasty, he provides some background information:

"[After Amenophis] came Sethos, and Ramesses, who had
an army of horse, and a naval force. This king appointed
his brother, Armais, to be his deputy over Egypt."
[In another copy[3] it stood thus: – After him came Sethos,
and Ramesses, two brethren, the former of whom had a
naval force, and in a hostile manner destroyed those that
met him upon the sea; but as he slew Ramesses in no
long time afterward, so he appointed another of his
brethren to be his deputy over Egypt.]
He also gave him all the other authority of a king, but
with these only injunctions, that he should not wear the
diadem, nor be injurious to the queen, the mother of his
children, and that he should not meddle with the other
concubines of the king; while he made an expedition
against Cyprus, and Phoenicia, and besides against the
Assyrians and the Medes. He then subdued them all, some
by his arms, some without fighting, and some by the terror
of his great army; and being puffed up by the great suc-
cesses he had had, he went on still the more boldly, and
overthrew the cities and countries that lay in the eastern
parts. But after some considerable time, Armais, who was
left in Egypt, did all those very things, by way of opposition, which his brother had forbid him to do, without fear;
for he used violence to the queen, and continued to make
use of the rest of the concubines, without sparing any of
them; nay, at the persuasion of his friends he put on the
diadem, and set up to oppose his brother. But then he who
was set over the priests of Egypt wrote letters to Sethos,
and informed him of all that had happened, and how his

---

3 Josephus must have had at least two versions of Manetho available to him.

brother had set up to oppose him: he therefore returned back to Pelusium immediately and recovered his kingdom again. The country also was called from his name *Egypt*; for Manetho says, that Sethos was himself called Egyptus, as was his brother Armais called Danaus."[4]

To summarize this account: Pharaoh Sethos had two brothers – Ramesses and Armais. At some point and for an unknown reason, Sethos killed Ramesses and then, while occupied in land and naval conflict with Cyprus, Phoenicia, the Assyrians and the Medes, he appointed Armais as his regent at home. Sethos had considerable success in his military endeavours. Meanwhile, however, Armais raped the queen, had his way similarly with the royal concubines, and declared himself king in opposition to his brother. Learning of all this, Sethos returned to Egypt, defeated Armais, 'and recovered his kingdom again'.

If Sethos is Seti II, as I have demonstrated above he must be, then it follows that we must have an account here of the conflict for the throne between Seti II and his brother Amenmesse, here called Armais. There is nothing in external sources to collaborate the existence of a third brother, Ramesses. Given Ramesses II's huge number of offspring, it may be that there is something historical here. Perhaps this is an indication that there were a number of other pretenders to the throne from among Ramesses' myriad sons and grandsons. On the other hand, as we saw in Figure 16, Josephus does get confused about different people called Ramesses. I say Josephus rather than Manetho because a close study of the text shows that not all of the account above is straight quotation from Manetho. The first two lines about the existence of the three brothers seems to be a quotation. But all the rest seems to be Josephus's paraphrase, not a direct quotation from Manetho. He says

---

4 *Against Apion* I:98-102.

'Manetho says' and 'This is Manetho's account' but the narrative is actually Josephus's. This is reassuring about Manetho's reliability because Josephus's account is clearly wrong in at least one important respect: the whole account of Sethos' overseas exploits does not reflect the history of the reign of Seti II at all. Seti II was beset by internal power struggles, not overseas adventures. On the other hand, they do reflect well the history of Ramesses the Great. No other pharaoh had exploits like these – they are the reason Ramesses II is known as 'The Great'. Josephus – not necessarily Manetho – is clearly getting muddled here. All I think we can take from this account with any assurance is that Manetho recorded the accession to the throne of Sethos/Seti II, and that Seti II had problems with an unknown number of pretenders attempting to usurp the throne, notably his brother Armais/Amenmesse.

But Josephus has not finished with Manetho. At this point in *Against Apion* he moves on over several chapters to discuss other evidence for his argument, but later on in the text he returns again to Manetho and picks up the story where he left off. And it is at this point that he introduces the second narrative from Manetho of which he strongly disapproves. Up to this point in our examination of the Josephus text, Josephus has been fully approving of the Manetho account. Nothing in it so far has conflicted with his understanding of the history of the Jews, and in the account of the Hyksos he sees solid evidence of the historicity of the Biblical account of the Sojourn, Exodus and Conquest. Like many others since, the chronological discrepancies do not trouble him – it is enough that both Manetho and the Bible recount similar events in a golden age of long ago.

But when Josephus here returns to Manetho, it is to confront much less congenial material: a narrative that seems to contradict his association of the Hyksos period with the Exodus, and worse still, to portray that event in terms that are an apparent slur and libel upon the Jewish race. It is worth reflecting for a moment on this. The narrative to which he objects so strongly must have been present in some form in the one or more version(s) of Manetho in front of him, otherwise why would he draw such attention to it and take so much trouble to refute it? He dismisses it as 'incredible narrations', essentially because it tells a different version of the Exodus from the Hyksos one; for Josephus, relying on the Bible, there was only one Exodus so one of the versions must be wrong; he likes the Hyksos one, so this other must be a malicious fiction. From a non-Biblical perspective, there is no rational reason to prefer one version of the Exodus over the other. Perhaps the Hyksos connection is erroneous. Or perhaps there was more than one Exodus and both accounts are valid. Let us see.

This second narrative picks the story up again where it left off – with the tale of the two brothers: Sethos/Seti II and Armais/Amenmesse. Josephus now[5] states that after expelling Amenmesse, Seti II reigned for 59 years and then his eldest son Rhampses reigned after him for 66 years. This is another muddle. We know that Seti II reigned only for about 6 years, not 59; that his son was Siptah, not 'Rhampses; and it was Ramesses II who reigned for 66 years. Let me stress again, this is *Josephus'* muddle: Manetho correctly attributes the 66 years to Ramesses II and does not give any reign length at all to Sethos/Seti II. It is at this point in the narrative that Josephus introduces a new pharaoh called Amenophis, who Josephus describes unequivocally as 'fictitious'.[6] He says that Manetho does not give him a regnal length and argues that Manetho is just recording hearsay rather than history. This 'floating' Amenophis is the one I referred to earlier as the cause of considerable confusion. Josephus clearly has

---

5 *Against Apion* I:231.

6 *Against Apion* I:232.

no real idea who he is or how he fits into the chronology. What I shall now demonstrate is that this mystery Amenophis is a puzzle for Josephus because he has got his different pharaohs called Amenophis in a complete muddle. We just saw that the two pharaohs he lists in the 19th Dynasty as Amenophis are, in fact, duplicates of Amenhotep III, who is, in reality, Merneptah. We shall now see that his mystery Amenophis is also a confusion between two pharaohs – Amenhotep III of the 18th Dynasty and Setnakhte of the 20th Dynasty. Let us see how this has happened.

Josephus has described three pharaohs called Amenophis. He clearly regards these as historical and, indeed, we have clearly identified them. To repeat:

Amenophis 1 = **Amenhotep I** who reigned at the beginning of the 18th Dynasty, from about 1525 to 1506 BC.

Amenophis 2 = **Amenhotep III** (the Magnificent), also of the 18th Dynasty, who reigned from about 1390 to 1353 BC.

Amenophis 3 = **Merneptah** of the 19th Dynasty who reigned *c.*1213–1203 BC.

Josephus clearly believes his new, 'fictional' Amenophis can be none of these, because he introduced him in the context of Seti II and Amenmesse who, coming at the end of the 19th Dynasty, postdate all these. But when he then goes on to describe his extra Amenophis, it becomes clear that he is describing Amenophis 2/Amenhotep III:

When Manetho therefore had acknowledged that our forefathers were gone out of Egypt so many years ago he introduces his fictitious king Amenophis and says thus:
"This King was desirous to become a spectator of the gods,[7]

---

7 Interestingly, one possible etymology for 'Israel' is 'He who sees God'.

as had Orus, one of his predecessors in that kingdom, desired the same before him; he also communicated that his desire to his namesake Amenophis, who was the son of Papis, and one that seemed to partake of a divine nature, both as to wisdom and the knowledge of futurities . . .

[This] namesake of his told him that he might see the gods, if he would clear the whole country of the lepers and of the other impure people; that the king was pleased with this injunction, and got together all that had any defect in their bodies out of Egypt; and that their number was eighty thousand; whom he sent to those quarries which are on the east side of the Nile, that they might work in them, and might be separated from the rest of the Egyptians . . .

There were some of the learned priests that were polluted with the leprosy; but that still this Amenophis, the wise man and the prophet, was afraid that the gods would be angry at him and at the king, if there should appear to have been violence offered them; who also added this further, [out of his sagacity about futurities,] that certain people would come to the assistance of these polluted wretches, and would conquer Egypt, and keep it in their possession thirteen years; that, however, he durst not tell the king of these things, but that he left a writing behind him about all those matters, and then slew himself, which made the king disconsolate . . ."[8]

To summarize this passage: Pharaoh Amenophis wants to emulate his predecessor Orus and to that end is advised by his namesake, another Amenophis – presumably a vizier – to gather up all the lepers and 'impure' people in Egypt, including any priests so inflicted, and enslave them in the Delta quarries. The vizier Amenophis then has visions of the future

---

8 *Against Apion* I:232-6.

in which he sees that as a consequence of this advice, Egypt would be invaded in support of the slaves for a period of thirteen years, and he commits suicide.

The Amenophis described here is certainly not fictional, as Josephus supposes, he is just an anachronism. We have met this Amenophis who shares his name with an adviser before: Amenhotep III of the 18th Dynasty, whose vizier was Amenhotep, son of Hapu. As we saw, that vizier later became influential, famous and was even deified. There can be no doubt at all that Papis and Hapu – the names of his father – are one and the same and that, therefore, the Amenophis referred to here *has to be* our Amenophis 2, who was Amenhotep III. The fly in the ointment here is that Josephus describes this pharaoh as seeking to emulate his predecessor, [H]Orus, who we have confidently identified as Akhenaten. That identification is reinforced by this passage: only Akhenaten could be described in this way as wanting 'to become a spectator of the gods'. But Amenhotep III *preceded* Akhenaten – indeed, it was Amenhotep III who initiated the Aten worship that Akhenaten then followed through:

*c.*1390 BC	Amenophis	37	Amenhotep III	37
*c.*1353 BC	Orus	36	Akhenaten	17

We can only conclude that Josephus has got muddled here. Orus must be Akhenaten and, *as described here*, Amenophis must be Amenhotep III. Let us set this as a stake in the ground:

> The Amenophis described as having a namesake vizier was the 18th Dynasty Amenophis 2/Amenhotep III, the father of Akhenaten/Orus. And it was that Amenophis 2/Amenhotep III who enslaved lepers and other impure people in the Delta.

So, with this established, why then does Josephus regard this Amenophis as fictitious? Because in further information that he now gives us about this Amenophis, he describes someone else entirely, someone that he has got confused with the 18th Dynasty pharaoh, Amenhotep III.

Josephus says this about his fictional Amenophis:

After which he [Manetho] writes thus, verbatim:
"After those that were sent to work in the quarries had continued in that miserable state for *a long while*, the king was desired that he would set apart the city Avaris, which was then left desolate of the shepherds,[9] for their habitation and protection; which desire he granted them. Now this city, according to the ancient theology, was Typho's city. But when these men were gotten into it, and found the place fit for a revolt, they appointed themselves a ruler out of the priests of Heliopolis, whose name was Osarseph, and they took their oaths that they would be obedient to him in all things. He then, in the first place, made this law for them, That they should neither worship the Egyptian gods, nor should abstain from any one of those sacred animals which they have in the highest esteem, but kill and destroy them all; that they should join themselves to nobody but to those that were of this confederacy. When he had made such laws as these, and many more such as were mainly opposite to the customs of the Egyptians, he gave order that they should use the multitude of the hands they had in building walls about their City, and make themselves ready for a war with king Amenophis, while he did himself take into his friendship the other priests, and those that were polluted with them, and sent ambassadors to those shepherds who had been driven out of the land by Themosis to the city called Jerusalem; whereby he informed them of his own affairs, and of the state

---

9 i.e., the 'shepherd kings' – Hyksos.

of those others that had been treated after such an ignominious manner, and desired that they would come with one consent to his assistance in this war against Egypt. He also promised that he would, in the first place, bring them back to their ancient city and country Avaris, and provide a plentiful maintenance for their multitude; that he would protect them and fight for them as occasion should require, and would easily reduce the country under their dominion . . ." [author's emphasis][10]

Notice that Josephus begins this passage with the phrase I have highlighted: *'After which . . .'.* The preceding passage is that relating the suicide of the vizier Amenophis. But we do not know if this second quotation from Manetho followed *directly* on in the original: perhaps there was an original passage between the two that has gone missing and that has led to Josephus's confusion, leading him to believe that what he now relates about Amenophis follows on *immediately* from the death of the Vizier. The hint that this might be the case is the second highlighted phrase in the first sentence of the Manetho quotation that follows: this is very clear that *'a long while'* passes between the lepers being gathered and enslaved by Amenophis 2/Amenhotep III, and their subsequent rebellion involving a character called Osarseph. I would argue strongly that this second passage describes a second Levantine invasion 'a long while' after the first, Hyksos invasion. In that case, the 'fictitious' Amenophis is a later pharaoh who has got confused with Amenophis 2/Amenhotep III. We shall call him for the moment, **Amenophis 4.**

We must presumably, therefore, look for the missing 'fictitious' Amenophis 4 in the period following the two brother pharaohs, Seti II and Amenmesse, because Josephus introduces us to his Amenophis 4 in that context. The final years of the

10 *Against Apion* I:237-242.

19th century BC were characterized by disruption and civil war, but we know in broad outline that, as we have seen, after Seti II the last two pharaohs of the 19th Dynasty, Siptah and Twosret, lasted just a few years before the dynasty came to a chaotic end. If we want to locate the mysterious Amenophis 4, we need to look in the next dynasty – the 20th Dynasty that follows on immediately from Twosret.

Fig. 17: Pharaohs of the 20th Dynasty

Date (BC)	20th Dynasty	Reign
1190	Setnakhte	4
1186	Ramesses III	31
1155 to 1077	Ramesses IV to Ramesses XI	78

It will be recalled that all the pharaohs of that Dynasty were called Ramesses except for the founder – Setnakhte. The various Manetho sources other than Josephus simply state this without bothering to list them all by number. Could Setnakhte be Amenophis 4? I shall now demonstrate that he is exactly that. The identity of the real Amenophis 4 has been obscured by Josephus's own confusion between different characters called Amenophis. And in that confusion, once unravelled, we shall find at last the reality behind both the 15th Dynasty Hyksos narrative and the 20th Dynasty Exodus narrative.

First, let us address Josephus's very obvious distaste about his 'fictional' Amenophis 4. What upset Josephus about all this will be obvious: here we have a second story from Manetho that seems to describe, better than the earlier Hyksos narrative, the enslavement of the Israelites in the Delta. It ties in that period of enslavement with the religious reforms of Amenhotep III and his son, Akhenaten. But it also suggests that the Israelites were lepers and other unclean persons, which for Josephus and just about everyone ever since, has seemed like a gross libel on the Jewish people (not unlike the one that the Israelites themselves made about their Moabite neighbours). The apparently libellous nature of this story has meant that scholars, following Josephus, have always dismissed this narrative as scurrilous fiction, rooted in anti-Semitic sentiment. I have set out in the Preface to this book my own rejection of racism of any kind, including anti-Jewish racism. So, I hope I can now examine this narrative dispassionately to see just how likely is this story of lepers and unclean persons being gathered up and enslaved.

First, we surely need not share Josephus' distaste for lepers and other unclean folk. Many civilizations have economies based on slavery and/or an underclass. And many civilizations justify the subjugation of such an underclass by denying their common humanity. I could cite the Dalits, the lowest denizens of the Indian caste system. Or more germane, the denial of Jewish humanity by the Nazis in justification of their horrific 'final solution'. Let us assume for a moment that Manetho's story is true and that we can deduce from it that the Israelites are descended from lepers. What is wrong with that? From our modern perspective, lepers are to be pitied and for a race of people to arise from that disadvantage should be a source of pride not shame. From the perspective of an Apion or a Manetho or a Josephus, the story is scurrilous. But it may reflect something historical, nonetheless.

In any case, Manetho's account is not as black and white as it is painted. We noted earlier the doubt whether references to leprosy at that time meant the disease that goes by that name today. Historical pathology is notoriously difficult to determine. There is very little specific reference to disease in the very limited literature (outside of the Pentateuch) surviving from the Bronze Age; and even then, it is hard enough for us today to interpret correctly the vague and imprecise descriptions of disease that prevailed until the advent of modern medicine in the 20th century AD – how much harder to interpret descriptions from over 3,000 years ago. And archaeology can only be of limited assistance: some diseases leave their traces in bone material that survives the millennia, but not all, and interpretation is often tendentious. Having said that, modern science suggests that true leprosy (Mycobacterium Leprae) is a bacterial disease that first emerged in China in the first millennium BC – that is, after the Bronze Age with which we are here concerned. It seems not to have arrived in Egypt until the mid-4th century BC, imported by the armies of Alexander the Great. The earliest case discovered in the Levant was even later – the early years of the first century AD. New discoveries may one day push these dates back, but right now the evidence would suggest that whatever afflicted the Israelites, it was not leprosy. As we noted earlier, it is in any case, from its description, more akin to psoriasis than leprosy.[11]

The Israelites used the Hebrew word 'tzaraath' to cover all manner of skin complaints, and that seems to be what this passage refers to. The story speaks of 'other impure people' and those 'that had any defect in their bodies'. So, this is not a leper colony, but something broader. But more important still: the period between a hypothetical enslavement of the Israelites following the Hyksos ejection from Egypt in the mid-16th century BC, and the rising up of Osarseph at the beginning of the 12th century BC, is about 350 years. Unless

---

[11] And I should know – I suffer from psoriasis myself. It manifests as white flakes of dead skin – not, raw, angry skin as in modern leprosy.

these 'impure' disorders were hereditary, we can assume that at the end of that time, the vast majority of the Delta slaves would be no more infected than any other Egyptian population. Nonetheless, I am not inclined to dismiss the idea of skin disease as a characteristic of these people. We saw in earlier chapters the Israelite obsession with ritual bodily purity, and the repeated associations of leprosy with Moses, who himself went around with his face covered. Why that obsession if not a reflection of some historical reality?

The Israelites were not the only people obsessed with ritual cleanliness. It seems to have been a significant issue in Egypt as well, to the extent that one must wonder whether the Israelites inherited their obsession from Egypt. Ritual purity was of utmost importance in Egypt. Everything and everyone coming into the presence of the gods had to be purified, so we can surmise that any pharaoh wishing to 'see' the gods would need such impurities removed. We are used to depictions of Egyptian priests with shaved heads,[12] but the requirements of purity went much further. Here is the daily routine of an Egyptian priest, centred entirely around the need for continual ritual cleansing of the body:

BEFORE DAWN: RITUAL ABLUTIONS

To be ritually pure, the priests bathed in the temple's sacred lake, shaved off all hair and gargled with salt solution, before dressing in linen robes and sandals.

SUNRISE: MORNING CEREMONY

The high priest entered the shrine and awoke the god's spirit in its statue. This was then cleansed, anointed and dressed, and offered the finest foods while frankincense was burned to purify the surroundings.

---

12 The Jewish Nazirite vow of ritual purity also involved shaving the head.

PRE-NOON: REVERSION OF OFFERINGS AND RITUAL ABLUTIONS

Once the god had its fill of food offerings, these reverted to the priests as breakfast. Then, to maintain ritual purity, the high priest bathed once again before re-entering the god's presence.

NOON: MIDDAY CEREMONY

At noon, the high priest re-entered the shrine, this time burning myrrh resin while sprinkling water to further purify the temple's shrines and sacred spaces.

EVENING: RITUAL ABLUTIONS

To maintain ritual purity, the priests had to bathe once again before re-entering the god's presence.

NIGHT: RITUAL ABLUTIONS

A fourth bath maintained ritual purity.

It does not seem wholly improbable, therefore, that a pharaoh, advised by a trusted priest, might conclude that ridding the country of 'bodily defect' would win the favour of the gods. It might also be attractive to such a pharaoh to have a convenient reason of this sort for providing slave labour in the quarries and mines. So does the account of the enslavement ring true in other respects?

The narrative is certainly concrete enough for us to identify the quarries concerned in the story. We are told that they were on the 'east side of the Nile' and that the workers were housed in Avaris and their leader came from Heliopolis. The location is therefore in the eastern Nile Delta, where we also know the Israelites/Canaanites were settled. The quarries were probably those of Gebel el Ahmar, located near Cairo on the east bank of the Nile, near the suburb of Heliopolis (see Figure 18).

Fig. 18: Map of the Nile Delta Area 2

The site was in full production in the times of Amenhotep III, Akhenaton, Tutankhamun and Ramesses III, so precisely in the period described by Manetho. The reference to 'Typho' is also indicative. Typho[n] was a Greek god, usually regarded as equivalent to the Egyptian 'Set', known as the god of the red desert, and Gebel el Ahmar translates as 'The Red Hill'. We saw earlier that Manetho regarded Avaris as a religious foundation; this passage confirms that he regarded it as associated with Set. So, whether or not you choose to believe the earlier passages about bodily impurity and prophecy, this passage describes a group of slave quarry workers, based in Avaris in the Delta who rise up in revolt. Surely this sounds a lot more like the Biblical Exodus story than the earlier one of 'shepherd kings'. And in that case, the identity of their leader Osarseph is as intriguing as the identity of the contemporary pharaoh Amenophis 4.

At this stage we are told that Osarseph was originally a priest at Heliopolis, an ancient and important Egyptian city, close to modern Cairo. We saw in the previous chapter that both Joseph and Chancellor Bay had connections to the same city. The name, of course, is Greek and means 'City of the Sun'. It was the key centre for the worship of the Egyptian sun gods Ra and Atum, which became syncretised as Atum-Ra. Akhenaten's monotheism was also based on the worship of a sun god – the Aten. That cult was abolished after Akhenaten's death. If we are here sometime after the end of the 19th Dynasty, then we are two centuries after Akhenaten, when it is usually assumed that all traces of his heresy would have been stamped out. But we have no proof of that, and to repeat the point, Manetho certainly seems to have known about him centuries later still. It may be that the Delta area remained unstable in religious affiliation as well as politically. It must also be remembered that priests of the New Kingdom were powerful individuals who rivalled pharaohs for power, and at times and in places ruled as pharaohs in their own right. It is not at all unlikely, therefore, that a Delta priest of the sun god, with a local history of heresy and insurrection, might have seized the opportunity offered by a slave uprising in Avaris to take control of the area. The narrative does not say that he started the revolt but that he was appointed to the leadership when the uprising had already taken place.

The narrative is clear that Osarseph rejected the Egyptian gods. It does not say whether he replaced that worship with something else, although it is inconceivable that he should have introduced atheism. The reference to sacred animals is interesting in this regard. The Egyptians held just about every animal, wild or tame, to be sacred in some way and many animals were regarded as manifestations of the gods. The passage here does not refer to the slaughter of real animals but to the destruction of sacred animal images – idols in other words. As the centre for the sun god Atum-Ra, Heliopolis was also a centre for the cult of the Mnevis Bull which was closely associated with Atum-Ra, as his physical manifestation. The Mnevis Bull was second only in veneration to the more famous Apis Bull of Memphis. It had two concubines – two cows that were the physical manifestation of the goddesses Hathor[13] and Iusaaset. The Mnevis cult was one of the very few to be tolerated by Akhenaten's religious reforms, precisely because of its sun god associations. When the Israelites were wandering in the desert after the Exodus, they are described as making and worshipping a 'golden calf', to the anger of Yahweh and Moses who were in the process of negotiating the new covenant at the time.[14] I would not be the first to suggest a link between that calf idol, and the worship of bulls, cows and calves in Egypt. Osarseph's rejection of sacred animals must have included or even focused on, the Mnevis Bull. And that rejection surely echoes Moses' similar rejection of the golden calf in the Sinai.

Whatever the case, a more immediate priority for Osarseph was to prepare for the inevitable armed response to his insurrection from the Pharaoh we have called Amenophis 4. According to Manetho, Osarseph invited the descendants of the Hyksos, now resident in Canaan, to come to his aid:

These shepherds were all very glad of this message, and came away with alacrity all together, being in number two hundred thousand men; and in a little time they came to Avaris. And now Amenophis the king of Egypt,

---

13 As worshipped by the Shardana.

14 Such worship seems to have endured for centuries among some Israelites – there were still such idols extant in Israel at the time of Jereboam.

upon his being informed of their invasion, was in great confusion, as calling to mind what Amenophis, the son of Papis, had foretold him; and, in the first place, he assembled the multitude of the Egyptians, and took counsel with their leaders, and sent for their sacred animals to him, especially for those that were principally worshipped in their temples, and gave a particular charge to the priests distinctly, that they should hide the images of their gods with the utmost care he also sent his son Sethos, who was also named Ramesses, from his father Rhampses, being but five years old, to a friend of his. He then passed on with the rest of the Egyptians, being three hundred thousand of the most warlike of them, against the enemy, who met them. Yet did he not join battle with them; but thinking that would be to fight against the gods, he returned back and came to Memphis, where he took Apis and the other sacred animals which he had sent for to him, and presently marched into Ethiopia, together with his whole army and multitude of Egyptians . . .[15]

The reference to 'shepherds' on the face of it refers to the 'shepherd kings' – the Hyksos. But there is no reference here to kings, just to 200,000 'shepherds'. This is not, I think, a replay of the Hyksos period. This is a period of weak rulership and dissension that a group of pastoral Canaanites seems to have exploited. There is clearly a kinship between Osarseph's followers and the Canaanite invaders, but this is a story of an invading rabble, not of Canaanite rulers seeking the annexation of northern Egypt. Earlier, Manetho refers to the rebels as a confederacy. Whatever the truth of the 'leprosy' story, Avaris at the time would have had a population of Canaanite descendants from the Hyksos period. Some, like Bay (Joseph),

---

15 *Against Apion* I:243-246.

even rose to positions of power. Over the intervening centuries, there would have been continuous trade contact between the Delta and Canaan as there always had been. The retreat south into Ethiopia suggests that Amenophis 4 allowed the invading Hyksos to overrun upper as well as lower Egypt.

The quotation from Manetho concludes thus:

... the king of Ethiopia was under an obligation to him, on which account he received him, and took care of all the multitude that was with him, while the country supplied all that was necessary for the food of the men. He also allotted cities and villages for this exile, that was to be from its beginning during those fatally determined thirteen years. Moreover, he pitched a camp for his Ethiopian army, as a guard to king Amenophis, upon the borders of Egypt. And this was the state of things in Ethiopia. But for the people of Jerusalem, when they came down together with the polluted Egyptians, they treated the men in such a barbarous manner, that those who saw how they subdued the forementioned country, and the horrid wickedness they were guilty of, thought it a most dreadful thing; for they did not only set the cities and villages on fire but were not satisfied till they had been guilty of sacrilege, and destroyed the images of the gods, and used them in roasting those sacred animals that used to be worshipped, and forced the priests and prophets to be the executioners and murderers of those animals, and then ejected them naked out of the country. It was also reported that the priest, who ordained their polity and their laws, was by birth of Hellopolls, and his name Osarseph, from Osyris, who was the god of Hellopolls; but that when he was gone over to these people, **his name was changed, and he was called Moses ...** After this, Amenophis returned back from Ethiopia with a great army, as did his son Rhampses with another army also, and that both of them joined battle with the shepherds and the polluted people, and beat them, and slew a great many of them, and pursued them to the bounds of Syria. [author's emphasis][16]

Now we get to the heart of things. If the reference to Moses is to be believed, then what we have here is indeed a story of the 'real' Exodus. Very few have ever taken this reference to Moses seriously. If the 'leper' story is an anti-Semitic libel, then the reference to Moses, it is argued, comes from the same scurrilous intent, either by Manetho himself or some later redactor. But, if the rest of this narrative can be shown to be plausible, then perhaps the Moses reference should be taken seriously after all. I have already addressed the 'leper' issue. It may well be a libel, but as I have sought to demonstrate, this is by no means certain or, even from a modern point of view, scurrilous. What about the rest of Manetho's story? There are a number of elements to be considered:

1. The historical evidence for a Levantine invasion at this time.
2. The historical evidence for a pharaoh – Amenophis 4 – who fled south rather than meet the invasion in battle but who returned with his son 13 years later to defeat Osarseph and eject the invaders.
3. The identity of Osarseph.

First then, was there an invasion? We saw the answer to this in Chapter 14: the narratives about Canaanite invaders from the *Setnakhte Stele* and the *Harris Papyrus* both suggest that this did indeed happen at the end of the 19th Dynasty. It will

---

16 *Against Apion* I:246-251.

be recalled that there is some debate about whether the turmoil described in the papyrus was internal or external to Egypt and I argued the latter on the basis of the stele evidence. We can now add the evidence from Manetho. All three sources are clearly describing a Levantine incursion to exploit the power vacuum left after the death of Seti II, and the power struggle between potential successors. If my conclusions about the Sea Peoples in Chapter 15 are correct, this should come as no surprise at all. Indeed, given the history of incursions by Levantine Sea Peoples from the time of Ramesses II down to Ramesses III, it would surely be surprising if those peoples had not had another go at invasion during the period of the 19th Dynasty decline. The motivation as always was food and plunder, as Manetho's narrative makes plain. Osarseph's personal motivation seems to have had a more religious slant as we shall see a little later.

Second, who was Amenophis 4? We are told here that he had a son, Sethos, also called Ramesses after his grandfather Rhampses (Ramesses). It was common practice at the time for royal sons to be named after their grandfathers in this way. This does seem to point to Setnakhte, who was probably descended in some way from Ramesses II, whose son was indeed another Ramesses (III), and who founded the Ramesside 20th Dynasty.

This would certainly match well with Manetho's account of the defeat of Osarseph and the ejection of the Levantine invaders. But how did Manetho and Josephus come to call him Amenophis? The answer lies in the muddle between Amenophis 2, who was Amenhotep III, and Amenophis 4, who was Setnakhte. Manetho's narrative describes two events and two pharaohs, separated by two centuries. Josephus confuses the two and assumes they are one, coming at the end of the 19th Dynasty. So far so good. But there is no evidence at all that Setnakhte was Pharaoh at the time of the invasion, let alone that he then retreated to Ethiopia (for which as always, read 'Cush' – the land south of the second cataract) for thirteen years.

Setnakhte's origins are a mystery, and it is tempting to think that Manetho's account provides a solution. One could, on Manetho's evidence, hypothesise that Amenmesse was not the only potential heir to challenge Seti II – Manetho mentions in passing one called Ramesses who was 'killed' by Seti – and that perhaps Setnakhte was one such. Intriguingly, one of Ramesses II's many sons was called Prince Senakhten-amoun. We know next to nothing about him, but one could hypothesise that he abandoned his pretensions to the throne on the invasion and bided his time in the south before returning and becoming Pharaoh Setnakhte. The thir-teen-year sojourn in 'Ethiopia' is not at all unlikely in itself: that land had been ruled by Egyptian viceroys for centuries and Manetho's remark that 'the king of Ethiopia was under an obligation to him' would reflect that. The thirteen-year period itself also has some basis in truth: it was roughly the period of time between the end of Merneptah's reign, when the wars of succession began, and Setnakhte's accession to the throne. The fact that Setnakhte's son was called Ramesses (as was Amenophis 4's son) might suggest that he was indeed one of Ramesses II's sons and thus a legitimate heir to Seti II. The evidence is that he regarded himself as such and had inscriptions mentioning Twosret and Siptah defaced.

Unfortunately, I cannot prove a word of all this. And there is another piece of evidence that might suggest a different solution to the problem. In Chapter 14 we described another son of 'The Great' Ramesses II: Prince **Setna Kh**aemweset, whose full name is very close to **Setnakh**te. He was the heir apparent for a time but he died, as far as we can tell, about five years before his father, and the next son, Merneptah, inherited the throne. We know that Prince Setna had two sons and a daughter. His eldest son, Ramesses, is mentioned on a block statue from Memphis, where he holds the title 'King's Son'.[17] His second son, Hori, followed in his father's footsteps to become High Priest of Ptah at Memphis during the latter part of the 19th Dynasty.[18] So again, it seems unlikely that Pharaoh Setnakhte can be traced back to this line. But nevertheless, it does seem to me that a lot of the story about Prince Setna has somehow attached itself to the Manetho narrative about his Amenophis 4. Much of that narrative is taken up with matters of religion; the Levantine invaders were motivated by venal concerns, but Osarseph seems to have had religious motivations, and certainly, Amenophis 4 as described by Manetho seems much more concerned with religion than invasion. Rather than offer battle, he gathers the sacred animals and sacred images and takes them into safety in Ethiopia. This sounds more like the actions of a high priest than a pharaoh and, more specifically, the High Priest of Ptah who had particular responsibility for the Apis Bull, which Manetho mentions specifically. Prince Setna held that office and was famed for enlarging the Serapeum to accommodate Apis Bull remains, and by the time Manetho was writing, he was as famous in myth and legend as any pharaoh.

In the final analysis, the connection between Setnakhte and these two sons of Ramesses II cannot be proven either way, but I suggest that there is enough evidence here to suggest strongly that however the heredity worked out, Setnakhte was a legitimate heir who traced his lineage back directly to Ramesses II (the Great) and more important still, was, one way or another, the historical reality behind

---

17 The title 'King's Son' was an honorific bestowed on favoured officials, so does not have ancestral implications.

18 Two viceroys of Cush called Hori I and II are recorded in the reign of Siptah and Setnakhte and Ramesses IV. Hori I is transcribed as 'son of Kama'.

Amenophis 4. Which leaves our third question – the identity of Osarseph. At this point, let me remind the reader of the character 'Irsu' from the Harris Papyrus: I would suggest that all the foregoing implies strongly that Osarseph was the same person as Irsu, which in any case sounds like a contraction of the former. Both characters were upstarts of non-royal lineage who rose to power at the end of the 19th Dynasty with the support of Levantine invaders. But was Osarseph/Irsu really the Biblical Moses, and was Setnakhte therefore the Pharaoh of the Exodus? Intriguingly, it will be recalled that the Levantine invaders were paid in 'gold and silver'; could this be reflected in the gold and silver that the Egyptians gave to the Israelites to spur them on their way out of Egypt?[19]

Josephus regarded his 'Amenophis' as fiction and on that basis could cast the same shadow over the whole Osarseph narrative. It is not hard to see why Josephus would argue this way: fitting his 'Amenophis' into the known history of the time, is as we have seen, while not impossible, certainly not straightforward. But, of course, that is not Josephus's real problem: he wants to hold onto the Hyksos ejection as the Exodus and to attribute the rest to anti-Semitism. His arguments in this regard have always been accepted and, indeed, as he shows at much length, the story is riddled with nonsenses of all sorts. At heart, his arguments amount to a judgement that Manetho's narrative has all the hallmarks of myth rather than history. And, of course, he is right. But to equate 'myth' with 'fiction' and leave it at that is the mistake that this book is seeking to redress. I want to suggest that behind the story of Osarseph and his people lies the roots of the story of the Exodus and the Israelites. But that is to beg the question of what those two words mean. Who exactly

---

19 Exodus11:2 and then, 12:35.

left Egypt at the time of Pharaoh Setnakhte and what was their relationship with the people who eventually became the Jewish nation?

CHAPTER 18

Apiru, Shasu and Levites

We have already determined some answers to those two questions: who left Egypt and were they 'Jews'? First, the Exodus could not have been what the Bible says it was. The story just is not credible at any level: common sense says that it did not happen, there is no archaeological evidence to suggest that it did, and there is every reason to believe that the story as we have it arose over a long period of time through the writings of various people and their many redactors. And second, whatever event it purports to describe, it did not eventuate in the establishment of the twelve tribes of Israel. Some, at least, of those tribes already existed and were in some way connected to something called 'Israel', long before the events of Setnakhte's reign. Manetho's story, I think, offers us a real clue as to what is going on here. Whatever the historical events surrounding the departure of Osarseph/Moses from Egypt, there was clearly a strong religious motive. The distinction between religious development and historical events is, in any case, necessary if we are to believe that the Exodus took place during Setnakhte's reign.

The historical problem is that dating the Exodus to the beginning of the 12th century BC leaves no room for all the subsequent history of the Israelites as described in the Bible.

It will be recalled that the destruction of Judah in the early 6th century BC is a firm, historical event. That means that the entire period between then and the Exodus would have to be squeezed into about 500 years: the wandering in Sinai; the Conquest; the period of the Judges; the United Kingdom period of the great Jewish Kings (such as David and Solomon); and the subsequent period of separate kingdoms. There is much debate about the length of this period, particularly over the Judges period, but most calculations allot about 1,000 years to these events. That is why the Exodus is usually regarded as taking place earlier. We saw that the mid-16th century BC Hyksos period is one favourite, and the mid-15th century BC is another. Both leave plenty of room. If the Exodus was an event in history as described in the Bible, there is no question at all that an early 12th century BC date is entirely inconsistent with the historical record, at least as set forth in the Bible. But as I shall now show, we are not dealing with a sequential historical account. The historical development of the Israelite nation has a timeframe of its own, to which whatever happened in Setnakhte's reign has no relevance at all. The Exodus at that time was an event in the history of *religious thought* not events, and one can be traced as an overlay over the other.

Any of the earlier dates for the Exodus would be consistent with a view that the Israelite nation evolved in Canaan over the second half of the second millennium BC. Those proto-Israelite tribes would have worshipped the Canaanite gods – notably El – at cultic shrines as described in Genesis. What I want to argue is that the Exodus was not an event in that evolution, but the key event in the introduction of monotheism in general, and the worship of Yahweh in particular, to the evolving Israelites. The Bible does not describe Moses as a military leader, responsible for an Israelite conquest of Canaan. He is a religious figure who 'sees god' in the way that Amenhotep III and Akhenaten wanted to 'see god'; who creates a set of religious rules and regulations; and who dies before the 'Conquest' ever begins. On this basis, there are elements of the Osarseph/Irsu narratives that make some sense. Osarseph is described as an Egyptian priest from Heliopolis; Irsu is a Levantine. Moses strangely combines the two: he is an Israelite, an Egyptian and a priest married to a priest's daughter, all at the same time.

Let us assume that the identification is secure – that Osarseph is indeed Moses and that we have here a memory of the 'real' Exodus. In that case, the people he leads must in some sense have had some role in the evolution of the nation of Israel. So, were they just a nameless rabble or can we identify them from the written record? In fact, I think we can. The Egyptians had a term for people like this; they called them 'Apiru'. The references to the Apiru in Egyptian and Asian documents of the period are legion. Scholars debate virtually every detail about them but are universally agreed that they were not an ethnic grouping, or a race or a nation. So, they weren't in any sense proto-Israelites. In fact, they seem to have had no ethnic affiliations at all and not even a common language. They are often found as servants or slaves, particularly as labourers, working in mines and quarries; sometimes they are hired as mercenaries generally, and bowmen in particular; and always they are described as rebels and outsiders from whatever civilization they find themselves in. They are, in other words, an untouchable caste, good for keeping the wheels of civilization turning by doing the work no one else wants to do, but not people one would want to introduce to polite society. For me, this sounds exactly the people that were consigned as slaves in the Delta, and also like their Levantine confederates who they invite into Egypt, not to rule like the Hyksos, but to pillage and burn.

The etymology of 'Apiru' is hotly contested and there is no real consensus. However, the two leading interpretations are 'one who has crossed over' – in other words, 'foreigner' or more precisely, 'immigrant' – and 'dusty' or 'dirty'. Perhaps the word had both connotations. Almost certainly, I think, it was pejorative. Evidence from the way underclasses are regarded in many cultures suggests that 'dirty immigrant' would not be an unusual way of describing such people. If you are reading this in North America, think 'spik'; if in the UK, think 'Paki'; if in Europe, think of whatever term you use in your language for 'immigrant worker'. And of course, yet again, the parallel with the way Jews were regarded in Nazi Germany comes immediately to mind. I have no difficulty seeing how such a social category from the second millennium BC should, by the end of the first millennium BC, emerge in the writings of Manetho and thus Josephus as 'lepers and unclean, polluted persons'. And there is concrete evidence that these Apiru were closely associated with the early Israelites. Scholars seem largely agreed that the Apiru are to be identified with a similar category of people called the 'Habiru'. The linguistic arguments are complex but the consonantal shift between 'b' and 'p' is a common one, as you will discover if you soundlessly shape those sounds. And most scholars are also agreed that 'Habiru' can be linguistically associated with 'Hebrew'. The term 'Hebrew' has, of course, become a synonym for 'Jew' and is the name of the Jewish language. But its use in the Pentateuch is always as a descriptor of social standing, caste or class and never of ethnic or racial affiliation. In other words, in the period of the Exodus, Apiru, Habiru and Hebrew were all descriptors of the Egyptian and Asian underclass.

It is in this context that the 'leprosy' libel should be understood. Manetho never says just 'lepers' – these are always just one example of the 'unclean' and 'polluted' people he is talking about. Remember that Amenhotep III's original concept was a religious one; that by segregating these people from polite society, he was engaging in an act of ritual purification that would enable him to 'see god'. And, insofar as the Biblical account of Pharaoh's intent towards the Israelites can be believed, what is described here has to be thought of as a variety of ethnic cleansing: a conscious decision to 'cleanse' society of undesirable elements who are regarded as in some way polluted and unclean and, therefore, in some sense less than truly human. Manetho says that some of the priests were 'lepers'. He does not specifically mention that Osarseph suffered from such an affliction, but if he did, and if he was indeed the historical basis for the Bible's Moses figure, then this would reinforce my earlier suggestion that Moses did indeed have some form of skin condition that caused him to keep his face covered and that lies behind the leprosy stories that surround him and his family.

My suggestion, therefore, is that Irsu was Osarseph was Moses, and this figure led a group of Apiru – indigenous and foreign – in a revolt from slavery or captivity or deprivation in the Nile Delta in the years between the end of the 19th Dynasty (1292 to 1189 BC) and the beginning of the 20th Dynasty (1189 to 1077 BC), exploiting pharaonic weakness brought about by the Bronze Age Collapse in general, and the concomitant activities of Canaanite Sea Peoples in particular. As a priest of Amun from Heliopolis, he would have been familiar with the concept of the Aten, and insofar as that represented a precursor to monotheism, he would have been familiar with that theological concept as well. Certainly, the narrative shows that he and his followers utterly rejected the Egyptian pantheon generally, and, in particular, the worship of graven images of animals – to the extent that extraordinary measures had to be taken to remove the most important of such down to safety in Cush/Ethiopia. This echoes the story of Moses' condemnation of Aaron's golden calf and the subsequent exhortations in the Ten Commandments and elsewhere in the Bible to eschew 'graven images'. According to the Egyptian sources, the Apiru rebels were eventually put down and thrown out of the Delta by Setnakhte and his son, Ramesses. The next question, therefore, is what happened to the foreign Apiru, the domestic Apiru and Osarseph/ Moses?

Manetho has no interest in what happened to the Apiru. His focus is Egyptian history, and we know that Setnakhte died soon after regaining the throne and his son, Ramesses III, soon had his hands full with the final assault of the Sea Peoples. If the Bible is to be believed, Osarseph/Moses led the indigenous Apiru into the Sinai desert, where they stayed for forty years. It should be noted in passing that whatever the truth of the pursuit of the fleeing Israelites and the destruction of the Egyptian army in the 'Red (or Reed) Sea', this sounds more likely as a memory of Setnakhte's eviction of warlike invaders than the pharaonic pursuit of Israelites who wanted to leave anyway. The Bible explains the forty years period as reflecting Yahweh's judgement that in punishment for disobedience, a whole generation had to pass before entry to the Promised Land. It is tempting to suggest that if leprosy and other 'Egyptian disease' was a factor in all this, then it would take a generation of cleansing practices, such as are set out in Moses' regulations for his people, to deal with the problem. But it is, perhaps, more germane to note again that according to the Bible, Moses wanted to lead the Israelites out into the desert to worship their God: in all Moses' dealings with Pharaoh, there is no mention at all of a permanent Exodus, let alone any intent to subjugate Canaan by force of arms.

It is at this point that we need to revert to the Midian connection. It will be recalled that Moses seems to have had triple nationality – Egyptian, Israelite and Midianite. His wife was the daughter of a Midianite priest, but we are not told of what religion. The Biblical account describes Moses leading the Israelites to the holy mountain in Midian to be reunited with his wife and to be advised by his father-in-law. So, who were these Midianite people; what was the mountain; and what God was worshipped there? Today, the Sinai Peninsula is entirely desert, inhabited by nomadic tribes of Arab Bedouin. At the end of the first millennium BC, things were no different, except, of course, that Islam lay 1,500 years in the future, so these nomads were not 'Arabs' as we know them today: they were known as the 'Shasu', from an Egyptian verb meaning 'to wander'. Unlike the Apiru, these were not a social caste; they were Semitic, semi-nomadic pastoralists who were fiercely independent, rarely if ever coming under any kind of Egyptian control and at times, when it suited them, allying themselves with Egypt's enemies, notably the Hittites.

The term Shasu is found in a variety of New Kingdom hieroglyphic texts. One of the most intriguing of the 19th Dynasty documents referring to the Shasu is a letter, dated 1192:

> Another communication to my Lord: We have finished letting the Shasu tribes of Edom pass the fortress of Merneptah Hotep-hir-Maat . . . which is in Tjeku, to the pools of Per Atum of Merneptah Hotep-hir-Maat, which are in Tjeku, to keep them alive and to keep their cattle alive . . .

This clearly places the Shasu in the Midianite area of Edom. There are two schools of thought among scholars about the extent of their nomadic wanderings. The traditional, and in my view correct, identifications place the Shasu squarely in the area between the Nile Delta in the west and Moab in the east – in other words, the Sinai desert and home of the Midianites. The alternative view regards the Shasu as much more widespread up into Phoenicia and beyond. This view has been promulgated by Ukrainian orientalist Michael C. Astour (1916–2004) based as much as anything on etymological derivations of tribal names. The problem is that, as with the names of the Sea Peoples, we only have consonants to work with, so all identifications are tentative. Egyptian sources describe six Shasu tribes, and I shall offer my own interpretations which I suggest, taken together, are more likely than Astour's and are consistent with an Arabian location and with the argument I am developing here.

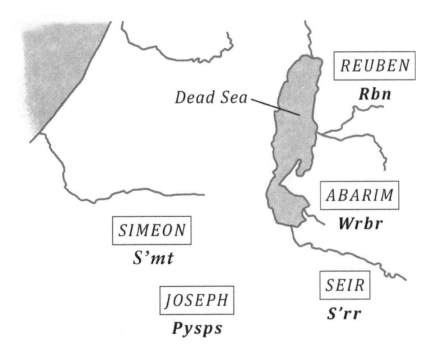

Fig. 19: Map of the Shasu Tribes

1 The Shasu of **Rbn.** This surely has to be the Israelite tribe of **Reuben**, the firstborn son of Jacob. Their allotted land was in Transjordan, just north of Edom and Moab, bordering the east coast of the Dead Sea.

2 The Shasu of **Sm't.** I suggest that this is another Israelite tribe – **Simeon**, the second son of Jacob. The Simeonites were allotted land opposite Moab and Edom to the west of the Dead Sea.

3 The Shasu of **Pysps.** My more tentative suggestion here would be that this is 'Pi-Ysp'. The prefix means 'House of' as in Pi-Ramesses; the suffix is the name 'Joseph', Jacob's eleventh son. The J and Y are interchangeable as in 'Jehovah' and 'Yahweh'. So **ysp** yields Joseph. As we have seen, there was no tribe of Joseph in Canaan: the 'House of Joseph' comprised two sons and two tribes – Ephraim and Manasseh – whose extensive lands were further north in Canaan. Perhaps this is an indication that there *was* originally a southern tribe called Joseph, with a location among the other Shasu, that eventually grew too large and moved north in search of room to expand. This conjecture could provide an explanation for the prominence of the Joseph narrative in the Pentateuch that otherwise seems enigmatic. Perhaps the historical 'Joseph' – Chancellor Bay, came from the tribe of Joseph?

So, before proceeding with the other three Shasu tribes, we have reasonably ascribed three of the tribes to 'Israel'. The etymological derivations are as valid as any others that have been offered and, of course, if correct, add to the accumulating evidence that Israel and its tribes was in existence long before Moses and the Exodus, reinforcing again the view that the Exodus was important for religious reasons rather than racial ones.

4 The Shasu of **Wrbr**. Probably the area known as 'Abarim' – a mountain range to the east and south-east of the Dead Sea, mentioned a few times in the Pentateuch. I suspect that both terms emerge in modern times as Arabia.

5 The Shasu of **S'rr**. Most scholars identify this, correctly in my view, with another mountain – Mount Seir – which we have encountered already as the area in which Esau settled. It is located in the area stretching between the Dead Sea and the Gulf of Aqaba in the northwestern region of Edom and southeast of Judah.

Interestingly, both the last two locations feature in the Biblical account of the itinerary of the Israelites on their forty-year peregrination in the Sinai desert. And, of course, Seir was, most importantly, regarded in Israelite tradition as the original home of Yahweh:

And he said, "Yahweh came from Sinai, and rose up from Seir unto them." [20]

Yahweh, when thou wentest out of Seir, when thou marchedst out of the field of Edom, the earth trembled, and the heavens dropped . . . [21]

These two quotations are absolutely critical. The southern Mount Seir has never been definitively identified. Neither have Mount Sinai or Mount Horeb, both of which also seem to have been the home of Yahweh. My own view is that all three names refer to just one place. Seir and Sinai refer to the general location, and Horeb is probably the correct name for

---

20 Deuteronomy 33:2, KJV, except I have translated correctly as 'Yahweh'.

21 Judges 5:4. KJV, except I have translated correctly as 'Yahweh'.

the mountain itself. Its etymology seems to be something like 'glowing/heat', reflecting its presumably volcanic nature, and the story of the burning bush.

All this is borne out by the sixth, last, and most significant of the Shasu tribes:

> 6 The Shasu of **Yhw**. Almost without exception, scholars translate this as **Yahweh**. It is the earliest written attestation to Yahweh outside the Bible and establishes unequivocally what the Shasu of Seir implies and the Bible actually states: the origin of the worship of the God Yahweh is in the land of the Midianites in Northern Arabia between Edom and Goshen. This is exactly where Moses grazed his flocks before meeting Yahweh and where Moses later leads the Israelites following the Exodus to worship the same God.

The term the 'Shasu of Yahweh' seems to imply that, like the other Shasu tribes, there was either a place called Yahweh or a tribe called Yahweh. But there is no evidence at all that such a place or tribe ever existed. I think that there is a different explanation: that the Shasu of Yahweh were a priestly tribe, providing religious services for the other tribes of Shasu. They were located at a mountain known as Seir, the same mountain as Sinai and Horeb: the sacred mountain where Yahweh showed himself to Moses from a burning bush and where Moses later obtained the Ten Commandments from Yahweh and brought them down the mountain to the waiting Israelites. If this is the case, surely, we can also conclude that Moses' father-in-law, Reuel/Jethro, was not just any old priest: he was a priest of Yahweh, also serving his God on the sacred mountain. If Manetho's account is to be believed, Osarseph/Moses led his Apiru/Habiru people out to that very spot to worship their God. They probably knew him as Aten but would have had no difficulty identifying him syncretically with Yahweh, just as they were later to do again when they identified Yahweh in turn as identical with El: the God of the Israelites.

The final question that then needs to be asked is how the worship of Yahweh was introduced to the various Israelite tribes already living in the Levant and Transjordan. In the case of four of them – Reuben, Simeon, Ephraim and Manasseh – we already know the answer: Semitic Shasu tribes already lived in those areas and over time came to self-identify as Israelite. Presumably the Yahweh priesthood took the message to them. That priesthood self-identified as Shasu but, under the leadership of Osarseph/Moses and with an influx of new believers from Egypt, transformed over a period of (perhaps) forty years into a nomadic Israelite priesthood. And we know how they then came to self-identify: as Levites. Could the Levites – the Jewish priestly tribe – have their origins in the Apiru of Osarseph?

One consideration must have been population size. Putting to one side the inflated numbers of the Biblical Exodus, even a relatively small number of Apiru (say hundreds or perhaps low thousands) would have been unable to live for long in the Sinai region. There just would not have been enough water or food; as ex-slaves in the mines and quarries, they would not have brought many possessions with them. But perhaps the Shasu priesthood represented a viable economic model, seeking a living from the other Shasu tribes in return for the priestly services they offered. It is a model followed by priests and monks in many other societies in modern Asia and the sub-continent and, of course, it is precisely the model adopted by the Levites, who had no land of their own but served the other tribes as priests.

The Biblical account relates that the Levites descended from Jacob's son Levi. But we have seen that this whole story is aetiological. If there was a Jacob, he was a Hyksos ruler whose offspring would have been Hyksos/Egyptian princes. And the mathematics of the twelve tribes gets very confused with the Joseph/Ephraim/Manasseh story. The Levites spread themselves through the Israelite tribes – as no doubt their predecessors had done through the Shasu tribes – and brought the worship of their God Yahweh to predominance in the Levant, and ultimately in Canaan itself, to become the truly monotheistic religion of the Jewish people. The idea that the Levites were the real people of the Exodus has been championed by Friedman, whose version of the Documentary Hypothesis we followed in earlier chapters. He adduces much evidence in support of the idea. Some of that evidence, although I personally find it convincing, I will put to one side here because it can be, and has been, challenged.

For example, in the Song of the Sea, he points out that there is no mention of Israel but just the 'people of Yahweh', who are bound, not for the promised land, but for Yahweh's mountain abode.[22] Similarly, with the Song of Deborah and the Blessing of Moses, he rightly shows that among all the Israelite tribes enumerated there is no mention of a tribe of Levi. The implication is that when these were written, the idea that the Levites were a tribe, descended from a son of Jacob, simply did not exist. And since, in Friedman's view, these are some of the earliest texts in the Bible, that would suggest that whatever the Levites were, they were not considered one of the twelve tribes. But as we have observed, Friedman's view on these texts have been challenged by scholars, who see them as late texts written deliberately in archaic style. It was this objection that prevented us from accepting their versions of the Red Sea Parting episode as the earliest. I believe that the Red Sea and Levite evidence combined supports Friedman's

22 Exodus 15:1-18.

view: but in both cases there is plenty of other evidence, so we do not have to rely on assumptions that are assailable.

First, the authors of Exodus seem oblivious to the obvious fact that whatever else Moses may have been, he was an Egyptian – as Manetho correctly asserts. Moses' name is irrefutably Egyptian. But also, as Friedman points out, the only other names in these Biblical texts that are Egyptian are the names of Levites. In one or two of the cases Friedman quotes, there have been suggestions of Hebrew etymologies, but the fact remains that no non-Levite has an Egyptian name. The 'Tent of Meeting' or Tabernacle that the Israelites carry with them in their wanderings, and where Moses removes his veil to meet daily with Yahweh, is described in great detail, as is the Ark of the Covenant which it contains. These are very clearly based on Egyptian models – the Battle Tent of Ramesses II and Egyptian Ritual boats respectively; yet the former, which is mentioned over 200 times in the sources with priestly connections, is not mentioned *even once* by the non-priestly J Source. Similarly, circumcision is an obsession in the priestly sources and was almost certainly adopted from the Egyptians, but the J source mentions it only twice. And all of the descriptions of Egyptian geography and customs come from the Levite sources – not the J source. Quite simply, the evidence of the Pentateuch Sources is unequivocal: it is the Levite priests alone who retain and record memories of Egyptian names, geography and ritual artefacts.

Most compelling of all, in my view, is the fact that none of the references to the plagues of Egypt can be found in the J Source; they too are remembered only by the Levites. J (admittedly, as we now have it), simply jumps from the demand to 'let my people go' in Exodus 5, to the Israelites wandering in the Sinai at the end of Exodus 13. And another point, not made by Friedman but of central importance to my argument, is that all the references to leprosy come from the Levite sources, and none from the J source. For example, Exodus 34 contains the story of Moses and the Ten Commandments. It all comes from J until the point where the text describes Moses' red face: that element is pure Levite. It is the Levites who remember not just the Sojourn in Egypt, but who remained sensitive to their 'polluted' origins. Perhaps the stories of the plagues in some way reflect that obsession. Even the name 'Levite' betrays that origin. So far from being derived from Jacob's son Levi, its root is in a Hebrew term for 'attached': the Apiru were outsiders from society who over time 'attached' themselves as priests to what became the Israelite tribes.

So, are we to imagine the Levites wandering around Canaan, peaceably converting the tribesmen to their religious beliefs, rather like the Jesus of the gospel wandering around Galilee doing something similar? Probably not. I suspect a more apt analogy would be the early apostles of Islam, who brought the word of Mohammed to Arabia and beyond by means of the sword and conquest. We know that the Conquest of Canaan did not happen as described in the Bible, but on the other hand there are plenty of indications in the Bible that the Levites were not a bunch of people you would want to fall foul of. They were involved in the slaughter at Shechem and the massacre following the Golden Calf incident. When an Israelite is caught having sex with a Midianite woman in the Tabernacle – a double desecration – a Levite with the Egyptian name Phinehas drives a spear through them both, *coitus interruptus*! And Jacob prophesied as much:

> Simeon and Levi are brethren: instruments of cruelty are in their habitations . . . Cursed be their anger, for it was fierce; and their wrath for it was cruel . . .[1]

---

1 Genesis 49:5.

Given my association of the Shasu of Sm't with the Simeonites, the description of these two tribes together is perhaps suggestive.

I could of course be wrong about all of this. There is no way any of it can be proved one way or the other. But as Friedman himself has observed, why would anyone have made all this up. The Midianite/Seir connection is not my construct – it is there in black and white in the Bible. It is even there at the very beginning – according to the early E Source, the Midianites are descended from Abraham's third wife Keturah. Sarah is the matriarch of the Israelites; Hagar is the matriarch of the Ishmaelites; and Keturah is the matriarch of the Midianites. Whoever wrote that regarded the Midianite connection to be as important as the other two. The Exodus narratives go to great lengths to give Moses an Israelite/Levite background, but the Egyptian and Midianite connections just obtrude themselves in a way that is inconvenient to say the least. This is almost certainly an indication that there is an uncomfortable truth lurking in there somewhere.

I have connected that uncomfortable truth to others – the Shasu, the Apiru and Manetho's account of an Egyptian priest who leads a slave uprising in the same area as the Israelite's Biblical slavery. The Shasu definitely had connections with Yahweh; the Apiru sound very like the Hebrews; and Manetho clearly saw his Osarseph as a Moses-like figure, even if Josephus utterly rejected the identification. None of this is really new. Scholars have known about the Apiru/Hebrew connection and the Shasu/Yahweh connection for decades or more. Manetho's account has been available, preserved by Josephus for more than 2,000 years. It is just that no one seems to have known what to do with the information. All I have tried to do here is put it all together in a way that respects all the various sources – Biblical and Egyptian

– and creates a coherent narrative that is in accord with the archaeological record. As I said at the outset, that emergent narrative is very different from that which we were taught as kids, and from that which is preached in churches and synagogues alike. But the amazing thing is that it is recognizable, nonetheless.

CHAPTER 19

Some Concluding Thoughts

We have worked our way through all the surviving textual evidence relating to the origins of Judaism and hopefully the outlines of a hypothesis have emerged. I have endeavoured as much as possible to base that hypothesis only on findings which would be accepted by most scholars, and where that is not the case, to point out that fact, summarize the competing views and argue my case. In this final chapter, I shall outline that hypothesis with some concluding thoughts in support of my arguments. As with the trilogy as a whole, I offer those arguments with due humility and the sincere hope that scholars will give them a fair hearing and engage with me on them. I am not holding my breath.

1. The Book of Genesis is almost entirely based on etymological and aetiological explanations of the core assumptions of Judaism:

   – monotheistic belief in Yahweh;
   – His Promise to the Israelites; and
   – their right to the land of Canaan.

   Our analysis of the different sources undermines all this. Scholars are divided about how and when monotheism

273

arose in Israel, but Yahweh was a later introduction; the Promise took a very long time to be fulfilled and was always tenuous; and there was no eviction of Hamites by Shemites – they were all there all along.

2. The stories of the Creation, the Fall, the Flood and the Tower of Babel are all Mesopotamian in origin, inherited by the Israelites from their Amorite ancestors who came from there. There is nothing unique or special about them.

3. The Jewish Patriarchs are all aetiological fictions: Abraham's history reflects Amorite history; Lot is an excuse for racial libel; Isaac represents a vague memory of real child sacrifice in Canaan; and Jacob's role is to be the mythical father of sons who themselves are aetiological explanations of later tribal realities. Early Hyksos rulers seem to have been called something like 'Jacob' and thus may lie behind his story.

4. Jacob, therefore, is the mythical Patriarch of the Israelites, and the story of Joseph, while undoubtedly ancient, does not belong chronologically where it is placed in Genesis. It probably reflects the career of a uniquely powerful vizier of Egypt – Bay – who ruled at the end of the 19th Dynasty, just before the 'Exodus'.

5. The Sojourn of the Israelites in Egypt reflects generally the way in which the fortunes of Canaan and Egypt intertwine throughout the New Kingdom period, and all the Israelite Patriarchs find themselves living in Egypt at one time or another. More specifically, the Sojourn is a memory of the period initiated by the Hyksos in which Asians wielded power in Egypt, followed by the period

in which, following the Hyksos expulsion, Canaanites in the Delta area lived in much reduced circumstances, many of them ending up as slaves. The so-called Long Sojourn reflects that whole period – from the Hyksos 15th Dynasty in the mid-17th century BC up to the Exodus – which I have dated to the beginning of the 20th Dynasty: a total of about 450 years. The Short Sojourn reflects the 200-year period of slavery from Amenhotep III to Setnakhte.

6. The Hyksos expulsion was not the 'real' Exodus, despite the fact that the Hyksos period is reflected in memories of Canaanite sojourn in Egypt. Josephus thought that it was, based on Manetho's apparent identification. But it is hard to tell what Manetho thought because he also tells the story of a later Canaanite expulsion – one that Josephus dismissed as 'fictional'.

7. We have independent evidence, however, that the later expulsion under Setnakhte was not fictional. The contemporary reference to 'Irsu' tells much the same story, so some elements of it at least must be true. The reader will reach their own conclusions about which elements to accept, but my core assertion is that in the eviction of Irsu/Osarseph and his followers from the Delta we have the roots of the 'real' Exodus.

8. Manetho's story of Osarseph/Moses has never been accepted as historical, despite the Irsu confirmation, because of the 'leprosy' libel. I have argued that this is not as scurrilous as it appears and, indeed, perhaps explains some things about Moses himself and the 'rules' he laid down for his people.

9. The 'real' Exodus was not about an enslaved race of people called the Israelites leaving Egypt for the Promised Land of Canaan. It is about a smaller group of people, known as Apiru – or Habiru/Hebrews – led by a religious leader who has Egyptian and Asian roots, who travel to Midian in search of their God. They find him and his name is Yahweh. From there, they spread their faith to the tribes of Canaan and Transjordan, many of whom were already known by the Israelite names that appear in the Bible.

10. Some of those Israelite tribes formed part of the 'Sea Peoples', who were not a *cause* of the Bronze Age Collapse but Levantine peoples who, in a time of extended famine, attacked Egypt for its grain stores. Etymological identifications for the Sea Peoples that range the length of the Mediterranean are unnecessary – equally convincing identifications are available for all of them closer to home in the Levant.

11. Other Israelite tribes were among the semi-nomadic, Semitic pastoralists known as the Shasu, who lived in the Sinai and surrounding areas. One tribe of Shasu constituted the priests of the Shasu religion – the worship of Yahweh. They were based around Yahweh's holy mountain, known variously as Seir, Sinai and Horeb.

12. Moses' 'Hebrew' followers adopted the Shasu priestly model as their own, and now called Levites, 'attached' themselves (with force if necessary) in that role to the Shasu and Canaanite 'Israelite' tribes. Centuries later, the Israelites rationalized their role as an unlanded tribe descended from Jacob's son Levi.

*

The biggest problem that anyone faces who tries to get to the truth behind the Bible, is that vocabulary trips you up all the time. In this case, words like 'Sojourn', 'Exodus' and 'Conquest' come to us trailing thousands of years of religious associations, as their initial capitals suggest. Thus, Jews and Christians of all persuasions, and Biblical scholars and Egyptologists alike, seek answers to questions such as 'When was the Exodus?', or 'How long was the Sojourn?', or 'Was there ever a Conquest?'. As I have tried to show, these are the wrong questions. They start from too many unspoken and unacknowledged prior assumptions. Here lies the value of the textual analysis approach that I use in this book. As I acknowledged at the outset, my only *a priori* assumption is that the supernatural does not exist. What *do* exist are texts that can be analyzed in the context of who wrote them, when, and with what objectives. As Josephus argued, Egypt and Israel are unique in having preserved texts that are thousands of years old – a miracle for which we can thank their respective priesthoods. But we no longer need be constrained in our understanding of those texts by the preconceptions and beliefs of those priests. We can see them for what they are – uniquely precious survivals from a long-forgotten past. And if we treat them with care and respect; if we do not adopt the stance of maximalist, or minimalist, or any other kind of -ist; if we are open to what they actually say, rather than what we have been told that they say, it is just possible that we can recover more of that forgotten past than we ever thought possible.

And all this matters – deeply. The past is not just the past – it casts a long shadow over the present and future. As I look back on my trilogy, I discern a single theme running through it all – the dangerous nature of 'prophecy'. In the second and third volumes, I shall dissect the prophecies surrounding the Judaeo-Christian concepts of Messiah and

Apocalypse and show that these have a pernicious effect on current affairs today. In this book, my theme has been another prophecy that we have been calling the 'Promise' Yahweh made to the Israelites. When 'prophecy' becomes 'promise' it becomes dangerous; it moves from the realm of religious idea to that of historical determinism – from amoral fiction to immoral fact. The prophecy that the Shemite Israelites have a right to Hamite Canaan, becomes justification for a genocide that the Pentateuch is obsessed with defending. And three millennia later, it underpins the Zionist movement with the results that we are only too familiar with. Whatever view one takes about the modern tragedy that is the Middle East, and whatever the rights and wrongs of the Israeli and Palestinian peoples, for many of us in the West, it is the assumption of moral right, based on a prophetic promise 3,000 years old that is so repulsive. And it is fuelled by the kind of racial bigotry that underlay the ancient story of Lot and the Moabites. Unfortunately, the pen has never been mightier than the sword. It was the sword that brought Yahweh to Canaan, and the sword that brought Allah to Arabia. My pen will do nothing to reverse that history, but, just maybe, will provide a little more rational perspective to those who have any power at all to influence the inhumanity that is enacted every day in the modern Levant.

Select Bibliography

PRIMARY SOURCES

The Bible, The King James Version, www.kingjamesbibeonline.org.

Whiston, William (Trans.) *Josephus: The Complete Works* (Nashville, TN: Thomas Nelson, 1998).

Waddell, William Gillian (ed.), *Manetho* in Loeb Classical Library (London and Cambridge: William Heinemann and Harvard University Press, 1940).

Breasted, James Henry, *Ancient Records of Egypt: Historical Documents from the Earliest Times to the Persian Conquest, Collected, Edited and Translated, with Commentary* (Chicago: University Press, 1906–7).

SECONDARY SOURCES

Albertz, Rainer, *History of Israelite Religion* (Westminster: John Knox Press, 1994).

Albright, William Foxwell, *The Archaeology of Palestine: Revised Edition* (London: Penguin, 1960).

Albright, William Foxwell, *The Biblical Period from Abraham to Ezra* (New York: Harper & Row, 1963).

Assmann, Jan, *Moses the Egyptian: The Memory of Egypt in*

Western Monotheism (Cambridge, MA: Harvard University Press, 1997).

Astour, M. C., 'Yahweh in Egyptian Topographic Lists' in 'Festschrift Elmar Edel' in Gorg, Manfred, *Aegypten und Altes Testament* (Bamberg, 1979).

Bard, Kathryn A., *Encyclopedia of the Archaeology of Ancient Egypt* (London: Routledge, 1999).

Berlandini, Jocelyne, 'Contribution aux <<Princes du Nouvel Empire à Memphis>> [Le Prince Thoutmes, Fils d'Amenhotep III/Le Prince Senakhtenamon, Fils de Ramses II]' in *Etudes sur l'Ancien Empire et la nécropole de Saqqara dédiées à Jean-Philippe Lauer*. OrMonsp IX (1997, pp. 99–112).

Blenkinsop, Joseph, 'The Midianite-Kenite Hypothesis Revisited and the Origins of Judah' in *Journal for the Study of the Old Testament* (33.2, 2008, pp. 131–153).

Breasted, James Henry, *A History of Egypt from the Earliest Times to the Persian Conquest* (New York: Charles Scribner's Sons, 1905).

Breasted, James Henry, *A History of the Ancient Egyptians* (New York: Charles Scribner's Sons, 1908).

Breasted, James Henry, *Ancient Times – A History of the Early World: Revised Edition* (Boston: Athenaeum Press, 1935).

Burns, Rita J., 'Has the Lord Indeed Spoken Only Through Moses? A Study of the Biblical Portrait of Miriam' in *SBL Dissertation Series 84* (Atlanta: Scholar's Press, 1987).

Cline, Eric H., *1177: The Year Civilisation Collapsed* (Princeton, NJ: University Press, 2015).

Coogan, Michael D., *The Oxford History of the Biblical World* (Oxford: University Press, 1998).

Coogan, Michael D., *The Old Testament: A Historical and Literary Introduction to the Hebrew Scriptures* (Oxford: University Press, 2006).

Cooper, Kenneth R., 'The Shasu of Palestine in Egyptian Texts', *Artifax* Vol. 21 (2006) and Vol. 22 (2007).

Cross, Frank Moore, *Canaanite Myth and Hebrew Epic* (Cambridge, MA: Harvard University Press, 1973).

Cross, Frank Moore and Freedman, David Noel, *Studies in Ancient Yawistic Poetry* (Grand Rapids, MI: Eerdmans, 1975).

Dumbrell, W. J., 'Midian: A Land or a League?' in *Vetus Testamentum*, Vol. XXV (May 1975), pp. 323–337.

Eissfeldt, O. (trans. Ackroyd, P. R.), *The Old Testament: An Introduction* (Oxford: Blackwell, 1965).

Finegan, J., *Handbook of Biblical Chronology* (Princeton, NJ: University Press, 1964).

Finkelstein, Israel and Silberman, Neil Asher, *The Bible Unearthed: Archaeology's New Vision of Ancient Israel and the Origin of Its Sacred Texts* (New York: Simon and Schuster, 2002).

Fishbane, M., *Biblical Interpretation in Ancient Israel* (Oxford: University Press, 1988).

Fohrer, G., *Introduction to the Old Testament* (Nashville, TN: Abingdon, 1968).

Friedman, R. E., *Who Wrote the Bible?* (London: Jonathan Cape., 1988).

Friedman, R. E., *The Bible with Sources Revealed* (San Francisco: Harper, 2003).

Friedman, R. E., *The Exodus* (New York: Harper, 2017).

Goedicke, Hans, 'Irsu the Kharru in Papyrus Harris' in *Wiener Zeitschrift ü die Kunde des Morgenlandes 71* (1979).

Habel, N., *Literary Criticism of the Old Testament* (Minneapolis, MN: Fortress Press, 1971).

Haupt, Paul, 'Midian and Sinai' in *ZDMG 63*, 1909, p. 506.

Herrmann, S., *A History of Israel in Old Testament Times* (London: SCM-Canterbury Press, 1975).

Herrmann, S., *Israel in Egypt* (Naperville, IL: Allenson, 1973).

Homung, Erik, (trans. John Bains), *Conceptions of God in Ancient Egypt* (Ithaca, NY: Cornell University Press, 1982).

Jenks, A. W., *The Elohist and North Israelite Traditions* (Decatur, GA: American Scholars Press, 1977).

Kahn, Dan'el, 'Who is Meddling in Egypt's Affairs?' in *Journal of Ancient Egyptian Interconnections*, 2(1) (2010, p. 14–23)

Kitchen, Kenneth, *The Third Intermediate Period in Egypt* (Warminster: Aris & Phillips, 1998).

Kitchen, Kenneth, *On the Reliability of the Old Testament* (Grand Rapids, MI: Eerdmans, 2003).

Knohl, Israel, *Where Are We From* (Tel Aviv: Dvir Press, 2008).

Knohl, Israel, *How the Bible Was Born* (Tel Aviv: Dvir Press, 2018).

Knohl, Israel, *Exodus: The History Behind the Story* (www.thetorah.com/article/exodus-the-history-behind-the-story}.

Knohl, Israel, *Joseph and the Famine: The Story's Origins in Egyptian History* (www.thetorah.com/article/joseph-and-the-famine-the-storys-origins-in-egyptian-history)

Lane Fox, Robin, *The Unauthorized Version* (London: Viking, 1991).

Lemche, Niels Peter, *The Israelites in History and Tradition* (Westminster: John Knox Press, 1998).

Leuchter, Mark, *Who Were the Levites?* (www.thetorah.com/article/who-were-the-levites).

Leuchter, Mark, *The Levites and the Boundaries of Israelite Identity* (Oxford: University Press, 2017).

Mazar, Amihay, *Archaeology of the Land of the Bible* (New Haven, CT: Yale University Press, 1990).

Metzger, Bruce M. and Coogan, Michael D. (eds.), *The Oxford Companion to the Bible* (Oxford: University Press, 1993).

Nicholson, Ernest, *The Pentateuch in the Twentieth Century: The Legacy of Julius Wellhausen* (Oxford: University Press, 1998).

Noth, Martin, (trans. B. Anderson), *A History of Pentateuchal Traditions* (Atlanta, GA: American Scholars Press, 1981).

Ockinga, Boyo, 'Amenophis, Son of Hapu: A Biographical Sketch' (*Rundle Foundation for Egyptian Archaeology Newsletter*, No. 18, Feb. 1986).

Pritchard, James B. (ed.), *The Times Concise Atlas of the Bible* (London: Times Books, 1991).

Pritchard, James B. (ed.), *Ancient Near Eastern Texts Relating to the Old Testament* (Princeton, NJ: University Press, 1955).

Redford, Donald B., *Egypt, Canaan, and Israel in Ancient Times* (Princeton, NJ: University Press, 1993).

Rogerson, J., *Old Testament Criticism in the Nineteenth Century* (London: S.P.C.K., 1984).

Romer, John, *Testament: The Bible and History* (London: Michael O'Mara, 1988).

Sassoon, H. I. S. D., 'Moses, Aaron, and Miriam: Were They Siblings? The (In)Significance of Biology and Heredity' (www.thetorah.com/moses-aaron-and-miriam-were-they-siblings).

Shaw, Ian, *The Oxford History of Ancient Egypt* (Oxford: University Press, 2000).

Whitelam, K. W., *The Invention of Ancient Israel* (London: Routledge, 1996).

Wright, G. E., (ed.), *The Bible and the Ancient Near East* (New York: Doubleday, 1961).

Wright, G. E., *Biblical Archaeology* (London: Gerald Duckworth & Co., 1962).

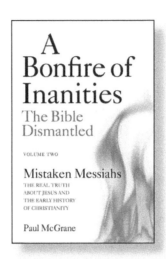

A Bonfire of Inanities: The Bible Dismantled offers, in three volumes, a revolutionary new understanding of the roots of Judaism and Christianity by way of a complete, rationalistic re-interpretation of the Bible, from Genesis to Revelation. There has never been anything like this – in scope, in approach, and in findings. It may be possible to continue in Jewish or Christian belief in the light of this trilogy, but it would be a very different kind of religious faith from the one normally espoused. Each volume has been written to stand alone, but there is a natural sequence to the arguments developed which is facilitated if they are read in order.

VOLUME TWO

AVAILABLE SEPTEMBER 2023

Mistaken Messiahs traces how Jewish messianic belief finds its way unrecognisably into the New Testament. It shows that the Jesus of the Gospels was a fiction disguising a more mundane reality. And that the entire chronology of 1st Century Palestine is shifted forwards by a decade, obscuring the real personalities and events behind the Christian story.

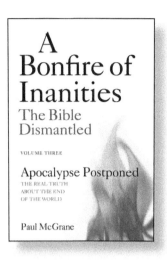

A Bonfire of Inanities: The Bible Dismantled offers, in three volumes, a revolutionary new understanding of the roots of Judaism and Christianity by way of a complete, rationalistic re-interpretation of the Bible, from Genesis to Revelation. There has never been anything like this – in scope, in approach, and in findings. It may be possible to continue in Jewish or Christian belief in the light of this trilogy, but it would be a very different kind of religious faith from the one normally espoused. Each volume has been written to stand alone, but there is a natural sequence to the arguments developed which is facilitated if they are read in order.

VOLUME THREE

AVAILABLE JANUARY 2024

Apocalypse Postponed focusses on the Christian belief in imminent apocalypse and traces how thoroughgoing mis-understanding of the relevant Old and New Testament texts has led to two centuries of fallacious expectation. It identifies the key apocalyptic themes and locates them, not in our future, but in people and events contemporary with the writer of Revelation.